D0168945

R00019 35680

Columbia Essays in International Affairs

VOLUME VII

The Dean's Papers, 1971

Columbia Essays
in International Affairs

VOLUME VII

The Dean's Papers, 1971

BY STUDENTS OF THE
FACULTY OF INTERNATIONAL AFFAIRS
COLUMBIA UNIVERSITY

EDITED BY ANDREW W. CORDIER

NEW YORK AND LONDON

Columbia University Press

1972

Andrew W. Cordier,
Formerly Dean of the Columbia University Faculty of
International Affairs and President Emeritus of
Columbia University, is a consultant to the Department of State,
Trustee of the Carnegie Endowment for International Peace
and the Dag Hammarskjold Foundation,
and Director of the Foreign Policy Association.

Copyright © 1972 Columbia University Press
Library of Congress Catalog Card Number: 66-14078
International Standard Book Number: 0-231-03667-1
Printed in the United States of America

Foreword

Each year, members of the Faculty of International Affairs, who provide instruction for the School of International Affairs and its Regional Institutes, select a number of student essays representing a large degree of originality and high quality of scholarship for possible inclusion in the annual volume of *Essays on International Affairs: The Dean's Papers*. The papers are presented to a review committee, appointed by the Dean, by the faculty member who originally encouraged the paper. The review committee selects the best papers for publication. It is a source of great satisfaction to the students whose papers are selected, to their instructors, and, indeed, to the entire Faculty to see these research efforts brought to fruition in published form. Readers of these volumes have often expressed great surprise at the quality of research and individual comprehension which these student essays frequently demonstrate.

The range of topics represented by these papers attests to the scope of concerns of students in the School of International Affairs and its regional institutes. They reflect an interest in the problems of ethnic and regional integration, political and social change in the Third World, economic planning and development, and the foreign policy-making process of nations.

The issue of land reform, so critical in many developing countries today, is dealt with in three papers. Mr. David A. J. Macey's discussion of "The Peasantry, the Agrarian Problem, and the Revolution of 1905–1907" is mainly historical in approach, but it deals with a problem which continues to plague the Soviet Union even today. Tracing the history of peasant unrest from emancipation through the agrarian uprising and mass movements of 1905–1907, Mr. Macey examines how peasant attitudes achieved conscious formulation and political significance which would ultimately lead to a victory for the peasant solution.

Taking a more current perspective, Norman Louis Cigar examines Soviet opinion of the agrarian reform carried out in Egypt from 1952–1961. Based on a study of original Russian sources dating from 1958–1963—a period in which land reform was treated in extensive ide-

301644

ological tracts—"The Soviet View of Egyptian Agrarian Reform: 1958–1963" suggests, among other things, that Russian criticism of the Egyptian policy was based more on its political implications than on its economic success or failure.

Comparative analysis is the approach of James Stepanek's "The Political Economy of Land Reform," which is concerned with the differential impact of land reforms on agricultural productivity and social problems in Taiwan and Colombia. Drawing upon his own first-hand experience in the two widely disparate countries as well as on literary sources, Mr. Stepanek finds some illuminating contrasts in in the way East Asia's long and unbroken cultural history and Latin America's relatively short, less well-developed cultural history have affected the course of local land reforms. Among the author's conclusions is that it is incorrect to argue that Taiwanese land reform can be a useful model for application in other less-developed countries.

Marie L. Rocca's, "The Negro in Colombia: An Historical Geography" is a well-researched and interesting study of the geographic distribution of the Negro population in Colombia from colonial times to the present. Well aware of the limitations imposed by available data, Miss Rocca has nevertheless come up with a clear if not detailed accounting of the Negro in Colombian history, which is particularly useful for relating the numerical distribution of the Negro to his differential cultural and economic impact on various regions of the country.

Felice Gaer's "A Cybernetic Reform Model for the Soviet Union" may afford a pleasant surprise for those who are skeptical of attempts to apply cybernetics to the study of the Soviet Union. Avoiding the trap of using technical verbiage to cover weak arguments, Miss Gaer does an excellent job of relating the cybernetic model to the problem of systemic reform, drawing a number of important distinctions often missed by past commentators, such as the way in which cybernetics is used by both centralizers and decentralizers in the U.S.S.R. Her discussion of East Germany is both appropriate and enlightened.

The study of the relationship between economic development and politics is exemplified by Michael Bucuvalas's case study of "The Breakdown of a Political System Experiencing Economic Development—Greece 1950–1967". In a skillful and rigorous application of complex analysis which was far wider implications than for Greece alone, Mr. Bucuvalas in effect describes the traditional political system in Greece represented by the old regime, the economic changes which took place under that regime, the obsolescence of the political institutions and styles on which the regime depended, the incompetence of the previous leadership to deal with the changed situation in Greece —and on these bases, explains the rise and consolidation of the Greek generals.

A well-conceived and totally original contribution to the study of modern Japanese political history and foreign policy decisionmaking is Michael K. Blaker's "Japanese Foreign Policy Decisionmaking in Middle Taisho Period: An Institutional Case Study of the Gaiko Chosa Kai." Making effective use of primary sources in the original Japanese, Mr. Blaker skillfully ties in the study of a specific Japanese institution to issues of broad interest to political scientists involved in foreign policy decisionmaking analysis.

Concerned also with foreign policy analysis is Stephen Adler's paper "The Cuban Missile Crisis: Strategic Theory in Practice" which focuses on deterrence relationships and why in this case they nearly broke down. Contradicting some former theorists, Mr. Adler concludes that the best deterrence relationship for the United States is not one in which the United States maintains a "favorable strategic balance" but rather one in which neither the United States nor Russia is allowed to get too far ahead of the other. In crisis situations, the author contends, too many external factors enter in the picture to distort events, such that "pure" deterrence theory gives way to the day-to-day exigencies of governments.

Mrs. Margaret Roff conducts with great sensitivity and sensibility her discussion of the origins and development of Southeast Asian institutions in "Disintegration and Integration in Southeast Asia." Showing clear evidence of her many years experience as a lecturer at the University of Malaysia, Mrs. Roff nicely combines international relations, "integrationist theory," and good empirical knowledge of the region in an interesting examination of the divisive and binding forces operating in the Southeast Asian state system.

The selection of these nine essays for publication in the Dean's Papers 1971 was based upon careful review. After being recommended by their sponsoring professors, the studies submitted were examined by committees appointed by the Regional Institutes or, in the case of subjects of a functional or nonregional type, by a committee designated by the Committee on Instruction of the Faculty. The final selection was made by a committee of the Faculty of International Affairs, consisting of Herbert A. Deane, Chairman, Lieber Professor of Political Philosophy, Charles Issawi, Ragnar Nurkse Professor of Economics, and Philip E. Mosely, Adlai. E. Stevenson Professor of International Relations, Associate Dean of the Faculty of International Affairs, and Director of the Institute on Western Europe. It is a pleasure to express my appreciation to this committee for the care they took in fulfilling this responsibility. I am happy, also, to express my thanks to Marguerite V. Freund, Administrative Assistant of the Institute on Western Europe, who again provided very efficient liaison between student contributions, faculty, the selection committee, and the Press.

Andrew W. Cordier
Dean

July 1972

Contents

Columbia Essays in International Affairs

VOLUME VII

The Dean's Papers, 1971

The Peasantry, the Agrarian Problem, and the Revolution of 1905-1907

DAVID A. J. MACEY

I

Russian agriculture after the Emancipation was in a state of constant crisis which ultimately exploded in the agrarian uprisings and mass movement of 1905–1907. However, neither of these two chronological limits fully encompasses the extent of this crisis.[1] Rather, they embrace a period during which the government and its supporters, having once reoriented their attitudes toward the peasant and rural Russia, were forced yet again to attempt a solution to the problems of the vast majority of the country's population and to those of the very basis of Russia's economic well-being. On the other hand, during this same period the peasants' attitudes toward these same problems achieved for the first time both conscious formulation and, through the offices of the revolutionary intellectuals, political significance. The path which the government ultimately followed after the 1905–1907 revolution proved to be its last opportunity for resolving the agrarian problem, and its failure was followed by the victory of the peasant solution—although even this did not resolve the problem, which continues to plague the Soviet Union today.

In essence, the crisis was an expression of Russia's general economic backwardness with respect to the rest of Europe and a symptom of her belated agricultural revolution. Thus, there developed a conflict between the traditional or "feudal" forms of agriculture and the modern or "capitalist" forms as the latter tried to usurp the for-

[1] Michael Confino, *Systèmes agraires et progrès agricole. L'assolement triennal en Russe aux XVIII–XIXe siècles* (Paris, La Haye: Mouton, 1969), pp. 361–66.

mer.[2] Together with this very broad dynamic which was the back-
cloth before which Russia's political and social problems played
themselves out, there was another dynamic which aggravated the economic and, therefore, the social and political problems. This was the
international grain crisis which developed in the late 1870s and
lasted until the late 1890s and which had a severely depressing effect
on the price of grain—and in particular of rye, the major product of
Russia's grain economy—on both the world and the Russian grain
markets. In addition to the aggravating effect of the crisis, however,
the end of the crisis and the following decade of increasing grain
prices had an even more abrasive effect on the general condition of
agriculture and of the peasantry.[3]

Turning to the peasant economy directly to search for the causes
and to examine the nature of the crisis one is confronted by a bewil-
dering slew of explanations, each of which tends to be a product of
the particular writer's political and social proclivities and all of
which center around the problem of change and how or if it is to be
accomplished. It would, however, be a mistake to enter the political
elements of these polemical arguments or to attempt to adjudicate between them since their statistical, let alone their theoretical, bases are

---

[2] As a result of Lenin's studies of the agrarian situation and his formulation
of the possibility of "two" paths, the Prussian and the American, of capitalist
development in Russian agriculture, subsequent Soviet works have tended to
be devoted almost exclusively to studying the manner in which the conflict between the *perezhitka* (remnants) of serfdom and the developing capitalist elements in agriculture resulted in the adoption of the Prussian or reactionary
form of capitalist development. See V. I. Lenin, *Collected Works* (Moscow:
Foreign Languages Publishing House, 1962–1963), XIII, 238–42 and XV,
141; A. Gaister, "Sel'skoe khoziaistvo" in 1905, Vol. I, *Predposylki revoliutsii,* ed. M. N. Pokrovskii, (Moscow / Leningrad: Gosudarstvennoe izdatel'stvo,
1925), *passim;* P. I. Lyashchenko, *History of the National Economy of Russia
to the 1917 Revolution,* tr. by L. M. Herman, (New York: The Macmillan
Company, 1949), pp. 470–72; S. M. Dubrovskii, *Stolypinskaia zemel'naia reforma* (Moscow: Izdatel'stvo ANSSSR, 1963), p. 46; A. M. Anfimov, *Krupnoe
pomeshchich'e khoziaistvo evropeiskoi Rossii* (Moscow: Izdatel'stvo "Nauka,"
1969), *passim.*

[3] Indeed, Gaister, *passim,* devotes most of his attention to the grain crisis as
the principal cause of the agricultural crisis. See also Lyashchenko, pp.
467–70; Anfimov, p. 93; Dubrovskii, *Stolypinskaia . . . ,* pp. 41–42; P. P.
Maslov, "Razvitiie zemledeliia i polozheniie krest'ian do nachala XX veka," in
Obshchestvennoe dvizheniie v Rossi v nachale XX.-go veke, eds. L. Martov,
P. Maslov and A. Potresov. Vol. I, (SPB: Tipografiia t-va "Obshchestvennaia
Pol'za," 1909), pp. 26–28, hereafter referred to as Maslov I.

rather too elusive to bear accurate analysis, even though the arguments themselves are not without logical consistency. Rather, an attempt will be made to give as broad and general a presentation as possible, referring only to partisan interpretations when they are relevant to the problem under immediate discussion.

II

Without question, land hunger was one of the root causes of the agrarian crisis and a major determinant of the features of the peasant economy in the period under review.[4] This land hunger had resulted from the interaction of two factors: the terms of the 1861 Emancipation and the rate of population growth. As is well known, the former *pomeshchik* (noble's) peasant as a result of the Emancipation received on average about 26 per cent less land than he had been accustomed to cultivating for his own benefit prior to 1861.[5] Furthermore, that land which he did receive was generally the least fertile and the most inconveniently located, while the "cut-off" land was principally composed of watering places, pastures, and forest land—all of which were vital components of the rural life cycle.[6] In

---

[4] The most ardent exponents of this theory are A. V. Peshekhonov, "Ekonomicheskoe polozheniie krest'ian v poreformennoe vremia," in *Velikaia reforma russkoe obshchestvo i krest'ianskii vopros v proshlom i nastoiashchem,* eds. A. K. Dzhivelogov, S. P. Mel'gunov and V. I. Pichet, Vol. VI (Moscow: Izdaniie T-va I. D. Sytina, 1911) pp. 201, 240, and 200–48, *passim;* and the peasants themselves.

[5] Generally the *pomeshchik* peasants will be the main subject of consideration throughout this paper, although as of 1861 they composed only 23 million out of the approximately 50 million rural inhabitants. Lyashchenko, p. 273; Terence Emmons, "The Peasant and the Emancipation," in *The Peasant in Nineteenth Century Russia,* ed. Wayne S. Vucinich, (Stanford: Stanford University Press, 1968), p. 41; Geroid T. Robinson, *Rural Russia under the Old Regime,* (Berkeley and Los Angeles: University of California Press, 1967) pp. 94, 288–89. Furthermore, the problem of "cut-offs" was one that particularly affected this category of peasant since the other groups of peasants were far better treated on their emancipation. Lenin, XV, 76–77; P. N. Pershin, *Agrarnaia revoliutsii v Rossii ot refomy k revoliutsii* (Moscow: Izdatel'stvo "Nauka," 1966), Vol. I, 20–25; A. A. Kaufman, *Agrarnoi vopros v Rossii,* 2 vols. (Moscow, Tipografiia T-va I. D. Sytina, 1908), I, 56.

[6] S. M. Dubrovskii, *Krest'ianskoe dvizheniie v revoliutsii 1905–1907 gg.* (Moscow: Izdatel'stvo ANSSSR, 1956), pp. 11–16, 13, 17; Pershin, I, 13–15; Lenin, XV, 58–59; Anfimov, pp. 32–34, 238–39; Peshekhonov, pp. 202–4; Kaufman, I, 48–49 and Ch. I for the effects of the Emancipation. See also

addition, to the mass of peasants who were emancipated in 1861 there were added some 600,000 *darstvenniki* who received only one-quarter of the average allotment for their region and who, consequently, suffered particularly from land hunger.[7]

Coupling the terms of the Emancipation with the gross figures on the size of the rural population of European Russia which show a growth rate of approximately 60 per cent between the years 1861 and 1897 and one of 20 per cent between 1897 and 1916,[8] it is clear that without any changes in the quantity of land owned by the peasant his economic situation was becoming considerably more precarious with the years compared to what it had been before the Emancipation.[9] However, the amount of peasant-owned land did not remain static. The quantity of allotment land in peasant ownership increased over the period by approximately 10 per cent, while there was added to this some 20 to 25 million dessiatines (2.7 acres) of privately owned peasant land, or approximately 20 per cent of the allotment land held in 1905.[10] The net result, nevertheless, was a reduction in

Leon Trotsky, 1905, tr. by Maurice Parijanine, (Paris: Les Éditions Minuit, 1969), pp. 34 and 37 and Confino, p. 367, who with Dubrovskii sees the Emancipation as the major cause of the economic distress. Marxists, however, generally cloak this by referring to the *pomeshchik* land surplus, thus introducing the element of class hostility. In fact the absolute proportions of land held by the peasantry and the *pomeshchiki* on the eve of 1905 were not particularly extreme when compared with other modernizing nations. See Bruce M. Russett, "Inequality and Instability: the relation of land tenure to politics," in *Quantitative History*, eds. D. K. Rowney and J. O. Graham Jr., (Homewood, Ill.: The Dorsey Press, 1969), pp. 365, n. 16 and *passim*.

[7] Pershin, I, 15; Dubrovskii, *Krest'ianskoe . . .*, p. 17.

[8] Robinson, pp. 94, 288–89; N. P. Oganovskii, *Sel'skoe khoziaistvo Rossii v XX veke* (The Hague: Europe Printing, 1968), pp. 18–21, 28–29; Anfimov, pp. 370–73; *Statisticheskii spravochnik; naseleniie i zemlevladeniie Rossii po guberniiam* (SPB:Knigo izdatel'stvo "Zemlia i Volia," 1906), pp. 14–17.

[9] Kaufman, I, 56; Peshekhonov pp. 202–4. It should be noted, however, that Marxist historians generally ignore the problem of population growth as irrelevant and Malthusian and attack those who make reference to it for hiding the essential social and economic basis of the problem. See Dubrovskii, *Krest'ianskoe . . .*, p. 13; Lenin, XIII, 231–34, 250. However, Anfimov, p. 48, does acknowledge the problem of rural overpopulation. On the other hand, he notes that the density of population in Russia was far lower than in European countries. *Ibid.*, p. 22.

[10] Oganovskii, p. 58; Robinson, p. 94. In 1883 the government founded a Peasant Land Bank to provide credit for purchasing land. However, the amount of land acquired made little impression on the problem and, in fact,

the amount of land cultivated both per household and per revision soul.[11]

A second major problem which contributed to the agrarian crisis was that of the "three-field system" which lay at the very basis of the purely economic aspects of the peasant's problems: the production of enough food to support the rural population.[12] This system of crop

worsened the situation by driving up the land prices due to the pressure from both increased demand and speculation while the beneficiaries were predominantly the more prosperous peasants or peasant associations and communes. See Peshekhonov, pp. 210–11, 213–14; Lenin, XV, 106; Gaister, pp. 72–75, 138–40; Dubrovskii, *Stolypinskaia* . . . , p. 24; Dubrovskii, *Krest'ianskoe* . . . , pp. 20–21; Pershin, I, 80–89; Maslov, I, 21–25; Kaufman, I, 93 ff.; Robinson, pp. 99–102, 131–33, 290–91, 296; Alexander Gershenkron, "Agrarian Policies and Industrialization, Russia 1861–1917," in *The Cambridge Economic History of Europe,* Vol. VI, Part II, (Cambridge: at the University Press, 1965), pp. 769–70; Francis M. Watters, "The Peasant and the Village Commune," in *The Peasant in Nineteenth Century Russia,* ed. Wayne S. Vucinich, (Stanford: Stanford University Press, 1968), pp. 147–51.

[11] Dubrovskii, *Krest'ianskoe* . . . , p. 25; Dubrovskii, *Stolypinskaia* . . . , p. 29; Watters, p. 149; Robinson, pp. 94, 102, 291; Peshekhonov, pp. 236–38; Maslov, I, 2–3.

[12] Indeed, the black-earth regions of the Center and the Left and Right Banks of the Ukraine did not produce sufficient grain to accomplish this. Dubrovskii, *Krest'ianskoe* . . . , p. 26. Over the whole period there was a decline in the production of grain per village inhabitant despite the fact that the average yield of grain per dessiatine increased in several regions and that there was a general expansion of the sown area. However, expansion was often at the expense of pasture land and led to decline in the quality and strength of the livestock and the quantity of manure. Lyashchenko, pp. 448–54; Dubrovskii, *Stolypinskaia* . . . , p. 30; Dubrovskii, *Krest'ianskoe* . . . , p. 26; Gaister, p. 109. The figures on yields are particularly treacherous. See Robinson, pp. 98, 290; Kaufman, I, 62–63; II, 12–13; Pershin, I, 44–62; Anfimov, pp. 216–17; Oganovskii, pp. 134–47; Gaister, p. 128. But when compared to Germany and other countries the dismally low yields achieved in Russia are clearly apparent. The wheat yield was one-half of that in Germany and one-quarter of that in England. See Dubrovskii, *Krest'ianskoe* . . . , p. 26; Anfimov, p. 375; Trotsky, p. 37. It should also be noted that it is on the basis of such evidence as this as well as on figures for the increasing levels of application of improved technology that Lenin, XV, 106–17, 135, claims that the agricultural crisis is not one of agricultural methods. Such statements must, however, be treated extremely carefully since the improvement of agricultural methods was indeed a basic problem—even if the solution to this problem *in vacuo* should not prove to be any panacea. Kaufman, II, 15, 55, cites the three-field system and its insufficiently high productivity—i.e., the technological backwardness of Russian agriculture—as the major cause of the agricul-

rotation which was in use over the greater proportion of the agricultural area of European Russia was one of poverty. It determined both the plan of rotation (winter-spring-fallow) and the types of cereals cultivated (rye-oats-fallow pasture) due to a combination of the demands of the growing cycle, soil quality, climate, and the labor, technology, and time available. Thus, these interrelated factors were, in essence, the only possible combination. The whole system was tied together by the association of ploughing and pasture which had to resolve the problem of providing animal fodder—although this was generally accomplished unsatisfactorily—for the animal power was at once the most essential and the weakest part of the economy. In toto, the three-field system was designed to feed both the animal and the human populations and as such was a closed system devoid of surplus. And, because of this lack of surplus, it became impossible to shift to a more nutritious cycle of crops, even within this system, such as wheat-barley-grass, since such crops required additional supplies of labor, manure, and time.[13]

The rigidities of the three-field system, however, were compounded as a result of their interaction with the *obshchina* or repartitional commune.[14] The most important consequence of this

---

tural crisis. See also the reports of the Special Conference under S. Iu. Witte in Dubrovskii, *Stolypinskaia . . .* , pp. 80–81. For Marxist criticisms of this view see *Ibid.*, pp. 32, 38, 40; Gaister, p. 159; Lenin, XV, 135–36, where the Kaufman type of approach is attacked for hiding the bankruptcy of the social relations of peasant agriculture which they consider to be the true crisis. For a curious reversal of the Marxist position to that of the bourgeois liberal, Kaufman, see Confino, p. 15, and the opinion of N. S. Khrushchev on the sources of agricultural backwardness.

[13] Confino, pp. 62–88; also see Peshekhonov, p. 204; Robinson, pp. 97–98.

[14] However, it must be noted that the three-field system and the *obshchina* were merely associated in many parts of European Russia and that the system of rotation cannot be considered to be the cause of the appearance of the communal structure, even though it was this *obshchina* which came to be seen by many, and in particular by the government, as the cause of the agrarian crisis. Confino, pp. 98, 296–97. See also S. Iu. Witte, *Vospominaniia tsarstvovaniie Nikolaia II,* (The Hague: Europe Printing, 1968), I, 467–73; V. I. Gurko, *Features and Figures of the Past, Government and Opinion in the Reign of Nicholas II* (New York: Russell & Russell, 1970) pp. 133, 157; Gershenkron, pp. 789–92; Dubrovskii, *Stolypinskaia . . .* , pp. 66–85. Confino, pp. 330–34, disputes the contention, held by the government, that the periodical redistributions were a source of insecurity and led to laziness and poor work. The source of this insecurity he finds, on the contrary, in the social regime. See also Robinson, pp. 97, 135–36, 200. Kaufman, II, 25–28 and

association was the fragmentation or division of the *obshchina*'s land into parcels for division among the peasants according to the number of *tiaglo*'s (work-units usually comprising one married couple), the number of fields in the rotation system (three), the number of different types of soil categories, and the relative distances of the various fields from the village. This was further complicated by the manner in which the peasant *mir* (the administrative unit or village) was split up into anywhere from two to twenty *obshchina*'s, depending upon the number of *pomeshchiki* in the area to whom the peasants had been attached as serfs, while this survival of pre-1861 relationships also led to the intermingling of *pomeshchik* and peasant lots.[15] Following from this fractionalization was the linear shape of the peasant fields, which in itself encouraged the use of the wooden and shallow ploughshared *sokha* and the light *kosulia* (harrow). But the consequence of this backward technology was a further depletion of the soil—which could not be compensated for by increased manuring—and an increased dependence on the rye/oats cycle for the basic crops since they were the only cereals that could withstand these poor conditions. Meanwhile the dependence on the *sokha* was strengthened by the unavailability of capital resources and by the fact that the peasant could make this kind of plough himself.[16]

Thus, from this brief survey can be seen the extremely low level on which this subsistence system of peasant agriculture operated. The major obstacle to progress, to the development of a more intensive system of agriculture, was the lack of any surplus resource that could be exploited—whether human or animal power or capital to obtain either of these or to increase the level of applied technology in the form of improved ploughs, seed, or fertilizer.[17]

Maslov, I, 28 32, 35, similarly do not see the *obshchina* as a cause of the crisis.

[15] Confino, pp. 99–106; Anfimov, p. 37; Dubrovskii, *Krest'ianskoe . . .* , p. 17. Indeed, it was this interdependence of peasant and *pomeshchik* land that resulted in part from this physical intermeshing which became one of the major stimuli arousing the concern of the nobility and of government circles for the state of both peasant and *pomeshchik* agriculture.

[16] Confino, pp. 111–13. See also Lyashchenko, pp. 442–44.

[17] Manuring, itself, was a problem since the land was often too distant to fertilize. In all, some two-thirds of peasant land was unfertilized. Anfimov, p. 210. In addition, the peasants had to utilize manure for fuel in winter due to their lack of forest land from which to gather firewood. Lenin, XV, 115. To make matters still worse, there was a general reduction in the quantity of live-

A further obstacle to the introduction of any small improvements on the agro-technical side was the simple fact that initially any changes, whether to new crops or new systems of rotation, would inevitably be accompanied by a reduction in the subsequent harvest for at least one and often as many as five or more years. Thus, any changes would create an unbearable food shortage that in itself would have adverse effects on the peasantry, the livestock, and the soil fertility, and would sabotage the attempted change at its weakest point.[18] On the other hand, while one might assume that the labor surplus that developed in the second half of the nineteenth century might act as a substitute for capital investment in order to help raise the productivity of the land available, in fact this merely increased the number of mouths to feed, made the problem of land hunger more severe, and produced lots too small to permit improvement.[19] In sum, the economic problem resolves itself into two parts: land hunger and low productivity. Meanwhile, the peasantry was becoming ever more impoverished and ever more "pauperized," although each member retained the right to an allotment of land in his community no matter how small that allotment might be.[20]

stock and of draught horses per capita of the population in the years after the Emancipation. Dubrovskii, *Stolypinskaia* . . . , p. 31; Gaister, pp. 61–62; P. P. Maslov, "Krest'ianskoe dvizheniie 1905–1907 g." in *Obshchestvennoe dvizheniie v Rossii v nachale XX.-go veke,* eds. L. Martov, P. Maslov, and A. Potresov, (SPB: Tipografiia T-va "Obshchestvennoe Pol'za," 1910), Vol. II, Part II, pp. 204–8 (hereafter referred to as Maslov, II); Maslov, I, 14; Anfimov, pp. 64–70; Pershin, I, 44, 60; Robinson, pp. 102–3.

[18] See Confino, pp. 303–20 for the problems which faced *pomeshchiki* before 1861 in relation to the introduction of improved methods but which also apply to some extent to the peasantry after 1861.

[19] *Ibid.,* p. 377. The labor surplus has been estimated by the government in 1901 to be some 23 million, or one-half of the adult working population. Dubrovskii, *Stolypinskaia* . . . , p. 31; Dubrovskii, *Krest'ianskoe* . . . , pp. 26–27; Pershin, I, 26. Trotsky estimated the surplus to number five million in the Central Agricultural Region (C.A.R.) alone and as having the effect of lowering productivity by 30 per cent (p. 36). See also Maslov, I, 32–34; Robinson, pp. 98–99.

[20] Maslov, I, 16; Anfimov, p. 377. One of the more perplexing problems that faces the student and one which pervades the Marxist literature is the determination of some relative or even absolute level in the decline of the peasantry's welfare as well as the choice of suitable indicators to demonstrate this development—the underlying assumption being presumably that some point will be reached at which time the peasantry should or would rise up in revolt

III

Although the purely economic aspects of the agrarian problem are very important, there is another aspect which in its political implications had a far greater impact, namely the social.[21] There are three elements to this side of the question: The problem of the peasants' relationships with the *pomeshchiki;* of the peasants' relations with the government and the bureaucracy; and of the internal relations among the peasantry—the problem of *rassloeniie* (class differentiation).

The sociàl dependence of the peasant on the local *pomeshchik* was not, as one might expect, abolished by the Emancipation. In fact, if anything, it increased considerably as a result of the severe economic straits into which the peasant was forced by his deteriorating economic situation. The economic interdependence of the peasant and

---

and usher in the new bourgeois-capitalist order. One such indicator would be the frequency of partial (every three years) and widespread (every ten years) crop failures. Dubrovskii, *Stolypinskaia . . .* p. 30; Dubrovskii, *Krest'ianskoe . . .*, p. 26. Perhaps the best figures to demonstrate the effects of the agrarian crisis on the peasantry are those for military rejects from Orel *guberniia* which rose from 16 per cent in 1875 to 36 per cent in 1890, while for all of Russia they rose from 11.2 per cent in 1874–1875 to 22.1 per cent in 1899–1907. Gaister p. 63. For figures on sickness, crippled, and death rates see Peshekhonov, p. 238. Also see Kaufman, I, 72; Robinson, p. 116.

[21] It is this aspect of the problem, i.e., the class struggle, with which the Marxists are most interested; see Lenin, XV, 93. However, the problem for them is closely connected with determining the nature of the emerging forms of economies, the level of capitalist development in agriculture, and whether this development will follow the Prussian (*pomeshchik*) or American (peasant) path as well as the socioeconomic factors that will support such interpretations. These problems, inseparable from a study of the *pomeshchik* economy, are treated excellently by Anfimov, *passim,* who concludes that the rural economy was right up to 1917 in a predominantly pre-capitalist stage. For Anfimov's dispute with Dubrovskii see both authors in *Osobennosti agrarnogo stroia Rossii v period imperializma,* eds. S. M. Dubrovskii *et al.* (Moscow: Izdatel'stvo ANSSSR, 1962), pp. 5–44, 64–85. For examples of the Marxist approach alluded to, see Lenin, XIII, 220–55; XV, 69–147; Pershin, I, 63–171; M. N. Pokrovsky, *Brief History of Russia,* tr. by D. S. Mirsky, (Orono, Maine: University Prints and Reprints, 1968), II, 23–37; Lyashchenko, *passim;* Gaister, *passim.* For a more balanced account and greater emphasis on social relations in an estate-bureaucratic order see Maslov, I, 1, 36 and *passim.*

the *pomeshchik* in the post-Emancipation period is now an acknowledged fact, and in itself was one of the major causes for the general
backwardness of all branches of Russian agriculture.[22]

This new cycle of peasant oppression was initiated by the fact that
the peasant in the vast majority of cases was forced to seek supplementary means beyond the cultivation of his own allotment by which
he could fulfill his requirements for food and other essential needs.
Primarily this meant renting either more arable land to cultivate or
supplementary pasture and/or forest land in order to enable his
economy to function. In sum, this was "hunger renting." [23] However,
since the peasant did not usually have the capital resources with
which to rent the land for cash, and since the *pomeshchik* himself
was customarily in need of a cheap labor force, the normal form of
payment was by means of labor services, *otrabotka*—essentially a
post-Emancipation form of serfdom's *barshchina*. An alternative
form of payment that was equally as widespread was *ispol'shchina*
—the working of the rented land for a share of the crop, usually
one-half.[24]

Another form of escape from the vicious cycle of poverty was to
turn to wage labor, usually on a *per diem* basis but more and more
frequently on a permanent basis. But this too, as in the case of rent-

[22] For *pomeshchik* agriculture see Anfimov, *passim;* for peasant agriculture
see Lenin, XIII, 234–38, 252, 254–55, 276–83 and *passim;* XV, 136, 144.
Also see Maslov, I, 4.

[23] Dubrovskii, *Stolypinskaia* . . . , pp. 32–38; Peshekhonov, p. 204. In
Marxist literature this problem is usually highlighted by a comparison of the
amounts of land owned by the peasants and the *pomeshchiki* in order to bring
out the social nature of the problem as opposed to the economic. See Dubrovskii, *Stolypinskaia* . . . , pp. 18–19; Lenin, XII, 220–29; XV, 71–75; Gaister,
p. 20; Anfimov, p. 47 and Chapter I.

[24] Anfimov, pp. 53–54; see also for figures Dubrovskii, *Stolypinskaia* . . . ,
p. 21; Peshekhonov, pp. 206–7; Kaufman I, 98; Pershin, I, 36, 89–96; Lenin,
XV, 85, 97–98. The vulnerability of the peasant was, needless to say, exploited to full advantage by the *pomeshchiki,* who were able to dictate the
conditions of renting, frequently setting the *otrabotka* ratio as high as the cultivation of two dessiatines of *pomeshchik* land in return for the use of one
rented dessiatine of arable land. In addition, leases were often highly restric-
tive while cash rentals frequently exceeded the rented land's net income. Further, competition among the peasants themselves for the available land drove
up the rents, which in the 1900s in the C.A.R. reached as high as fifteen rubles
per dessiatine. Dubrovskii, *Stolypinskaia* . . . , pp. 17–23; Dubrovskii,
Krest'ianskoe . . . , pp. 18–19; Anfimov, pp. 89–93; Maslov, I, 13; Gaister,
pp. 145–48; Pershin, I, 89–96; Robinson, pp. 99–100, 290–91.

ing, was a product of need rather than as a result of market forces, while the *pomeshchik*'s exploitation of the situation as well as the huge labor surplus resulted in very long hours averaging from seven hours a day in December to fourteen and one-half hours per day in June. Sometimes it reached as high as twenty hours a day. Concomitantly, wages were held at very low levels, averaging in the 1902–1904 period sixty-four kopecks a day.[25] Another form of wage labor was *otkhodnichestvo,* whereby peasants sought to bring in extra income to the family by means of seasonal or even full-time employment in nonagricultural occupations away from the village. This departure of a proportion of the adult male members of the community, on the one hand, relieved the surplus-labor and the food problems but, on the other hand, often led to a deterioration in the family's productivity. Needless to say, the wage levels for these migratory workers were also quite low, although this depended on where they found work. The total proportion of peasants engaged in such labor was approximately ten million at the turn of the century; yet, while this figure might appear large, it also was no solution to the problem of poverty.[26]

The peasants' relationships with the government were conducted on two levels: the political or administrative and the fiscal. In the first arena there were two institutions of importance, the *mir* and the *zemskii nachal'nik,* both instruments of the exclusive estate structure of society. The government, in part out of its concern for social stability, had with the Emancipation bound the peasant to the land, to which he was granted an inalienable right through his membership in the *mir.* However, the other side of this coin was the fact that the peasant was all but unable to separate from this institution either with or without his share of the land, while to leave it either temporarily for seasonal or permanently for full-time employment in other

[25] Dubrovskii, *Stolypinskaia . . . ,* pp. 27–31; Pershin, I, 120–23; Dubrovskii, *Krest'ianskoe . . . ,* p. 24; Lenin, XV, 118–24; Anfimov, pp. 50–53, 60–62; Robinson, pp. 105–7, 292.

[26] Gaister, pp. 152–58; Kaufman, I, 80 ff.; Lenin, XV, 122–25; Pershin, I, 121–24; Anfimov, pp. 48–49; Robinson, pp. 106–9; Sula Benet, translator and Editor, *The Village of Viriatno, an Ethnographic Study of a Russian Village From Before the Revolution to the Present* (Garden City, N. Y.: Doubleday and Co., 1970), pp. 28–41. For other forms of *pomeshchik* exploitation, see Anfimov, pp. 54, 58–59, 62; Dubrovskii, *Stolypinskaia . . . ,* p. 26; Dubrovskii, *Krest'ianskoe . . . ,* p. 23; Peshekhonov, pp. 204–5; Pershin, I, 33–35, 41.

localities he had to obtain a passport through the *mir* authorities.[27] By freezing the peasants' mobility this system was, thus, responsible for the surplus of labor in the countryside and as such both a cause and a perpetuater of the peasants' impoverished existence.

The *mir,* although nominally an instrument of peasant self-government, was in fact nothing more than an extension of the government bureaucracy. Nor was it any longer an autonomous institution, for in 1889 it had been placed under the almost complete control of the *zemskii nachal'nik,* a local official exercising both police and judicial as well as executive authority. Thus, the door was opened to all kinds of legal abuses of the peasant and the exploitation of his position as a member of a special and subordinate estate. Like many other aspects of rural life, this situation bore a remarkable similarity to that which the peasant had endured before the authority of the *pomeshchik* in the days of serfdom.[28]

The other level of the peasants' relationship with the government was fiscal,[29] and made up of two components: redemption payments for the land which they had been alloted with the Emancipation, and taxes. These latter included the poll tax (abolished in 1886), the government land tax (reduced by one-half in 1896), *zemstvo* land taxes

[27] The instrument by which this totally embracing control of the peasant *mir* was exercised was that of *krugovaia poruka* (mutual responsibility, abolished in 1903) which in itself was the government's method for securing its financial interest in the peasant. Thus, each member of the commune was mutually responsible for every other member's fulfillment of his share of the *mir*'s taxes and redemption payments and, therefore, had a vested interest in the retention of all of its members. The problem of migration to Siberia is particularly instructive, for, while this could provide no long-term solution to the problems of European Russia, it exemplified the government's obsession with peasant immobility. Thus, not until the 1880s did resettlement become legally permissable, while the doors to Siberia were not finally thrown open until 1906. Peshekhonov, pp. 212–13; Maslov, I, 17–21; Kaufman, I, 87 ff.; Lenin, XIII, 247–54; Oganovskii, pp. 30–53; Robinson, pp. 109–10.

[28] Dubrovskii, *Stolypinskaia* . . . , pp. 27, 66–85; Maslov, I, 5–9; Gershenkron, pp. 765–67, 768–76, 785; Robinson, pp. 78–80, 124–25, 131–32; Dubrovskii, *Krest'ianskoe* . . . , p. 24.

[29] Writers such as Peshekhonov cite the government's tax policies as one of the major causes for the disintegration of traditional peasant life and for the transfer of the peasant economy from a state of natural economy to one of a market or money economy since the peasants were forced to sell their labor and goods in order to meet their taxes. Thus, it was on the backs of the peasants that the government ushered the country into the industrial era (pp. 224–25). See also Kaufman, II, 29; Confino, pp. 367–68.

and duties, *mir* duties, other special duties such as the recruitment tax, and a whole series of indirect taxes on items such as vodka, sugar, tobacco, salt, kerosene, and matches. The most important taxes were the indirect, which comprised approximately two-thirds of the peasants' tax burden. Figures on this aspect of the peasants' life are extremely difficult to analyze and compare. However, two statements it seems can be made. First, that the tax burden borne by the peasantry increased over the period in question while the assessment placed on the peasant was anywhere from ten to fifty times more than that placed on the noble agriculturalist. As a result the peasant payed about 90 per cent of the tax levied on agriculture as a whole, although this was in effect an indirect tax on the *pomeshchiki* themselves. Further, in most areas the peasant assessment exceeded the ability of the allotment alone to pay, while on average it probably consisted of upwards of 50 per cent of the peasant's gross revenue. The most significant indicator of all, however, is the growth of peasant tax arrears, which by 1900 had reached 119 per cent of the average annual assessment between 1896 and 1900. And this took no account of local taxes, the extent of which little is known.[30]

Finally, we must turn to the problem of intrapeasant social relations, to *rassloeniie*.[31] The only conclusion that it seems possible

[30] This indicator is frequently used also as one of the peasantry's general economic decline. One must, however, be cautious in the utilization of this tool, for as Emmons, pp. 70–71, notes, arrears were permitted to accumulate by the state without there being any open confrontation, and as such they served as a safety valve and as a substitute for agrarian disturbances. On the other hand, the peasants had frequently to sell their crops at harvest time when the prices were lowest in order to pay taxes. Thus, they were forced into still greater dependence on their local nobility when by the beginning of winter they had to borrow grain—often their very own grain that the *pomeshchik* had hoarded for just this speculative purpose. See Dubrovskii, *Stolypinskaia* . . . , pp. 24–26; Lyashchenko, pp. 424–44, 446–47; Robinson, pp. 85–96, 110–11; Gershenkron, pp. 786, 768–69, 779–81; Maslov, I, 4–5; II, 203; Gaister, pp. 60, 104, 164–65; Peshekhonov, pp. 215–35; Dubrovskii, *Krest'ianskoe* . . . , pp. 21–23; Lenin, XV, 109–12.

[31] This problem is one of prominent concern to the Marxists, who raise it in connection with almost every presentation of statistics concerning the peasantry and who relate it to every problem that has been discussed so far in this paper in their attempt to give evidence of the precipitation of a bourgeoisie and a proletariat out of the mass of the peasantry and of the ripeness of the countryside for the bourgeois-capitalist revolution. However, the major theoretical question—whether in fact one can determine the formation of a bourgeois class of peasants by means of statistics concerning the amount of land

to draw with any validity from the data presented in the literature in this field is that the peasantry in European Russia fell into three groups: the prosperous (20 per cent), the middle (30 per cent), and the poor (50 per cent). Similarly, it may be concluded that the poorer peasants were harder pressed by the agricultural crisis while the more prosperous were able through their initially better circumstances to accumulate more resources—including larger families. For it is clear from the statistics that greater supplies of one resource encouraged the accumulation of greater supplies of others. On the other hand, one finds that those peasants with improved implements or who possessed machinery were frequently more heavily exploited by the *pomeshchiki* than their poorer brethren.[32]

IV

Having thus covered the economic and social backgrounds of the agrarian problem in Russia at the turn of the century, we are now brought face to face with the ultimate expression of rural despair as the peasants sought one final path of escape from their increasingly burdensome situation—the path of peasant revolution. Prior to a discussion of the revolution of 1905–1907, however, we shall turn to those preliminary events of 1902 which took place in the *gubernii* of Poltava and Khar'kov on the Left Bank of the Ukraine.[33] The significance of these events for the study of the peasant movement is quite clear. For the "miniature revolution" on the Left Bank brought into

---

held in allotment, rental, or ownership, the number of horses owned and the proportion of improved agricultural implements possessed—is left completely unresolved and brings into question the whole undertaking. This problem is further compounded by the fact that in many instances, as for example in the case of the Cossacks, the prosperous were geographically separated from the pauperized.

[32] Lenin, XIII, 220–31 and *passim;* XV, 80, 96, 101, 105, 112, 117 and *passim;* see also Lenin's *The Development of Capitalism in Russia* (Moscow: Foreign Languages Press, 1956), *passim;* Pershin, I, 108–34 and Chapter II; Maslov, I, 15–16, 25, 34–35; Dubrovskii, *Stolypinskaia . . . ,* p. 29; Dubrovskii, *Krest'ianskoe . . . ,* pp. 27, 30–31; Gaister, pp. 29–35, 70–83, and *passim;* Lyashchenko, pp. 455–61; Anfimov, pp. 69–72; Robinson, pp. 111–16.

[33] For a study of the whole pre-1905 period, including Saratov, where 1902 was also a year of exceptional disorders, see S. M. Dubrovskii and B. Grave, "Krest'ianskoe dvizheniie nakanune revoliutsii 1905 goda (1900–1904 gg.)" in M. N. Pokrovskii (ed.) *1905,* Vol. I, *Predposylki revoliutsii* (Moscow/Leningrad: Gosudarstvennoe izdatel'stvo, 1925), pp. 233–392 *passim.*

sharp focus the economic and social aspects of the peasant's discontent as he was caught in the vise of advancing social and economic exploitation brought on by the rapidly developing modernization and market orientation of the surrounding *pomeshchik* agriculture. This had begun, as has already been indicated, in the second half of the 1890s and was a consequence of the improving market conditions that accompanied the end of the international agricultural crisis. Thus, this "buffer zone" which was caught between the most backward (the Central Agricultural Region) and the most advanced areas (the Southern Steppe) of grain production exemplified the worst aspects of both pre-capitalist and developing capitalist forms of exploitation. Above all, it was the dynamic rate of change that was affecting *pomeshchik* and consequently also peasant agriculture which acted as the catalyst for these disorders rather than any particular level of impoverishment.[34] Thus, we will examine first the economic conditions in this area, then the dynamics of economic and social change, and lastly the psychological dynamic that finally brought on the disturbances.[35]

The mass movement broke out between March 25 and April 2, 1902, in Konstantinograd and Poltava uezds in Poltava *guberniia* and Valkovskii and Bogodukhovskii uezds in Khar'kov *guberniia*. The economic conditions in these four uezds were among the most oppressive in European Russia. At the time of the Emancipation many of the peasants had been freed without any allotments while many others were *darstvenniki* who had received only one-quarter of

[34] We will return to this problem again in this section, but see Anfimov, pp. 148–57, 182–84; Dubrovskii, *Krest'ianskoe . . .* , pp. 28–30; B. B. Veselovskii (ed.), *Krest'ianskoe dvizheniie 1902 goda* (Moscow / Leningrad: Gosudarstvennoe izdatel'stvo. 1923), pp. 4, 49, 50–51, 107; Dubrovskii and Grave, pp. 237–49 and especially pp. 246 and 301. Dubrovskii and Grave, pp. 242, 304, specifically identify the threat of proletarianization and the imminent separation of the petty producer from the means of production (the land) as the cause of the 1902 disorders. However, this does not seem to be borne out by the evidence. The problem was one of pauperization rather than one of proletarianization.

[35] For excellent descriptions and analyses of the causes see the letters of Kovalenskii and Semenov and the testimony of the *starost'* of the village of Maksimovka concerning the robbing of one of the properties of the Karlovka estate in Veselovskii, pp. 47–56, 58–60, 61–63, 64–113. For an English language summary and narrative, see Craig Merle Dean, "Poltava Guberniia, 1900–1917: A Case Study of Revolution in the Provinces," (unpublished M.A. Essay, Columbia University, 1966), pp. 1–54.

the standard allotment. Thus, with the increase in population, and despite considerable migration, the average allotment sizes at the time of the outbreaks were often less than one-quarter of a dessiatine of arable per male soul and even as little as the *usad'ba* (household) plot alone. There were also severe shortages of pasture and forest land.[36] At the same time, however, this shortage of land must be contrasted with the great concentrations of *pomeshchik* land which surrounded and enveloped the peasantry in these areas.[37]

The alternatives that were open to the peasantry were limited. Land was extremely expensive to rent, with prices rising as high as eighteen rubles per dessiatine for cash rentals. In the case of *otrabotka* renting, dues were as high as the harvesting and cartage of the grain on two-three dessiatines in return for the use of one dessiatine of arable or pasture land.[38] In addition, the purchasing of land was particularly hard, for prices had risen to 300 to 350 rubles per dessiatine.[39] The other alternative for the peasants was wage labor on the surrounding capital intensive and semimechanized *pomeshchik* properties, where wages were as low as five kopecks a day.[40] Then, to further aggravate the situation, there was a harvest failure in 1901—and this in a zone where in normal years there was insufficient grain produced to feed the inhabitants.[41] There was also a crop

[36] For example, in Maksimovka village in Konstantinograd uezd, 657 persons in the first village had only 28 dessiatines of land while 413 in the second village had 32 dessiatines. Fifteen of the communities that participated in the disorders had no allotments at all. Veselovskii, p. 75. See also *Ibid.,* pp. 8, 50, 54, 56; Pershin, I, 228; Dubrovskii and Grave, pp. 301–3. The conditions were only slightly less severe in Khar'kov *guberniia.* Veselovskii, pp. 76–79.

[37] For example, the 5,549 private landowners (those with properties exceeding fifty dessiatines) in Poltava in 1910 averaged 193 dessiatines each, while the 442,900 peasants in that *guberniia* averaged only 6 dessiatines each. The 351 largest properties averaged 1,460 dessiatines each while, the ten properties of the Herzog Meklenburg-Strelitskii totaled 123,800 dessiatines. Anfimov, pp. 151, 384.

[38] Veselovskii, pp. 8, 56, 59, 76–77; Dubrovskii and Grave, p. 304.

[39] Veselovskii, pp. 80–81; Pershin, I, 85; Pokrovsky, II, 58–59.

[40] Veselovskii, p. 56. The wages were so low in fact that even day laborers starved. See also Dubrovskii and Grave, p. 305.

[41] In 1901 the area was short by some seven million *pud* @ 50 kopecks, a total of 3.5 million rubles. 75% of all economies in Konstantinograd uezd—the center of the disturbances—had insufficient grain and 54% in Poltava uezd. Veselovskii, p. 75. For figures on yields see Pershin, I, 46–47, 48–49, 55, 228; Pokrovsky, II, 60; Dubrovskii and Grave, p. 304.

failure in potatoes, an important item in the peasant diet of this area.[42] As a consequence people had to engage in such destructive practices as feeding their livestock the straw from the roofs of their houses.[43]

Another factor of considerable importance was the conjunction of this economic crisis among the peasantry with the industrial recession which had begun in 1899 and which had had the effect of returning large numbers of *otkhodniki* from the cities to the Left Bank, increasing the competition for work and lowering the wage levels. The impact of the recession was also felt by the sugar processing industry, which was of vital significance in this region, and that also contributed to lowering wage levels and raising competition among the peasants for the available jobs.[44]

As bad as the economic situation was, however, the most important aspect from the point of view of how the disturbances began was the fact that the *pomeshchik* economies in these areas—as also in the South-West and the Southern Steppe—had since the late 1890s been undergoing a process of intensification and modernization. This was particularly important in Konstantinograd uezd, the center of the movement, where the Karlovka estate of Meklenburg-Strelitskii, one of the most advanced capitalist estates in all Russia, was located. In 1899 there had been only one distilling plant and steam-mill on this property. But from that year on there began construction on sugar-beet, starch, and brick plants. Between 1893 and 1914 the value of all of the estate's inventory rose five times to 2.314 million rubles while the arable land cultivated by the estate increased between 1899 and 1913 from 12,400 to 25,500 dessiatines (out of a total area of 57,000 dessiatines), of which 3,760 dessiatines were under sugar-beet and 12,000 under wheat. There were also large increases in the numbers of daily, periodical and permanent workers employed (some 140 workers were employed in the workshops to service the agricultural machinery alone). Similarly, the estate adopted the newest agro-technical systems of rotation and the use of mineral fertilizers. However, *otrabotka* was not abandoned, especially in relation to harvesting, where the absolute area harvested by this means increased—although the proportion was reduced between 1893/94 and 1913/14 from 95 per cent to under 50 per cent. Thus, between

[42] Dubrovskii and Grave, p. 307.   [43] Veselovskii, pp. 54, 58, 61.
[44] *Ibid.*, p. 99; Dubrovskii and Grave, pp. 251, 305.

1893 and 1914 the estate's income multiplied ten times to 3.2 million rubles and profits doubled.[45]

The result of these changes was not only to increase peasant exploitation but also to rupture the rather precarious equilibrium that had existed in peasant/*pomeshchik* relations until their appearance. The introduction of multicrop rotation systems led to reductions in fallow land for the pasturing of peasant livestock while the cultivation of new crops led to a reduction in the area available for the production of the vital grain/food supply. Since this was generally accompanied by an expansion of *pomeshchik* arable land such changes inevitably led also to a sharp reduction in the amount of land available for renting. And it was these kinds of changes which were so significant. For while the peasant might tolerate land hunger it seemed that he could not accept the fact that there was no longer any land to rent.[46] Just as with the violation of their pattern of life by the Emancipation in 1861, the peasants had reacted with unrest and disturbances, so now with the new violations to their traditional system of values and the new patterns of impoverishment they again responded with uprisings. And it is just this difference which explains, for example, why there were virtually no disorders following the famines of 1872 and 1891/92. The peasant's value system in more normal times accepted such acts of fate as inevitable and as a natural part of his life, and death.[47] And these aspects of a traditional way of life were reinforced by the religious order which accepted such natural disasters as the will of God and His punishment for the sins of mankind.[48] But with the turn of the century and the new violations of the traditional *pomeshchik*/peasant relationship the ground was set for the peasant to stop recognizing the *pomeshchik*'s right of private property and to take decisive action in order to regain the utilization of that land which it seemed had been taken from him by the *pomeshchik*.[49]

[45] Anfimov, pp. 75, 152–54, 199. Similar details can be seen for the two uezds in Khar'kov *guberniia* in Veselovskii, pp. 8, 50–51.

[46] Maslov, II, 232.

[47] See L. A. Owen, *The Russian Peasant Movement, 1905–1917* (New York: Russell and Russell, 1963), pp. 9–10; Benet, p. 37; Mary Matossian, "The Peasant Way of Life," in *The Peasant in Nineteenth-Century Russia*, ed. Wayne S. Vucinich (Stanford: Stanford University Press, 1968) pp. 39–40.

[48] Pershin, I, 59–60.

[49] The importance of the factor of economic "change" in the 1902 disorders is confirmed by an analysis of the social composition of the owners of 68 es-

Thus, we have summarized the economic factors which were of decisive importance in the appearance of the outbreaks. However, three further elements were necessary in order to make these outbreaks possible—for, indeed, while the economic conditions on the Left Bank were similar to, if more severe, than those which afflicted other areas, especially the Central Agricultural Region, a mass movement broke out only in 1902 in Poltava and Khar'kov *gubernii*. These factors were : (1) a loss of faith in the authorities; (2) the appearance of revolutionary propaganda; and (3) the development of an ideology to justify the illegal actions that the peasants were about to undertake.

The first of these, the loss of faith in the authorities, state, zemstvo, local and clerical, was a consequence of their total inability and unpreparedness to assist the peasantry in its hour of need as well as of the uselessness of the palliatives of the past fifty years.[50] And even when the peasants sought out assistance from the authorities directly —and they had seen the local *zemskii nachal'nik* perhaps once or twice since his office had been established—the authorities were unable and unprepared to respond and so contributed to the peasants' sense of alienation and helplessness. Left with no alternative, the peasants were forced to turn to the neighboring *pomeshchiki* for help. But with few exceptions they too responded with apathy to peasant demands for more land to rent, for lighter renting conditions, and for distributions of grain, potatoes, and fodder for cattle.[51] Thus, all of the peasants' traditional authorities, but especially the government, had failed them when they were needed most.

To this already smoldering fire there was added the fuel of revolutionary propaganda.[52] That some subversive activity was being conducted in the area of the disorders during the months of February and March 1902 was evidenced by the fact that the police had found

---

tates that were robbed of grain. Thus, 60 per cent were owned or operated by *raznochinets* landowners and renters; 10 per cent by absentee *dvoriane;* and 30 per cent by *dvoriane* who lived on the properties—and three of whom were women and employed managers. This 30 per cent included all who had transferred to new types of agriculture. Veselovskii, p. 84.

[50] This breakdown and loss of faith is well documented in Veselovskii, pp. 9, 52, 53, 54, 60, 61, 71–73, 85–98, 103.

[51] *Ibid.,* pp. 9–10, 23, 53, 58, 61, 64–65; Owen, pp. 10–12; Pershin, I, 227.

[52] Much information on this aspect is given in the reports and letters of Lopukhin, procurer of the Khar'kov *sudebnaia palata,* who with Pleve, the Minister of the Interior, felt that propaganda was the major cause for the Ukrainian disorders. Veselovskii, pp. 17–39.

revolutionary proclamations in some six uezds, and two groups had been placed under surveillance, a Ukrainophile group and the Poltava committee of the RSDRP (Social-Democrats).[53] More important than this, however, was the presence of the two brothers Alekseienko, who had been expelled from the University of Khar'kov for their participation in the December 3, 1901, disorders and who had returned to the village of Licich'ia immediately afterward to live with their mother. These brothers subsequently became the center of a small revolutionary group—presumably of the *kruzhok* variety—that was not apparently affiliated with any of the regular party organizations.[54] Thus, into the very center of the troubles was introduced an outside element which, in combination with the other elements, acted as a catalyst to impel the peasants to action in defense of their interests.[55] The next stage of the process was the crystallization in the peasants' consciousness of an ideology to justify the proposed actions against the surrounding landowners.

The peasants' own experience, as we have seen, had led them to lose faith in the authorities. To this was added the impact of the propaganda, much of which was antigovernmental in nature. The result was a search for a new authority that would permit them to escape from the oppressive conditions. This new authority they "discovered" in many guises, depending on their own predilections. Some found it

---

[53] *Ibid.*, pp. 19–20, 17–21. In addition there had been police reports concerning the presence of Moscow students in the area. For examples of revolutionary literature see *Ibid.*, pp. 29–31. See also Dubrovskii and Grave, p. 306.

[54] Veselovskii, p. 28; Pokrovsky, II, 61–62.

[55] S. R. (Social-Revolutionary Party) participation was not revealed by the authorities or by the documents, although S. N. Sletov in his *K istorii vozniknoveniia P.S.-R* (Petrograd: n.p., 1917), pp. 56–57, noted that there had been S. R. activity in the area for some twelve years prior to these events. See O. H. Radkey, *The Agrarian Foes of Bolshevism* (New York and London: Columbia University Press, 1962) p. 57. One should also beware of such assertions as those of Pershin, I, 229, who claims that 1,859 illegal publications were distributed in Poltava *guberniia* between January 1 and August 1, 1902, since it is most probable that the majority of these were distributed after the disorders and in particular during the trials of the participants. Finally, the presence of propaganda activity should not lead one to suppose that the movement was an organized one. On the contrary, it was purely spontaneous, while its spread to other uezds was accomplished mainly through the process of example and imitation. In this connection see Veselovskii, pp. 24, 63; and Dubrovskii and Grave, pp. 364–77.

in the rumors which began to circulate in the area shortly before the outbreaks.[56] According to one report there was in existence a letter which granted to the peasants all the moveable property of the *pomeshchiki* while at the same time it proclaimed that the courts would cease to function for the next three years.[57] In another it was claimed that the Tsar, whose will was frustrated by the bureaucratic and clerical authorities, had gone abroad to visit his mother-in-law and had ordered Prince Mikhail, and/or the generals, to carry out his will and distribute land to the peasants.[58]

Clearly, then, a process of selection had taken place in the peasant's mind as he chose those elements of the propaganda and rumors that conformed to his own consciousness, desires, and dreams. Two elements of the peasant's traditional system of values, his belief and trust in the Tsar, and the belief that the land was somehow his [59]— or at least that he had a right to the *pomeshchik*'s grain—combined with his dissatisfaction toward the landowners and the authorities, here distinguished from the Tsar, and with all of his most unrealizable hopes and expectations for a distribution of land. Thus, the peasant was able to reconcile his loyalty to the Tsar with his opposition to the authorities, and he began to interpret revolutionary proclamations as Tsarist ukazes. In this manner all of his wildest dreams and chimeras seemed to be sanctioned by the Tsar, and the time for their realization seemed to have arrived.[60] Then, as the disorders began to break out, the pressures upon the peasants became so intense that they convinced themselves that these rumors and stories actually did show a path of escape, and so created for themselves a form of justi-

[56] One must not, however, exaggerate the belief of the peasantry in rumors since this was in part a defensive ruse adopted by the peasants when they were brought to task by the authorities and when it served them best to appear ignorant. At the same time the more conscious among them exploited the rumors to attract support from the less conscious. Dubrovskii and Grave, pp. 361–63.

[57] Veselovskii, p. 47.

[58] *Ibid.*, pp. 51–52, 63, 103–4. Note also how the Prince wore an overcoat and was recognizable only to the initiated.

[59] A conception that had been if anything strengthened by the whole experience of the Emancipation and confirmed by the practice of renting. See Sir John Maynard, *Russia in Flux Before the October Revolution* (New York: Collier Books, 1968), p. 43.

[60] Veselovskii, pp. 51–52, 103; Owen, p. 13; see also Emmons, pp. 47–71 for a discussion of peasant psychology with regard to the peasant's reactions to the Emancipation.

fication for their actions.[61] Further, when it became clear that they were able to rob the estates with impunity—especially in Poltava *guberniia* where the disturbances subsided before the intervention of any authorities—they were only encouraged in their belief that the robbery was justified.[62] Then the disorders broke out on a hitherto unprecedented scale. In all, some 174 communities and 38,000 peasants participated in the disorders, which were characterized by a widespread solidarity of all layers—although it is true that the poorest peasants participated more frequently than the more prosperous.[63]

V

The social and economic conditions which served as the background and which helped bring about the disorders on the Left Bank of the Ukraine in 1902, while perhaps unique in their intensity, nevertheless held much in common with those in every region of Euro-

---

[61] Veselovskii, pp. 9–10, 63, 101, 103–6.   [62] *Ibid.*, p. 48.

[63] Pershin, I, 227. These figures do not agree with and are somewhat lower than those given by Dubrovskii and Grave, p. 311. Perhaps the best proof that the ultimate origin of these disorders lay in need is the fact that of the 78 estates seized by troubles only six suffered the destruction of their *usad'by*. Veselovskii, p. 62. On the other hand, Dubrovskii and Grave, pp. 310–11, assert that the destruction of property was considerable—the goals being the destruction of the *pomeshchik*'s material basis for economic dominance, the acquisition of his land, and the driving out of the *pomeshchiki* from the countryside. However, while this may have been true of Saratov, it does not apply to the Ukraine at this time. See also in this connection Maynard, p. 62. The impact of the disorders was not limited to the Left Bank of the Ukraine, as has already been suggested. Echos were heard in the *gubernii* of Kursk, Voronezh, Ekaterinoslav, Chernigov, Saratov, Stavropol'ia, Georgia, and elsewhere. But, while these areas may have shared some of the same conditions, nowhere did the movement achieve more than a sporadic and isolated nature. Pershin, I, 230; Dubrovskii and Grave, p. 315. One important point in relation to the 1902 uprising concerns the nature of peasant landownership in Poltava, for government officials considered that a major factor in these troubles was the instability of repartitional land tenure. In fact, however, hereditary-household (*podvornyi*) tenure predominated in Poltava, comprising 82.1 per cent of the total number of households and 85.4 per cent of the cultivated land area. Dubrovskii, *Stolypinskaia* . . . , p. 572; Dean, p. 8; Watters, pp. 146–47; Jerome Blum, *Lord and Peasant From the Ninth to the Nineteenth Centuries* (New York: Atheneum, 1965) p. 522; Robinson, p. 145.

pean Russia.[64] By 1905 they had only been given an opportunity to become more developed. However, we shall not again go over those economic aspects which have already been covered in the earlier sections of this paper.[65] Rather, we shall turn our attention to some of the more important differences between 1902 and 1905–1907, as well as consider some of the new elements.

Two aspects are particularly important and are closely interrelated in their catalytic roles: the general expansion of the horizons of peasant knowledge and experience and of contact with the other worlds that made up Russia; and the role of the Russo-Japanese War in the total loss of faith and belief in the government and in the breakdown of authority. The importance of the war, and of the mass mobilization of the reserves for the first time, cannot be underestimated. Initially, its effect was the removal of the strongest working hands from the villages and the loss of the heads of families—which of course had deleterious economic consequences. Then, as the war progressed, special collections of taxes began to increase. The two factors together began to accelerate the rate of economic disintegration while identifying the war with the peasants' ever-increasing oppression. To the significance of these events, however, the fact was added that with the war large numbers of newspapers and other informatory materials began to penetrate the countryside and to reach the proverbially "dark" peasantry. At first, their curiosity was spurred by a sense of patriotic interest and concern for a war in which so many of their compatriots were fighting. But with the ceaseless news of retreats, defeats, and casualties these papers served to turn the peasants toward

[64] The differences in the economic characteristics of the various regions of European Russia are quite considerable. See Anfimov, pp. 94–176; Pershin, I, 67–79, 240–43; Maslov, I, 9–12; *Agrarnoe dvizheniie v Rossii v 1905–1906gg.* III otdeleniie imperatorskago VEO ottisk iz "Trudov I.E.V.O." 2 Vols. (SPB: Tipografiia t-va "Obshchestvennaia Pol'za," 1908), *passim,* hereafter referred to as *Agrarnoe dvizheniie.* . . .

[65] For details and examples of the role of economic and social change as catalytic factors in the revolution of 1905–1907 similar to those already discussed in connection with 1902, see *Agrarnoe dvizheniie,* I, 39, 50, 59, 96, 178, 231; II, 9, 10, 19–20, 27–29, 309–12, 425–26, 429, 431; and on the role of landed relations in general, *Ibid.,* I, 7–10, 15, 19, 152, 165–66, 359, 362; II, 291–92, 424. For reports concerning the role of revolutionary propaganda and agitation, see *Ibid.,* I, 41, 49, 77–78, 87, 174, 363; II, 25–26, 290, 417; for rumors see *Ibid.,* I, 3, 6, 41, 49, 86–87, 95; II, 16, 26, 302 and particularly I, 169 and II, 314 and 326; also see Owen, p. 2.

politics. And the popular mind, beginning to search for those on whom it could place the guilt of these disasters, started turning, unwillingly at first but nevertheless turning, toward those for whom they had already built up large reserves of hostility—the *pomeshchiki* and the authorities.[66]

However, the war was not all that the countryside read about in the newspapers, which also contained news of the growing opposition movement in the cities, of assassinations of government ministers, of workers' strikes, of the hopes that were raised by Sviatopolk-Mirskii's "spring," and all of the other events of a political nature that were stirring the country. Then, with the events of "Bloody Sunday," the tempo speeded up while the newspapers became freer in their ability to report about and comment upon the news. There followed the final and humiliating defeats at Mukden in March and Tsushima in May 1905. From every side it appeared that the government was totally useless, inept, corrupt, inefficient, and completely divorced from the needs and expectations of the country. This newly developed consciousness concerning the government as a whole, fed to some extent by the activity of the opposition movement, combined with a similar consciousness concerning the authorities on the local level to bring about a complete and utter loss of faith and trust in the constituted authority and a belief in its total breakdown, similar to that which had occurred in 1902 on the Left Bank of the Ukraine but on a far wider scale.[67] Similarly, this breakdown was reflected in the religious sphere, where at first the peasants' traditional value system had sustained them in their acceptance of the war and the accompanying suffering as an inevitable and unchangeable part of their life. However, here too the burden was too great and acceptance became transformed into rejection, support of the authorities into hatred, and respect into fear.[68]

Apart from the newspapers, there were several other aspects of Russian life in the countryside which contributed to the broadening

---

[66] *Narodnoe Delo. Sbornik.* (Paris: Izdaniie Ts.K. Partii Sotsialistov Revoliutsionnerov, 1909–1912) 7 vols., II, 62–63, 77; VII, 183–84; Pershin, I, 249; Owen, pp. 17–18; Dubrovskii, *Krest'ianskoe . . . ,* pp. 144–45; *Agrarnoe dvizheniie . . . ,* I, 49, 123.

[67] See *Narodnoe Delo,* II, 62–63, 77; II, 183–84; *Agrarnoe dvizheniie . . . ,* I, 5, 13, 46, 170, 223, 239, 362; Owen, p. 18. See also concerning the role of newspapers *Agrarnoe dvizheniie . . . ,* I, 6, 41, 49, 150, 174; II, 290.

[68] Benet, p. 161; Maynard, p. 91.

of peasant consciousness. One of these was, of course, the expansion of literacy which followed the Reforms of 1864 and the gradual if ineffective penetration of primary education to the village level either through the church or the zemstvos.[69] This increasing literacy, while measured at a rate of only 17 per cent in 1897 in the countryside, was far higher among such strategic sections of the peasantry as the youth and the migratory workers or *otkhodniki*—two groups that often overlapped and which played an important role in the development of peasant consciousness.[70]

As has been suggested by this account, the agrarian movement of 1905 generally broke out spontaneously and spread by example, while the active role which the oppositional and revolutionary parties played was minimal—although it increased significantly in 1906.[71] Nevertheless, it would be wrong to deny the fact that contact with industrial centers, with the cities and with workers as workers and/or as members of the RSDRP or the P.S.-R had any influence.[72] However, while there is evidence of party activity in some *gubernii,* it seems more correct to note that this work was sporadic, developed mostly after the revolution had got under way, and was in the main limited to rural areas around the major cities or around factories, plants, or mines.[73] The only major exceptions to this were in the Baltic provinces, the Caucasus, the CAR, and Saratov, where the role of revolutionary parties was quite significant.[74]

[69] See for example J. S. Curtiss, "The Peasant and the Army," in *The Peasant in Nineteenth-Century Russia,* ed. Wayne S. Vucinich, (Stanford: Stanford University Press, 1968), pp. 129–30; Radkey, p. 60.

[70] Benet, pp. 129, 161 and Chapter VI. For the role of youth in 1902, see Dubrovskii and Grave, pp. 309, 348–50, 354; Pokrovsky, II, 58, 66.

[71] The various Marxist attitudes toward this question can be seen in Lyashchenko, p. 741; *Istoriia SSSR,* Pervaia Seriia, Vol. VI, ed. A. L. Sidorov and others, *Rossiia v period imperializma 1900–1917 gg.* (Moscow: Izdatel'stvo "Nauka," 1968), p. 142; Pershin, I, 269; Trotsky, p. 171 ff. Dubrovskii, *Krest'ianskoe . . . ,* pp. 47–48, comes closest to calling it organized. See also *Agrarnoe dvizheniie . . . ,* I, 6, 7–9, 174, 363; II, 288–89, 290, 418.

[72] See, for example, *Agrarnoe dvizheniie . . . ,* I, 7–9, 169, 364.

[73] Dubrovskii, *Krest'ianskoe . . . ,* pp. 130, 132, 133, 140, 158, and Chapter VI; Pershin, I, 238; Maslov, II, 250; Radkey, pp. 60–64.

[74] Dubrovskii, *Krest'ianskoe . . . ,* p. 35; Pershin, I, 235; Robinson, p. 158. Also see Dubrovskii, *Krest'ianskoe . . . ,* pp. 47–48, 163, for an extreme statement of the importance of RSDRP propaganda activity. An additional work on this question is P. I. Klimov, *Revoliutsionnaia deiatel'nost' rabochikh v derevne v 1905–1907 gg.* (Moscow: Izdatel'stvo Sotsekgiz, 1960).

VI

The events of 1905–1907 bear out what has so far been said in relation to 1902 concerning the socioeconomic origins of the revolutionary movement. Thus, from the available data [75] it can be concluded that the movement was most severe in those areas with the highest levels of development of capitalist agriculture but which were at the same time most highly dependent on such exploitative, precapitalist forms as renting and *otrabotka*—that is to say, the areas with the greatest interdependence of *pomeshchik* and peasant agriculture and with the most highly developed peasant/*pomeshchik* class struggle. Specifically, this category is composed of the Ukraine, the Volga, and the Southern Steppe. Similarly, areas with the highest proportions of pre-capitalist survivals, such as the CAR and Georgia, were also particularly subject to uprisings. The major exceptions to these conclusions are the Baltic provinces, which were characterized by a highly developed large-scale *pomeshchik* capitalist agriculture on the Prussian model and conducted with a very high proportion of wage labor. However, the extremely high degree of activity on the part of the revolutionary parties was undoubtedly the cause of this anomaly, and together with the role of the cities and the *otkhodniki* was also responsible for the severity of the movement in the Lake region. However, both of these regions tended to have more in common with the workers' movement rather than with that of the peasants. [76] In this connection it should be noted that the higher the level of capitalist development and the more the struggle centered around the problems of wages and, secondarily, of renting, the more organized was the movement and the greater the proportion of agricultural strikes. Similarly, the greater the survivals of pre-capitalist forms, the more the struggle centered around the problems of land utilization and, secondarily, renting, and the greater was the proportion of destructive and violent forms of the movement. Correspondingly, where the struggle was less severe, as in the Urals, the CIR, and the North, the forms of the movement were more moderate. [77]

---

[75] Dubrovskii, *Krest'ianskoe* . . . , pp. 38, 42, 60–61; Pershin, I, 239–41; Maslov, II, 204–8, 277; *Agrarnoe dvizheniie* . . . , II, 162–64.

[76] Dubrovskii, *Krest'ianskoe* . . . , pp. 60, 62; Pershin, I, 245–46; Anfimov, pp. 187–88. See also Pershin, I, 67–79, 240–43.

[77] Pershin, I, 245–46; Maslov, II, 229. See also Pershin, I, 67–79, 240–43.

An important feature of the peasant movement was that many of its forms had a symbolic function behind which were hidden the true goals of the peasantry.[78] Thus, the *razgrom* (destruction of property) movement, as well as the burnings which frequently accompanied it, had as its main goals the liberation of *pomeshchik* land for distribution to the peasantry and the driving of its owners from the countryside. In addition, by the destruction of buildings, inventory, and machines it was hoped that the *pomeshchik* could be prevented from conducting his estate in a normal and profitable manner and so forced to offer land for rent.[79] These same goals can also be seen behind the widespread destruction of sugar-beet and distilling plants, although such actions also had the more specific goal of liberating land under potatoes and sugar beets for renting and for the cultivation of grain.[80]

The other great symbolic form was the strike which, in essence, was quite dissimilar from that of the urban workers. Here the aims of the peasantry were twofold. First, there was the goal of attempting to improve working conditions, including a reduction in the number of hours and an increase in wages. However, in many instances such demands were accompanied by one of two other elements. In some localities demands for improved conditions were conjoined with demands for the release of more land for renting and for improving rental conditions. In other localities the demands for wages and improved conditions were pitched so high, or the demands for reduced rents pitched so low, as to make their fulfillment impossible. Their goal was similar to that of the *razgrom* movement, the hope being to make it impossible for the *pomeshchik* to conduct his economy, to

[78] Geographically, the different forms of the movement were distributed as follows: actions in relation to rented land predominated on the Left and Right Banks of the Ukraine, in the Southern Steppe, and in the CAR and were frequently related to the *razgrom* movement which was concentrated in the CAR, the Ukraine and the Volga region. The struggle for forest land occurred in all areas where there were forests, since nearly all such land was owned by private landowners or by the state. It was especially predominant in the North. Strikes by agricultural workers were most widespread in the Baltic, the Ukraine, the Southern Steppe, the Don, the Kuban, the Lower Volga, and the CAR—although in the CAR they did not appear until 1906. Dubrovskii, *Krest'ianskoe* . . . , pp. 72, 75–78; Maslov, II, 210–28, 231, 242–60, 275; Pershin, I, 240–43; *Agrarnoe dvizheniie . . . , passim.*

[79] Dubrovskii, *Krest'ianskoe* . . . , pp. 67, 71, 72; *Agrarnoe dvizheniie,* I, 92; II, 405.

[80] Dubrovskii, *Krest'ianskoe . . . ,* p. 71.

drive him out of the countryside, and to liberate his lands for the benefit of the peasantry.[81]

Thus, above all else, it seems, the peasants' cries were for land, land, and still more land, while in the struggle with the *pomeshchiki* they apparently strove to abolish his right to private property in land and to prevent him from further exploiting them by means of his privileges and their disabilities.[82]

From the foregoing it is obvious that the main target of the agrarian movement was the *pomeshchik* landowner.[83] Further, it seems that not only were the disturbances directed predominantly against the peasants' former owners, but that they were also directed equally against members of the *kupechestvo* (merchantry) or other social groups who had rented or purchased land from neighboring *pomeshchiki*.[84] It is interesting to note that despite the fact that 75 per cent of the peasants' actions were directed against those persons to whom they had been for so long bound in a position of dependence, there were relatively few cases of murder.[85]

The other side of the agrarian movement's social nature is the problem of which sections of the peasantry participated. The general picture presented is one of widespread unity and solidarity of the peasantry in the struggle, although it should also be noted that in most cases only 10 to 30 percent, and rarely 50 per cent, of a community participated in a given action.[86] Within this unity, however, there were some peculiarities about the participants that are worth

---

[81] *Agrarnoe dvizheniie* . . . , I, 73–76, 92; II, 11–18, 159 ff., 405; Maslov, II, 231, 275; Dubrovskii, *Krest'ianskoe* . . . , p. 79.

[82] See Robinson, p. 174; Pershin, I, 246.

[83] Dubrovskii, *Krest'ianskoe* . . . , p. 65; see also *Agrarnoe dvizheniie* . . . , I, 10, 19, 51, 79–80, 88, 95, 170, 231, 359, 360, 364; II, 18, 27–29, 307, 314, and *passim*.

[84] See *Agrarnoe dvizheniie* . . . , I, 231, for example.

[85] Dubrovskii, *Krest'ianskoe* . . . , p. 80. With regard to the role played by the *kulachestvo* (rich peasants) it is clear that intrapeasant conflict was only in its infant stages. Those instances of anti-*kulak* struggle which did occur were mostly in Novorossiia, the Don, the Caucasus, the lower Volga, and some Central Industrial (CIR) *gubernii*. Dubrovskii, *Krest'ianskoe* . . . , pp. 4, 65, 83; see also *Agrarnoe dvizheniie* . . . , I, 10, 22, 51, 87; II, 413, 438. Also see *Osobennosti* . . . , pp. 5–44, 64–85. With regard to peasant conflict with other social groups, see Dubrovskii, *Krest'ianskoe* . . . , pp. 65, 83; and Pershin, I, 261.

[86] Dubrovskii, *Krest'ianskoe* . . . , p. 83; *Agrarnoe dvizheniie* . . . , I, 62, 65–66, 165–166, 173, 364; II, 18, 21–22, 26, 290, 408.

mentioning. The agricultural workers played a major role in areas where capitalist forms of agriculture were most highly developed, such as the Baltic, the Don, the Kuban, and the Volga regions.[87] Beyond these areas the *bednota* (poor) were the most revolutionary, especially the *darstvenniki*. On the other hand, the poor frequently did not participate in areas where the movement was weakly developed and where they were more cowed by the authorities.[88] The middle layers of the peasantry were also very active.[89] With regard to the prosperous, they were particularly active where the illegal cutting of timber was most important, due in large measure to the greater numbers of horses which they owned and which made it easier for them to cart away wood. In some areas they even sold such wood on the open market.[90] Similarly, in the CAR and the other black-earth regions where natural rents predominated, the prosperous peasants were the main elements who rented, and, therefore, they also participated in these areas with greater interest than elsewhere.[91] On the other hand, peasants who had purchased land almost without exception abstained from the movement, apparently seeing it as a threat to their right of private property in land.[92]

Another characteristic feature of the movement's social nature was the general lack of solidarity between the peasantry and farm workers, particularly those who were not native residents of the area.[93] Clearly, the locals considered that the outsiders were depriving them of their ability to supplement the earnings of their allotments and were thereby in part responsible for their impoverished circumstances. There were innumerable examples of outside workers being dismissed from the estates by the local peasants and being driven out of the area altogether.[94]

Perhaps the most important split within the peasantry—despite all of the concentration on the social—was the generational. Without exception, all sources indicate that the young peasants played a

[87] Dubrovskii, *Krest'ianskoe . . .* , p. 84.

[88] *Ibid.,* p. 85; see also *Agrarnoe dvizheniie . . .* , II, 23.

[89] See Dubrovskii, *Krest'ianskoe . . .* , p. 86; *Agrarnoe dvizheniie . . .* , II, 291 and *passim.*

[90] Dubrovskii, *Krest'ianskoe . . .* , p. 76; *Agrarnoe dvizheniie . . .* , I, 94, 170.

[91] Maslov, II, 229, 282; *Agrarnoe dvizheniie . . .* , II, 23.

[92] *Agrarnoe dvizheniie . . .* , I, 77, 87, 175, 364.

[93] *Ibid.,* I, 49, 62, 173; II, 18, 290, 408.

[94] *Ibid.,* I, 2, 70; II, 11, 12, 409, 429.

preeminent leadership role in the agrarian movement. The reasons
for this have already been outlined. In part, it was a product of the
participants' youth itself. In addition, they were the beneficiaries of
the expanding literacy rates and were, therefore, more open to the influence of the press. And it was this literate and conscious youth
which served as the main conduit for the transmission of news and
political views to the rest of the village. In addition, the youth were
also in large measure those who left the village to seek employment
in other regions, and especially the cities and industrial centers where
they would come into contact with the workers' movement. Similarly,
they were also the group which was in the main called upon to serve
in Manchuria—an experience which was perhaps more radicalizing
than any other. Thus, with the massive return of these *otkhodniki*
and *Manchurtsy* to the villages during 1905 and 1906 they not only
brought with them the discontent of the cities and the army toward
the government and the war, but they also began to struggle against
the deplorable conditions that faced them at home.[95]

However, yet another struggle was being played out in the commune, namely the struggle for power between the young, who were
not permitted to take part in the village *skhoda* (assembly), and the
old, who as the heads of families had the right of representing their
households. This conflict was a direct product, it would seem, of the
different worlds to which the two groups belonged: the young, born
as long as two decades after the Emancipation to a world of expanding horizons and of rising expectations; and the old, the vast majority
of whom were born before the Emancipation and who remembered
how things had been then.[96]

The character of the agrarian movement went through four major
stages in the two years of its existence. The first of these was between
January and October 1905, when it was distinguished by predominantly economic demands. As the movement progressed, however, it
began to advance political demands, in part under the influence of
revolutionary parties but also in part, as we have suggested earlier,
under that of a spontaneous process that had received its initial im-

[95] *Ibid.*, I, 5, 49, 71, 93, 150; II, 24, 290, 391; for the role of *otkhodniki,*
see *Ibid.*, I, 41, 49, 174, 364; II, 25, 290–91; 370; for the role of *Manchurtsy*
Ibid., I, 49, 93, 165–66, 174, 364; II, 25, 290, 295.

[96] Benet, p. 44; *Agrarnoe dvizheniie . . .* , I, 69; Owen, pp. 14–15; for the
passivity of the older generation in the disorders see *Agrarnoe dvizheniie*
. . . , I, 49; II, 290.

petus from the press.[97] During this first period, the highest point was reached in the month of June, when there were 492 outbreaks, while the total for May through July was 1,039 cases. These disorders were undoubtedly related to the ever-worsening course of the Russo-Japanese War and to the final humiliating defeat of the Russian Navy at Tsushima on May 15.[98]

The second stage developed after October, when the movement became more political and as political demands began to be joined with economic ones. The months of November and December were the time of the revolution's highest intensity, with 796 and 575 outbreaks recorded respectively.[99] The crucially important events which it seems the peasants were responding to at this time were the October general strike and the publication of the October Manifesto. The latter appears to have been the more important of the two, however, and many correspondents of the Free Economic Society of St. Petersburg reported that the Manifesto's publication was the force behind the beginning or intensification of the movement. Thus, it appears that the peasants misunderstood this document, at first believing it to have granted freedom—including apparently the freedom to take the *pomeshchik*'s land. However, when the peasants discovered that their expectations concerning an imminent distribution of land were not fulfilled by the Manifesto, which made no mention of the land problem whatsoever, they again turned to direct action.[100] Similarly, the government's attempt to placate the peasantry with the abolition of redemption payments on November 3 clearly did not go far enough and, by ignoring the land question, had the opposite effect from that the government had hoped for.[101]

In 1906 the movement took two new tacks. First, the peasants'

---

[97] Maslov, II, 228; Dubrovskii, *Krest'ianskoe . . .* , pp. 50–51.

[98] Dubrovskii, *Krest'ianskoe . . .* , p. 44. Dubrovskii attempts to correlate the peaks of the peasant movement with those of the workers' in order to prove a causal relationship between them. However, such an exclusive factor of causation ignores other major political developments. *Ibid.*, pp. 51–52. Similarly the SRS almost exclusively attribute the peasant movement's swings as responses to governmental actions. *Narodnoe Delo*, II, 67; VII, 201, and *passim*. Maslov, II, 240 uses a combination of these factors together with crop failure to explain the upsurge of activity. See also Maynard, p. 84.

[99] Maslov, II, 261; Dubrovskii, *Krest'ianskoe . . .* , p. 44.

[100] *Agrarnoe dvizheniie . . .* , II, 289; also *Ibid.*, I, 3, 48, 171; II, 288, 400; Maynard, p. 81.

[101] Robinson, p. 170.

struggle for land was transferred from the countryside to the Duma, a process that was accompanied by a rise in the petition movement.[102] At the same time there was a more massive development of the strike movement and its extension to the agricultural regions of the Baltic, the Ukraine, the Volga, and the CAR.[103] Accompanying this change in tactic a new peak was reached in June, with 739 outbreaks, and to a lesser extent in July, with 682 outbreaks.[104] This high point was related to two phenomena: first, the gradual loss of faith in the Duma as a solution to the peasants' problems—reinforced by the Duma's dissolution on July 8; and second, the beginning of the summer work season and the organization of agricultural strikes to coincide with this moment in the agricultural calendar. A fourth and final stage was reached in 1907 with a return to more destructive forms which seemed to express the peasants' sense of frustration and despair at the failures of the past two years.[105]

Thus, there is left, finally, the question of the political attitudes and consciousness of the peasantry. First of all it must be emphasized that despite the many changes in the course of events the peasantry in the vast majority maintained its traditional belief in the Tsar.[106] As one S. R. writer described it, the Russian peasant was far too used to thinking of himself as a slave before authority and to placing his hopes not in himself but in such authorities as God, the Tsar, and the government; and later in the Duma, the students, the revolu-

---

[102] The petition movement, one of several forms of the political side of the peasant revolution, seems to corroborate the general findings of this paper. Thus, a breakdown of some 146 *prigovory* sent to the Peasant Union between November and December 1905 showed that all of them demanded the transfer of all nonallotment land to the peasantry and the abolition of private property. Of these, 78 per cent demanded that the conditions of transfer be regulated by the Duma or a Constituent Assembly. Other economic demands that were expressed were: the aboliton of hired labor (59 per cent); the abolition of indirect taxes, and the substitution of a direct income tax (84.2 per cent); and the abolition of redemption payments (78.7 per cent). In addition, 74.6 per cent demanded the abolition of *sosloviia* and the equalization of the peasantry with the other classes before the law. Dubrovskii, *Krest'ianskoe . . .* , pp. 111–15; see also Maslov, II, 231–32, 277; Pershin, I, 244, 248, 250, 252, 253–59; *Agrarnoe dvizheniie . . .* , I, 28–37, 41, 48, 87, 153, 174, 399; II, 26, 439; Robinson, p. 205.

[103] Maslov, II, 262–63, 272; Dubrovskii, *Krest'ianskoe . . .* , p. 57.

[104] Dubrovskii, *Krest'ianskoe . . .* , p. 44.

[105] Maslov, II, 279; Dubrovskii, *Krest'ianskoe . . .* , p. 73.

[106] Pershin, I, 249; and see *Narodnoe Delo,* I, 39–62.

tionary parties, the committees, the strikes, and individual deputies to the Duma. And this was so despite the efforts of the revolutionary parties to the contrary.[107] On the other hand, the peasantry had redefined its relationship to the *pomeshchiki* as well as toward the outside world of all-Russian affairs.[108]

With regard to the peasants' attitudes toward the two Dumas, it is clear that a large proportion of them saw behind this new legislative institution the figure of the Tsar. But even if this were not always the case, as far as the peasantry was concerned the First Duma was the Duma of "popular hopes," and all of their dreams and hopes and expectations for a rapid solution to the land problem rested with this body.[109] The peasants often sent their representatives to the First Duma with instructions not to return unless it was with the land.[110] Similarly, delegates to the Second Duma were instructed to obtain land by any means possible, but, having learnt their lesson from the dissolution of the previous one, they were also instructed not to attack the Tsar in their speeches. However, there was among the peasantry a period of sharp disillusionment with and loss of faith in the Duma following that first dissolution, as was evidenced by the sudden surge in rural disturbances. Then, with the failure of the Second Duma and the June 3 coup d'état, the last vestige of belief was lost.[111] No longer could it be believed that the Duma would give them the land, while at the same time it would appear that the peasantry no longer possessed any illusions about the true nature of the government, whether represented by the Tsar and his ministers or by "Society" and the Dumas.[112] Nevertheless, all the experiences of the revolutionary period, of direct action and of the petition movement, as well as those of a more passive nature, such as the expansion of horizons consequential with the penetration of newspapers into the countryside and their proliferating points of contact with the world at large—all contributed to the peasantry's political education and the development of a revolutionary consciousness.

[107] *Narodnoe Delo,* II, 78–83; VII, 212; Pershin, I, 249.

[108] See *Narodnoe Delo,* II, 75–76, and *passim;* VII, *passim.*

[109] *Ibid.,* VII, 212; *Agrarnoe dvizheniie . . . ,* I, 16, 28, 40, 44, 104, 151, 251, 365; II, 295, and *passim.* This placing of trust in the Duma is what the Marxists call "constitutional illusions"; see Pershin, I, 247; Dubrovskii, *Krest'ianskoe . . . ,* p. 120.

[110] Dubrovskii, *Krest'ianskoe . . . ,* p. 121.

[111] *Ibid.,* pp. 116, 119; Pershin, I, 251; Robinson, p. 179.

[112] See Pershin, I, 248, 251, 270.

An example of the persistence of the peasantry's loss of faith in
the authorities is their widespread distrust and even outright hostility,
at least through 1907, to those measures which the government began
to take, mostly with the aid of Article 87, and which are known
collectively as the Stolypin reforms, for the resolution of the agrarian
problem.[113] It is true that many of the peasants were unaware of the
government's ameliorative measures. But among those who were,
there were widespread expressions of hostility toward the Peasant
Land Bank, boycotts of the land settlement commissions, and general
opposition to the law of November 9, 1906, which encouraged peasants to leave the commune. One of the oft-cited reasons for this
mood among the peasantry was the fact that it made no sense for
them to buy what would eventually be given to them.[114] At the same
time, the government's programs revealed the existence of a potential
split within the peasantry. Thus, the more prosperous, and especially
those who had purchased land, appeared more favorably inclined toward these measures. Similarly, it was the same groups who accounted for the slight increases in migration to Siberia that were recorded in some areas after the relaxation of the regulations on
resettlement.[115] But the rank-and-file peasant remained totally un-
satisfied by these measures—or indeed any that fell short of his demand for the nationalization and redistribution of all privately owned
land—while he continued to express positive and widespread support
for both the *obshchina* and the *mir*.[116]

Thus, the peasant emerged from the revolution of 1905–1907
without any solution to his most immediate concern—the land

[113] We have already noted the peasant response to the abolition of redemption
payments in November 1905. There were four main changes which were em-
bodied in laws of November 3, 1905, March 4, 1906, October 5, 1906, and
November 9, 1906. These were respectively the expansion of Peasant Land
Bank activities; the establishment of local land settlement commissions for the
supervision of land problems, and after November 6 the administration of that
law; the relatively complete equalization of the peasant's legal position with that
of the other classes of the population; and finally, the granting to the peasant of
the right to leave the *obshchina* and to settle on separate economies. This latter
was the core of the Stolypin reform and was considered by many to be equivalent
to the forcible destruction of the commune.

[114] See *Agrarnoe dvizheniie* . . . , I, 5, 6, 11, 13, 16, 21, 27, 40, 55, 101,
102, 103, 180, 365; II, 295–96, 436–37; *Narodnoe Delo*, II, 85; Robinson, pp.
198–200.

[115] See *Agrarnoe dvizheniie* . . . , I, 11, 54, 381, 390, 394, 399; II, 44, 435.

[116] See, for example, *Narodnoe Delo*, II, 72–74.

problem—and without any prospects for a solution in the near future. The expectations that had been raised and fostered over the preceding two years had been crushed—in truth almost physically, as the government had regained its self-confidence and strength. And the peasant seemed once again to return to his fatalistic and traditional system of values in order to make it possible for him to continue living in this epoch of reaction. But the loss of faith remained —a loss of faith that could be restored only by satisfaction of the peasant's demand for land. And that demand the Tsarist government never met. Thus, the only path that remained lay outside the constitution in a "second peasant war."

The Negro in Colombia:
An Historical Geography

MARIE L. ROCCA

If the Indian in the New World is the stepchild of a European-dominated society, the Negro is its orphan—his heritage unknown or obscured by a socioeconomic system which placed him on the lowest level of a hierarchically-ordered social structure, his role in the creation of that society ignored, his very existence often outrightly denied. Even today the view of many Latin Americans, Colombians as well as Argentines and others, is that, "We are Europeans, without any mixture of Indian or Negro blood."

Yet, there can be no denying that, as in most countries of Latin America, the present population of the Republic of Colombia is derived from three parent stocks—Indian, white or European Caucasoid, and Negro. Currently about 8 per cent of the Colombian population is black and 20 per cent is mulatto.[1] However, these figures obscure important facts, since the three racial groups are not distributed uniformly throughout the country. From the lowlands of the Caribbean Sea and the Pacific, eastward through some of the densest rain jungles of South America, upward into the highlands of the western and central prongs of the Andes and in the river valleys which separate the chains, the Negro has made a home in Colombia. As late as 1971 that home may be nothing more than a decrepit shack or thatched hut in the swamp or jungle, as is the case in Buenaventura, Colombia's only Pacific port (and as such tremendously important to the national economy), where about 90 per cent of the population is black. A recent report paints a picture of squalor in the port city, where:

[1] From *Latin America,* by Preston E. James, copyright © 1942, 1950, 1959, 1969, by Western Publishing Company, Inc., reprinted by permission of The Bobbs-Merrill Company, Inc., 4th ed. (1969), p. 392.

Though enormous riches in oil, coffee, cotton, sugar and frozen shrimp pass through every day, the wealth never seems to rub off on Buenaventura, nor has it in the past. Unemployment is estimated at 80 per cent, and theft and prostitution are the two most conspicuous forms of livelihood. . . . These people still live essentially as slaves, working for the handful of white landowners.[2]

In future social and economic development, the black in Colombia can thus be ignored only to the whole nation's detriment.

A comparison of the figures given above for the percentage which the Negro constitutes in the total population of the nation as a whole and in the Buenaventura region reveals an important fact: that there are distinct areas of Colombia where the black population is heavily concentrated today. This population has its historical roots in the Negro slaves imported into the area which is now the Republic of Colombia by the Spaniards when, by the end of the first century after the Conquest, the aboriginal Indians, who were exploited as a source of labor supply by the conquerors, had either been wiped out or had withdrawn to remote areas of the country.

Objectives

This paper seeks to establish the relative numerical importance of the Negro population of Colombia from colonial times to the present, as well as its geographical distribution and concentration throughout the period. Tracing the distribution patterns of this population introduced from Africa should also reveal whether areas of occupation were stable or whether there were migrations, and whether there is a correlation between areas of relatively heavy Negroid concentration in the twentieth century and areas where Negroes were important in earlier times. Since the Negro was brought to Colombia for essentially economic reasons, and the need for his labor determined the areas into which he was initially brought, his role in the economic life of the Viceroyalty of New Granada, later the Republic of Colombia, is also reviewed.

[2] Malcolm W. Browne, "Riches Pour Into Colombian Port, but Poverty Reigns," *The New York Times,* April 3, 1971, p. 8. © 1971 by The New York Times Company. Reprinted by permission.

The First Blacks

Although the Negro in the history of Colombia dates from the time of the early Spanish explorers, he has been for the most part a very neglected subject of historical research, and the lack is all the more appalling when one considers that the Granadine city of Cartagena was one of the major slave trade ports of the Spanish empire. The arrival of the first Negro in the territory that would in 1739 become the Viceroyalty of New Granada went unnoticed, but the presence of Negroes in the territory was noticed when in 1529 certain rebellious Negro slaves in the city of Santa Marta set fire to the straw huts of the new town. The decade of the 1530s saw the beginning of the issuance by the Spanish crown of *licencias* to individual explorers or *adelantados* to allow them to bring slaves into the new territory as domestic servants (personal and household) or to work on farms. These *licencias,* together with the regular slave trade which soon grew up, resulted in a considerable Negro population along the Caribbean coast of New Granada. In the agricultural regions along the sparsely settled Caribbean plain at the mouth of the Magdalena River, the narrow littoral of Santa Marta and Río de la Hacha, and the rugged Isthmus with its interoceanic trade route, Negroes and their descendants comprised the greater part of the population. Here they were employed in the production of local commodities— dyewoods, tropical food crops, mules and other livestock—for domestic consumption or exchange for imported goods, or as workers who helped the merchant class in trade with Spain which supplied the interior of the Viceroyalty and the Pacific coast areas. Also, "among the merchants of Cartagena and Panama, the only two centers of any size in the region, domestic slavery was extremely common." [3]

Negroes also had a role in the *entradas* into western Colombia, as in the party of the explorer Jorge Robledo, who employed them in the extraction of gold. This employment of Negroes in the extraction of gold is an early manifestation of a pattern which would reach its climax in the seventeenth and eighteenth centuries, for while in other parts of the Spanish empire slavery was predominantly agricultural

[3] James Ferguson King, "Negro Slavery in the Viceroyalty of New Granada" (unpublished Ph. D. dissertation, University of California at Berkeley, 1939), pp. 51–52.

and domestic, only in New Granada were Negroes consistently used in large numbers during a long period of time as the chief source of labor in the mines. Western Colombia was, in fact, "the largest mining area in the Spanish colonies in which Negro slaves eventually replaced Indian labor." [4]

Negro Slavery

It was mainly in the three great gold-mining provinces of the western Andes where slavery was conditioned by mineral exploitation. In these three provinces which lay west of the Magdalena River, the gold occurred in stream beds and other alluvial formations in the form of dust and nuggets which could be easily extracted by the primitive methods of the day: digging out auriferous sand or soil and washing out the gold in running water by means of a panning process. The first area in importance was the province of the Chocó, considered to be the richest gold-mining region in the Spanish Indies. Extending south along the Pacific coast from the Isthmian Kingdom of Tierra Firme (present-day Panama) to the borders of Popayán province, it was a sparsely settled wilderness of tropical jungle, rain forest, and river valleys until after 1654 when white miners followed missionaries, who had undertaken pacification of the dangerous Chocó Indians, into the area. Second in importance was Popayán, centered about the capital of the same name in the upper Cauca valley (including the Pacific subprovince of Barbacoas). And in the heart of the mountain country of the central Andes between the Magdalena and the Atrato rivers, one of the most rugged areas of the Viceroyalty, Negroes came to be the principal source of labor in the gold washings of the third province, Antioquia.

Although Negro slave labor came to be the main labor base of New Granada mining, Negroes were imported only when Indian labor was no longer adequate, and introduction of Negro slaves, begun in the last quarter of the sixteenth century, only reached a mass scale in the seventeenth century with intensive exploitation of mines and haciendas. The Indian population was, to start, sparse, especially in the mining and agricultural regions of New Granada. A large labor force was needed to wash gold from gravel in the placer

[4] Robert C. West, *Colonial Placer Mining in Colombia* (Baton Rouge: Louisiana State University Press, 1952), p. 83.

mines and dig ore from veins, and where possible the Spaniards used the *encomienda* system [5] of forced labor to obtain Indians to work the mines of New Granada. During the sixteenth century *encomiendas* were most numerous around the mining center of Popayán, Anserma, Mariquita, Zaragoza, and Cáceres. The Indians were then preferred as mine laborers by the Spaniards because they were seasoned miners, and in 1565 more than 8,000 Indians in *encomienda* were engaged in the extraction of gold in the province of Popayán (which at the time included the area from the upper Patía basin northward to Antioquia).[6] But the sixteenth century saw a disastrous decimation of the Indians of the Cauca and Magdalena drainages. Among the reasons put forth in archival documents for the decline of the Indian population are excessive work, malnutrition, flight, segregation of the sexes, ill-treatment, cruelty, conscription for expeditions, enslavement, and the *mita*.[7] As one author has summarized it,

The more primitive Indians . . . were proving to be quite inadequate to meet the labor demands of the conquerors whether in the placer mines or on the plantations where the new commercial crops, sugar cane and indigo, were cultivated. The native peoples were ravaged by imported diseases against which they had no immunity and were unable to adapt themselves easily to the hard work demanded by the Spaniards. By the

[5] To receive Indians in *encomienda* meant that the Spanish colonial *encomendero* or trustee received rights to tribute payments and unrestricted personal services from a stipulated number of Indians living in stipulated villages. In return the *encomendero* was expected to render military service and to provide for the Christianization of the Indians committed to his charge, as well as to defend their persons and property. This system as instituted by the Spanish Crown proved an effective means of mobilizing available Indian labor to work the Spanish-owned mines and lands. The rendering of services was abolished in 1549 and thereafter the *encomendero* could only receive tribute payments from a given number of Indian villages.

[6] West, *Colonial Placer Mining*, p. 79.

[7] The *mita* was a pre-Conquest Andean system of draft labor to which the common people were subject. On a rotating basis, a certain proportion of the members of a village were required, for a specified number of days each year, to perform post service on roads, serve in the army, work in mines and on the construction and maintenance of irrigation works, roads, temples, palaces, and other public edifices. The Spaniards later employed this native type of labor levy to secure Indians, who were to be paid wages, for the mines and *haciendas*. It should be noted that *mita* was a local name for the system of labor *repartimiento* which was used throughout the Spanish empire, and which, after the aboliton of services in the *encomienda* in 1550, became the main institution of labor.

end of the first century after the conquest, the more primitive tribes of Colombia had either been wiped out by epidemics or had withdrawn to the remote selvas of the Pacific slope.[8]

Spanish authorities early responded to the Indian population decline by prohibiting in 1546 forced Indian labor in the mines, but the law was unenforceable and in 1567 the Audiencia of Santa Fe allowed that Indians might work in the mines provided they did so by their own choice and were paid a just wage. But as the population decline continued, the Negro, who was readily available, came to be viewed as a superior worker whose labor was necessary to sustain the area's economy. The superiority of the Negro over the Indian seems to have been an axiom of the period, and it was widely maintained that one Negro was worth four Indians in working a mine. Colonial officials strongly advocated substitution of Negro slaves, "one hundred of whom would produce more in a year than five hundred Indians," for Indian mine workers to revitalize the mining economy languishing for lack of laborers. An edict abolishing forced Indian labor in the mines was issued on July 7, 1729.

But the gold mines suffered no severe economic blow from this prohibition, for by this date Negroes had been working in the mines for some time. As early as the 1530s slaves were brought into the Sinú area (the valley of the Sinú River, between the eastern and middle prongs of the Cordillera Occidental) from Cartagena to dig gold from Indian graves, and in 1549 a royal order specified that only Negroes were to be employed in grave robbing. By 1544 blacks were working in the Popayán mines to supplement Indian labor and by 1550 Spaniards had introduced gangs of Negro slaves into the mines of Buriticá.[9] In Santa Fe de Antioquia, there were approximately 1,500 Indian workers, 300 Negro slaves, and over 200 Spanish residents in 1583.[10] Since reliable data are incomplete and scattered, estimates of the number of Negroes brought into New Granada during the colonial period are extremely hazardous. However, one who has made a study of colonial placer mining in Colombia has estimated that by 1590 at least 1,000 slaves were imported annually through Cartagena, and most were sold to miners in lowland Antioquia and the Cauca and Magdalena river valley areas, where the Indian element had been severely reduced.[11] Mine registers kept during the colonial

---

[8] James, p. 395.
[9] West, *Colonial Placer Mining*, p. 83.   [10] *Ibid.*, p. 82.   [11] *Ibid.*, p. 84.

period indicate that near the end of the sixteenth century there were
some 150 Negroes in the mining center of Cáceres, 1,000 in that of
Anserma, and 2,000 each in those of Zaragoza and Remedios; Negro
slaves in the mining center of Buriticá increased from 300 in 1583 to
600 around 1590.[12]

In the lowlands of the Pacific coast, Spanish mining activity in the
Chocó began in the 1570s, but Indian hostility prevented intense pla-
cering and importation of many Negroes for more than a century. By
1680 practically all of the most important gold placers of the Chocó
had been discovered and most were being worked by small gangs of
Negro slaves. The rebellion of the Chocó Indians in 1684, however,
forced most of the Spanish miners and their slaves to retire to the
highlands until peace once more was established in 1688. In the following year miners from the upper Cauca around Anserma, Cartago,
Cali, and especially Popayán, began to bring slaves into the upper
San Juan drainage (the area known as the province of Nóvita). At
the same time importation of Negroes into Barbacoas began on a
large scale. During the colonial period at least three mining districts
in the lowlands became centers of Negro slave population: (1) the
eastern tributaries of the upper San Juan and the Atrato drainages
—the heart of the Chocó; (2) the Barbacoas district, including the
Telembí and Magüí rivers and their tributaries; and (3) the upper
and middle courses of the numerous rivers that cross the narrow
coastal plain between Buenaventura and the Bay of Guapi. From
these three core areas, Negroes and mixed bloods spread to all parts
of the lowlands.[13] Table 1 opposite presents available statistics for the
number of slaves in the three main gold-producing provinces of Antioquia, Popayán, and the Chocó for a twenty-year period in the late
eighteenth century.

The growth of the Negro population of the Chocó from the beginning of the eighteenth century through the mid-nineteenth century is
given in Table II. It should be noted that by 1778 freedmen constituted about 35 per cent of the Negro population of the area.

It is by now apparent that the Negro slave was important in mining in New Granada, but in order to underscore the importance of
Negro slavery in the economy of the Viceroyalty as a whole, it is
important to remember that the external trade of the Viceroyalty de-

[12] *Ibid.*
[13] West, *The Pacific Lowlands of Colombia: A Negroid Area of the American Tropics* (Baton Rouge: Louisiana State University Press [c. 1957]), p. 98.

Table I. Number of Slaves in Mines, 18th Century[a]

Year	Antioquia	Popayán	Chocó[b]
1770	1,462	4,765	4,297
1778	4,896	6,320	–
1788	4,296	–	3,534[c]
1789	–	9,313	5,916[d]

[a] All calculations should be reduced by one-third, who were either children or employed in the domestic service of their masters. Source: Aquiles Escalante, "Notas sobre el Palenque de San Basilio, una comunidad negra en Colombia," *Divulgaciones Etnológicas* (Colombia), III, No. 5 (June 1954), 213–214.

[b] Includes the subprovince of Barbacoas.

[c] Source for this figure alone is Robert C. West, *Colonial Placer Mining in Colombia* (Baton Rouge: Louisiana State University Press, 1952), p. 97.

[d] Source for this figure alone is James Ferguson King, "Negro Slavery in the Viceroyalty of New Granada" (unpublished Ph.D. dissertation, University of California at Berkeley, 1939), p. 36.

Table II. Negro Population of the Chocó, 1704–1843

Year	Slaves	Freedmen	Total
1704	600	?	–
1759	3,915	?	–
1778	5,828	3,160	8,988
1789	5,916	3,342	9,258
1806	4,608	?	–
1843	2,505	[18,000] *	–

* As the 1843 census gave no information on freedmen or mixed bloods, this figure, suggested as an estimate, was derived by the author by assuming that 80 per cent of the total 1843 population was Negroid.

Source: Robert C. West, *The Pacific Lowlands of Colombia* (Baton Rouge: Louisiana State University Press [c. 1957]), p. 100.

pended almost exclusively on the export of gold. In a letter to King Charles III in 1783, the *procurador* of Popayán, don Vicente Hurtado, wrote:

The general and almost sole means for the subsistence of this Kingdom and its commerce with Spain, which keeps it alive and nourishes it, is the gold which is extracted from the many mines of that precious metal which are worked in the provinces of Popayán, the Chocó and Antioquia. . . . And there is nothing of royal revenue, commerce or individual interests which does not depend on and have its stability in the gold from the mines of this Kingdom.[14]

At the end of the eighteenth century the Viceroy Espeleta calculated that exports from the port of Cartagena in the decade 1784–1793 were valued at 21,052,594 *pesos,* and of this amount 19,209,035 *pesos* represented gold. From 1802 to 1804 exports through Cartagena were valued at 7,105,783 *pesos,* two-thirds of which derived from gold.[15] Gold remained the mainstay of external market relations for a long period despite the primitive technology used. As late as 1832 the British Captain Cochrane observed that,

As yet the mines have been worked entirely without machinery. They have not even a common pump to draw the water from the pits they make; and to remove a very large stone sometimes requires the whole force of many negroes for three weeks. Did they but know the use of gunpowder to blast the rocks; or had they but proper patent cranes for removing the pieces, and pumps for drawing off the water, the mines might be worked to much greater advantage . . . [16]

Given the primitive techniques of Granadine mining and the importance of manual labor in the mines, it is readily seen that the work of the Negro slave was quite an important factor in productivity. This is so despite the fact that, quantitatively, Negro slaves were never a large part of the total population of New Granada in the territory that today constitutes the Republic of Colombia.

[14] Aquiles Escalante, *El negro en Colombia* (Bogota: Universidad Nacional de Colombia, 1964), p. 122. Translated from the Spanish by Marie L. Rocca.

[15] Jaime Jaramillo Uribe, "La controversia jurídica y filosófica librada en la Nueva Granada en torno a la liberación de los esclavos," *Anuario Colombiano de Historia Social y de la Cultura,* I, No. 4 (1969), 63–64.

[16] Charles Stuart Cochrane, *Journal of a Residence and Travels in Colombia, During the Years 1823 and 1824* (2 vols.; London: Henry Colburn, 1825), II, 420.

Population Statistics in the
Colonial Period

In attempting to establish the numerical strength of the Negro in the Colombian population as a whole, some difficulties are encountered. During the colonial period the Spanish government never made a precise determination of the population of the Viceroyalty of New Granada, the heart of which forms present-day Colombia. We are thus for the most part forced to rely for at least general impressions for the early period on the calculations and estimates of various authorities. Ángel Rosenblat has assembled the following figures for the year 1570: in a total population of 825,000 the indigenous population constituted 96.96 per cent; whites, 1.21 per cent; and Negroes, mestizos, and mulattoes, 1.81 per cent.[17] His figures for the mid-seventeenth century are more detailed and Negroes are listed in a separate category, although no mention is made of the *zambos,* the offspring of Negroes and Indians. In a total population of 750,000, whites constituted 6.66 per cent; Negroes, 8.00 per cent; mestizos, 2.66 per cent; mulattoes, 2.66 per cent; and Indians, 80.00 per cent.[18]

There is one set of figures from the colonial period, however, which is more accurate and comprehensive. These are the figures, based on a 1778 census in the Viceroyalty of New Granada, given by the colonial official Francisco Silvestre. According to these figures, there were a total of 51,999 Negro slaves in New Granada out of a total population of 738,523. This number represented 7.04 per cent of the total population. However, the four provinces of Antioquia, Popayán, the Chocó, and Cartagena had over half of the total slave population, as can be seen in Table III to follow.

Since it is difficult to obtain extensive statistics for the colonial period, Silvestre's 1778 figures have been used to make a graphic representation of the racial distribution of the population of the Viceroyalty, shown on the map below. His figures for the four provinces of Cartagena, Antioquia, Popayán, and the Chocó have been used to construct tables showing population distribution by *castas* in absolute numbers (Table IV) and percentages (Table V).

[17] Ángel Rosenblat, *La población indígena de América desde 1492 hasta la actualidad* (Buenos Aires: Institución Cultural Española, 1945), p. 81. Mestizos are the offspring of Europeans and Indians, mulattoes the offspring of Europeans and Negroes.

[18] *Ibid.,* p. 57.

Marie L. Rocca

Table III. Distribution by Provinces of Slave Population, 1778

Province	Slaves	% of Total Population
Santafé	1,468	1.47
Tunja	6,047	2.33
Mariquita	4,083	8.66
Popayán	12,441	19.29
Neiva	450	3.94
Antioquia	8,791	18.08
Girón	–	–
Santa Marta	4,467	10.15
Cartagena	8,143	6.80
Darién	85	6.71
Chocó	5,916	38.70
Gobierno de los Llanos	118	0.53
Total	51,999	

Source: Jaime Jaramillo Uribe, "La controversia jurídica y filosófica librada en la Nueva Granada en torno a la liberación de los esclavos," *Anuario Colombiano de Historia Social y de la Culture,* I, No. 4 (1969), 65.

Table IV. Population of Colombia in 1778 (Selected areas only)

Area	White	Indian	Libres	Slave	Total
Cartagena	11,716	10,928	77,920	8,721	119,285 [119,647]
Antioquia	8,523	2,534	28,246	8,931	48,234 [48,604]
Popayán	13,351	15,692	22,979	12,441	64,463*
Chocó	335	5,687	3,342	5,916	15,280 [15,286]

* Excludes about 6,000 people in the province of Barbacoas.

Source: Francisco Silvestre, *Descripción del Reyno de Santa Fe de Bogotá* (Panama: Imprenta Nacional, 1927), pp. 12–69, *passim.* Totals given have been adjusted; bracketed totals are those published by Silvestre.

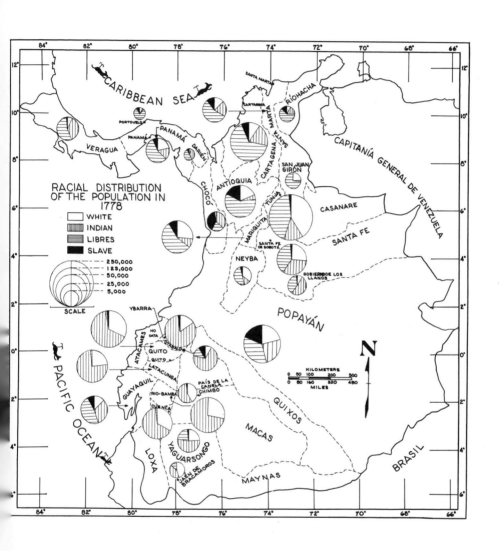

Table V. Population of Colombia in 1778—Percentages

Area	White	Indian	Libres	Slave
Cartagena	9.83	17.54	65.32	7.31
Antioquia	17.67	5.25	58.56	18.51
Popayán	20.71	24.34	35.65	19.29
Chocó	2.19	37.21	21.87	38.71

Note: these percentages are based on figures presented in Table IV.

We should note here that the classification *libres,* the largest segment of the population in each of the areas except the Chocó, probably included mestizos, mulattoes, and free blacks. The figures reveal that the white element was not very strong, as has been the case throughout Colombian history, since the *conquistadores* in the area were not numerous, settlers from Spain did not come in any great numbers, and immigration from European countries other than Spain has been negligible. Throughout the eighteenth century the population of the province of the Chocó consisted only of a handful of whites, for the most part *señores de cuadrilla* who directed the mining activities; a sparse and imperfectly reduced native Indian population [19] which produced limited crops of maize and plantains, virtually the only local food supply; an increasingly large class of free mixed bloods; and the Negro slaves, the largest single element in the population. Also, in Popayán and Antioquia slaves and free men of color predominated.

It is generally believed that males consistently formed by far the larger part of the cargoes of the slave ships coming to New Granada and because of this many left no issue,

for their social status made unions with white women impossible and even placed mulatto wives largely beyond their reach. On the other hand, *bozal* negresses, particularly children, drifted into domestic servitude,

---

[19] Robert Cushman Murphy, who has studied "Racial Succession in the Colombian Chocó," has written that indications are that the first black *cimarrones* to come among the Chocó Indians were hospitably received, "doubtless because of common enmity toward Spanish slaveholders," but later the Chocó developed so strong a sentiment against miscegenation that they became intolerant of association with either Negroes or *zambo* half-breeds (*The Geographical Review*, XXIX [July 1939], 466).

which increased the probability of their having children by white or mulatto fathers.[20]

Yet, the distribution by sex in these four provinces, shown in Table VI below, reveals a much closer over-all correspondence between the sexes than is usual for slave societies where males may have outnumbered women two to one. This may be due to the fact that female as well as male slaves were used in mining and agricultural operations in New Granada.

Table VI. Sex Ratio—1778 (Males / 100 Females)

Area	White	Indian	Libres	Slave	Total
Cartagena	104.5	92.7	94.0	96.9	94.8
Antioquia	92.3	104.0	148.1	121.3	128.6
Popayán	83.5	84.1	85.8	85.2	84.8
Chocó	155.7	104.4	114.0	113.4	110.9

Note: These figures are based on the statistics presented in Table IV.

It is also noteworthy that sex ratios differ more widely between provinces or geographical regions than between racial groups within a particular province. For example, the two provinces with the highest ratio of males per 100 females, Antioquia and the Chocó, are the two provinces whose terrain and climate, respectively, are the roughest.

Because of the lack of data, it is impossible to establish, either for society as a whole or for individual groups, such statistics as population growth rate, mortality rate, birth rate, and legitimacy-illegitimacy rate.

Economic Roles

We have seen that of the 7.04 per cent that was the Negro element in the Colombian population of 1778 more than 50 per cent was concentrated in the mines, with smaller concentrations in areas of sugar growing (cane sugar, brown sugar, and honey) and cattle raising (for example, the Cauca Valley). Some of the escaped Negroes from the Chocó took to the brush where they became self-sufficient,

[20] King, Ph.D. dissertation, p. 239. Reprinted by permission of the author.

hunting, fishing, and practicing patch agriculture. In the Cauca valley Negroes who had filtered in from the Chocó became patch agriculturalists in an economy based largely on sugar cane and cattle raising and ultimately gave up their self-sufficiency to the extent of raising some produce for the local market.[21] In transportation on the Magdalena and Cauca rivers, the *cargueros,* or freight carriers, were Negroes. In occupations, the Negro slave in Colombia also played a role in artisanal positions: carpentry, tailoring, hairdressing, shoemaking, commerce, domestic administration, and direction of the mine gangs. While no figures are available on occupation distribution, in the *barrio* of Mercedes, in Cartagena, on analyzing the population pattern of 1777 it was found that the majority of artisans in the above trades were Negroes.[22] Colonial documents reveal that possession of skills increased the value of slaves: slaves skilled in masonry and carpentry, for example, who were purchased for 250 *pesos* were sometimes sold for 500 or 600 *pesos.*[23]

Mining remained, nonetheless, the industry in which the work of the Negro slave population was concentrated, and the majority of Negro slaves lived in mining settlements. The basic colonial mining settlement in New Granada was a shifting placer camp, consisting of a group of small temporary huts with wattle walls and thatched roofs, placer workings, the surrounding forest, and adjacent agricultural lands. The camp also had a blacksmith shop, a storehouse for food and tools, and occasionally a stable for mules and burros; larger camps sometimes had a small church, visited by a circuit priest. Few camps exceeded a population of 150; most ranged from 15 to 20 people.[24] In these settings Negro slaves were organized into *cuadrillas* or gangs ranging from five or six to more than one hundred, depending upon the extent of the workings and the capital of the *señor* or mine owner. The overseer of the mine was either a white man or a mulatto, but the *capitán de cuadrilla,* or head of the slave gang, whose duties included the disciplining of his gang, the distribution of food and collection of the weekly take of gold for his overseer, was a

[21] Raymond E. Crist, *The Cauca Valley, Colombia: Land Tenure and Land Use* ([Gainesville?] Florida: n.p., 1952), pp. 18–19.

[22] Escalante, *El negro en Colombia,* p. 131.

[23] Jaime Jaramillo Uribe, "Esclavos y señores en la sociedad colombiana del siglo XVIII," *Anuario Colombiano de Historia Social y de la Cultura,* I, No. 1 (1963), 17.

[24] West, *Colonial Placer Mining,* p. 87.

Negro slave. At any one time only half of a slave gang would be employed in mining—the others, called *piezas de roza,* were required to
grow food for the camps in nearby fields. Both mining and farming
cuadrillas were composed of men and women, the women being used
as divers [25] and panners in the placer mines.

The Social Ambient: Colonial Policy
and Negro Reactions

Treatment of slaves depended on two controlling factors—law and
custom, with the former supplementing the latter. As one author has
put it, "By and large it was those provisions of slave legislation that
most nearly coincided with the popular attitude toward slavery which
commanded respect." [26] In the mining camps, food was rationed and
a slave's ration generally consisted of plantains, maize, salt, and fresh
or salted meat. Disease seems to have been rampant in such areas,
the principal ones being yaws, various intestinal diseases, syphilis,
leprosy, and tuberculosis. There was a fairly high mortality rate, such
that "a continuous influx of new slaves was necessary to replace the
dead, and when such were not available, gold production decreased
sharply." [27]

Social legislation which sought to regulate slavery in New Granada
chiefly took the form of sporadic royal *cédulas* addressed from time
to time to the governors and viceroys. General *cédulas* of universal
application in the Spanish empire also had the force of law in the
Viceroyalty. Thus, in New Granada, as in other areas, restrictions
were placed on Negroes, both slave and free: they could not walk at
night in cities or villages; could not carry arms or umbrellas; and
could not have Indian servants. Black women were prohibited from
wearing gold, silk, and certain types of cloaks or pearls, but free
black or mulatto women married to Spaniards might wear small
pieces of gold or silver jewelry, with pearls or a choker, and might

[25] Diving is a stream placer mining technique in which the diver, or *zam-bullidor,* weighted with a heavy stone tied against the buttocks, sinks to the
river bottom to scoop up gravel laden with gold. When the *batea* (a wide,
shallow bowl, counterpart of the tin pan used in the western United States) is
filled, the diver disengages the stone and swims to the surface with the load.

[26] King, "Negro Slavery in New Granada," *Greater America: Essays in
Honor of H. E. Bolton* (Berkeley: University of California Press, 1945), p.
310.

[27] West, *Colonial Placer Mining,* p. 88.

use velvet trimming on their skirts. The fact that much of the colonial legislation is, however, penal in character reveals the fact that the Negro slaves in New Granada were not an entirely submissive group. Rather, they resorted to violence, rebellion, and flight in protest against their social position. Documents from the colonial period in New Granada reveal that some female slaves killed their children to save them from a life of servitude; others committed suicide; and still others killed their masters.[28] Other forms of social protest were rebellions and runaways, the first rebellion noted being that of slaves in the newly founded city of Santa Marta in 1529.

The *cimarrones,* or runaway slaves, often established *palenques* or fortified village settlements in inaccessible places. From *palenques* in the swampy jungles between the Cauca and Nechí rivers, runaway Negroes raided outlying mining camps and preyed on shipping on the rivers. The *palenque* of Castillo de Popayán, in the extreme west of the Patía valley, was engaged in struggles with the Spanish for more than thirteen years before its Negroes were finally defeated in 1745. There were several *palenques* in Antioquia, but by far the most famous and enduring was the *palenque* of San Basilio established in the hinterland early in the seventeenth century. Within this *palenque* African language, dances, and customs were retained, but political organization showed a decidedly Spanish influence (although other *palenques* did establish themselves as kingdoms supposedly outside the Spanish monarchy). The members of the *palenque* elected their own officials, which were a *capitán de pueblo* who was in charge of civilian matters, a *capitán de campo* in charge of the military, and an *alcalde*. However, all officials had to be approved by the Spanish governor of the province. The *palenqueros* also organized their own fiestas, religious cults, and *cabildos*. San Basilio did have a Catholic priest who administered to its "178 families with 396 souls" in the eighteenth century, but the survival of Africanisms in religion was quite pronounced.[29] Until the end of the nineteenth century, the *palenqueros* lived almost totally isolated from Colombian society at large. They developed a closed economy based on rudimentary agri-

[28] Documents published by Roberto Rojas Gómez, "La esclavitud en Colombia," *Boletín de Historia y Antigüedades* (Colombia), XIV, No. 158 (May 1922), 92–101.

[29] Aquiles Escalante, "Notas sobre el Palenque de San Basilio, una comunidad negra en Colombia," *Divulgaciones Etnológicas* (Colombia), III, No. 5 (June 1954), 230–231.

culture centered on the cultivation of rice, corn, bananas, peanuts, and the yucca, and on cattle raising. They rarely left the settlement to exchange products, and when they did come to traditional festivals they would generally commission someone to buy goods in Cartagena.

The Provenance of Colombian Negroes

Because of a Spanish law of 1526 which banned all Negroes from the colonies except *bozales,* Negroes landing at Cartagena were fresh from Africa. These *bozales,* considered to be more adaptable to a new environment, more docile, peaceful, and obedient, were cheaper than creole slaves (those born and raised in the New World), and *piezas de Indias,* or "prime Negroes" (Negroes seven Spanish *cuartas* in height, a *cuarta* being a span of about eight inches), usually about eighteen years of age, commanded the best prices in New Granada, being valued at 300 *pesos* on the average. Young female slaves were often valued as highly as males, for they were used not only for breeding and as household servants, but also as agricultural workers and mine laborers, particularly in the placers.[30] Certain African groups were thought to provide better workers, while others possessed the reputation of producing offspring of superior physique. The Congo and Guinea Negroes, for example, were generally regarded as docile and capable of being driven to great exertion, though the fugitive tendencies of the former sometimes rendered them unpopular. The Gold Coast Negroes, on the other hand, though strong, intelligent, and well-built, were feared for their cunning and valor.[31]

The tribal origins of the Negroes who came to the Viceroyalty have been fairly well researched and established as a result of the influence of Melville Herskovits. In this sphere some emphasis has been placed on establishing the type of culture which the Negro population had at the time of importation from Africa in order to determine what social and cultural elements the Negro has contributed to the formation of the Colombian nation and to analyze the process of transculturation. Determination of the tribal background of the slaves that entered the mines of New Granada has relied heavily upon anal-

[30] West, *Colonial Placer Mining,* p. 85.
[31] King, Ph.D. dissertation, p. 207.

yses of slaves' surnames, for customarily the Negro slave was given the surname corresponding to the name of his tribal language, although care must also be exercised here, for the slave was sometimes given the name of the slaving station from which he was obtained. Lack of careful records makes it impossible to determine the relative numbers of the different Negro strains which were imported into New Granada; but study of importation records and other documents has revealed that most of the Colombian Negroes came from western Africa—Guinea, the Congo, Angola, and Senegal. Within these geographical limits, Negroes destined for Granadine mines came from a variety of tribes and language groups. The most common surnames indicate some of these: Angola, Lucumí, Mina, Chamba, Carabalí, Mandinga, Arará, Biáfara, Cetre, Bran, Congo, and Luango.[32] Less is known about where members of specific tribes were settled in Colombia. Robert West has indicated that such names as Mina, Congo, Mandinga, and Cangá abound in the region of Yurumanguí in Colombia; Biáfara, Cambindo, Mina, and Cuenú in Guapi; Carabalí and Congolino in the region of Iscuandé.[33] In his study on the *palenque* of San Basilio, Aquiles Escalante cites a funeral song which helps to identify the regions of origin of its dwellers:

>   Chi man congo
>   Chi man luango
>   Chi man rui luango de Angole.[34]

[32] *Angola* probably comes from the Portuguese colony of that name on the west coast of Africa. *Lucumí* were Yoruba from Nigeria. Arboleda asserts that the *Mina* came from Fanti territory near Dahomey, while West states that the surname derives from the slave mart of the Portuguese, São Jorge de Mina, where slaves collected from the Ashanti area, between the Bandama and Volta rivers on the Gold and Ivory Coasts were kept for shipment. The *Chamba* were of a tribe north of the Ashanti on the Gold Coast. The *Carabalí* came from the Calabar coast, east of the Niger Delta. The *Mandinga* came from the French Sudan, and their name has become a word in the Spanish language used to designate the devil. The *Arará* were a tribe in Dahomey, while the *Biáfara* were a Bantu-speaking group on the Gulf of Biafara, Cameroons. The *Cetre* were a Kru tribe living on the coast of eastern Liberia and the western part of the Ivory coast. *Congo* refers to the many Bantu-speaking groups in the lower Congo basin, the *Luango* possibly being one of those groups. *Bran* refers to the Brong Negroes of the Guinea coast. (José Rafael Arboleda, "Nuevas investigaciones afro-colombianas," *Revista Javeriana* (Colombia), XXXVII, No. 184 [May 1952], 204. Robert West, *Pacific Lowlands*, pp. 89, 102, 230–31.)

[33] West, *Pacific Lowlands*, p. 102.

[34] Escalante, "Notas sobre San Basilio," p. 214.

The peoples living along the Guinea coast and Islamic hinterland and other nearby areas, who contributed a large portion of the slaves that came to New Granada, were among the more developed African cultures. They were familiar with systems of agriculture, animal husbandry and cattle raising, iron and bronze work, textile manufacture, art, music and dance, and religious and political organization.[35] In spite of the shock and hardships borne by the Negroes in the capture, the "middle passage," and the seasoning and sale,[36] members of these African tribes transported to the New World managed to maintain a substantial number of cultural traits in those pockets where they were concentrated in large numbers—such as the Caribbean and Pacific coastal lowlands and their immediate hinterlands, along the course of the San Juan River and other small rivers which cross the Pacific lowlands area, and along the courses of the Atrato, Sinú, Magdalena, and Cauca rivers. (General areas where Negro influence is notable in Colombia are indicated on the map following.) For example, Artur Ramos has noted that a study of the *diablito* songs heard during the carnival which began each December 28 in the city of Cartagena during the colonial period reveals certain Bantu, Congolese, and Angolese traces.[37] The Negro or African influence in Colombia is still seen in art, music, dance, and funeral customs.[38]

Negroes and the Independence Movement

The lot of the Negro in Colombia during the colonial period was surely a difficult one, but the period was marked, legal and social barriers notwithstanding, by the constant growth in the population of mixed groups of one kind or another relative to the parent stocks. During the colonial period mine owners had obtained slaves chiefly through itinerant merchants who purchased the Negroes in the port of Cartagena and shipped them, together with other goods, up the rivers into the interior in canoes. This high cost of transport into the interior had often made the price of slaves prohibitive to many miners, and by the last decades of the eighteenth century importations of

[35] Jaramillo Uribe, "Esclavos y señores," p. 9.

[36] These are described in detail by Stanley Elkins in *Slavery* (2nd ed.; Chicago: University of Chicago Press, 1968), pp. 98–103.

[37] Artur Ramos, *Las culturas negras en el Nuevo Mundo* (Mexico: Fondo de Cultura Económica, 1943), p. 222.

[38] In his work, *El negro en Colombia,* Escalante devotes three full chapters to Negro influences in dance, music, and funeral customs (pp. 145–69).

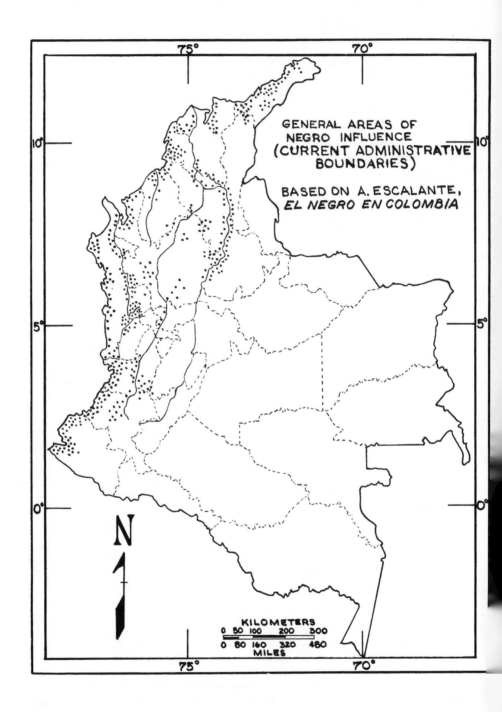

GENERAL AREAS OF
NEGRO INFLUENCE
(CURRENT ADMINISTRATIVE
BOUNDARIES)

BASED ON A. ESCALANTE,
EL NEGRO EN COLOMBIA

KILOMETERS
0 50 100 200 300
0 80 160 320 480
MILES

new African slaves became more and more difficult, at about the time of the Napoleonic wars and the beginning English attempts to abolish the slave trade. In 1791 the free importation of slaves was proclaimed for the ports of Cartagena and Ríohacha, but so little came of it that it was repealed the following year. The Viceroy Espeleta informed the Spanish crown that during the year covered by the decree only 29 slaves had been imported for the province of Antioquia and none for either Popayán or the Chocó.[39] The New Granada property owners were also in economic straits, which prevented them from buying new slaves and even paying for ones purchased on credit in prior years. This situation remained much the same until the period of the Independence movement, when the urgent need for soldiers in both Spanish and patriot armies led to promises of freedom and political rights to the slaves and free Negroes in return for their enlistment in the armies. The Liberator Simón Bolívar was committed to the emancipation of slaves, but he was, on the other hand, aware of the danger of permitting large groups of men in bondage to exist in a free society and saw in armed service an opportunity to lessen the number of Negroes.

For an estimate of the racial make-up of the population at the time of the start of the Independence movement, we have the estimates of the geographer Vergara y Velasco: in a total population of 1,095,000, he estimates the whites at 20.5 per cent, Indians at 15.9 per cent, Negroes at 6.6 per cent, and mixed groups at 57.1 per cent.[40] Ángel Rosenblat merely states that in a population of about one million there were 12,000 Spaniards, 300,000 *criollos blancos,* and 406,000 *hombres de color.*[41] After independence was accomplished, the Colombian Constitution of 1821 decreed that representation of the individual districts of the country should be according to population. A series of censuses was taken under this authorization, in 1825 for Gran Colombia, and in 1835, 1843, and 1851 for New Granada.[42] These censuses were taken by enumerators in the dis-

[39] Jaramillo Uribe, "Controversia en torno a la liberación de los esclavos," p. 66.

[40] T. Lynn Smith, "The Racial Composition of the Population of Colombia," *Journal of Inter-American Studies,* VIII (1966), 215.

[41] Rosenblat, p. 142.

[42] An historical sketch of Colombian censuses from 1825 to 1938 and Library of Congress reference numbers is provided in the U.S. Department of Commerce, Bureau of the Census publication, *Colombia: Summary of Biostatistics* (Washington, D.C.: December 1944), pp. 5 ff.

tricts, who compiled the returns and sent only summaries to the central government. The figures must be used with caution, however, since the use of the results for determining representation tended to maximize returns while the usual fears of taxes and military service led to underenumeration. Ángel Rosenblat has published the following figures from the 1825 census for New Granada: in a total population of 1,373,110, *libres* accounted for 1,182,500, *esclavos* 45,839, and *indios independientes* 144,771.[43] In percentage terms, *libres* were 86.11 per cent of the total population, *esclavos* 3.33 per cent and *indios independientes* 10.54 per cent. The figures of the French traveler Gaspard Mollien provide a more precise categorical breakdown for the year 1823, but his information was acquired at a time when the data were rough approximations at best. He calculated the number of whites at 250,000 or 14.3 per cent of the total population; mestizos at 400,000 or 22.9 per cent; Indians at 450,000 or 25.8 per cent; mulattoes at 550,000 or 31.5 per cent; and Negroes, freemen and slaves, at 94,600 or 5.4 per cent.[44]

It was to the male segment from fourteen to sixteen years of age of the Negro population that Bolívar's numerous emancipation edicts were directed. They did help to recruit Negroes in western New Granada for the patriot armies, but they also touched off between 1816 and 1821 a series of Negro rebellions in various parts of the lowlands on the part of those who misinterpreted some of the proclamations as meaning immediate and unconditional manumission. In 1821 the first legislation respecting freedom of the slaves, a free-birth law, was passed. The new constitution, also adopted in that year, removed all legal restrictions on people of color: schools were opened to the colored population; Negroes were appointed to lower government posts; and some mulattoes served in Congress. Not many Negroes were able to vote, but neither was a good part of the rest of the population, because of literacy requirements. Holding government and armed forces positions became the chief methods through which the Negro could rise socially and economically on the basis of ability, and José Padilla, who became an admiral in the Colombian armada, is one example. Prejudice, though, had not entirely disappeared.

[43] Rosenblat, p. 143.

[44] G. Mollien, *Voyage dans la République de Colombia, en 1823* (2nd ed.; Paris: Imprimerie de Level, 1825), II, 195.

The Abolition of Slavery

Neither had slavery disappeared, for that matter. In 1821 there were believed to be some 90,000 slaves in all of Greater Colombia.[45] And although Cochrane in 1832 had gloried in the thought that, because of the free-birth law and the manumission committees set up to purchase the freedom of some slaves, "in about 30 years there will not be a slave in Colombia," [46] at mid-century there was still a considerable slave population in Colombia. One estimate placed the number as high as 16,468, of which 7,046 (42.8 per cent) were men and 9,422 (57.2 per cent) women.[47] The distribution of these slaves in the Colombian republic is shown in Table VII below.

Table VII. Distribution of Slaves at Time of Abolition, 1851

Province	Slaves of Both Sexes	Province	Slaves of Both Sexes
Antioquia	546	Pamplona	20
Azuero	82	Panamá	320
Barbacoas	2,520	Pasto	86
Bogotá	216	Popayán	2,160
Buenaventura	1,132	Ríohacha	283
Cartagena	1,377	Santa Marta	304
Casanare	0	Santander	34
Cauca	2,949	Socorro	111
Córdoba	342	Soto	174
Chiriquí	33	Tundama	5
Chocó	1,725	Tunja	6
Mariquita	198	Túquerres	56
Medellín	870	Valle Dupar	270
Mompox	168	Vélez	106
Neiva	237	Veraguas	60
Ocaña	150	Territorio del Caquetá	0

Source: José Manuel Restrepo, *Historia de la Nueva Granada,* II (Bogota: Editorial el Catolicismo, 1963), 210.

As can be seen from the above, the immense majority of the slaves in 1851 still belonged to the miners and *hacendados* of the six prov-

[45] Eduardo Posada, *La esclavitud en Colombia,* Vol. I of *José Felix de Restrepo* (3 vols.; Bogota: Imprenta Nacional, 1933), p. 69.

[46] Cochrane, II, 419.

[47] José Manuel Restrepo, *Historia de la Nueva Granada,* II (Bogota: Editorial el Catolicismo, 1963), 188.

inces of Barbacoas, Buenaventura, Cartagena, Cauca, the Chocó, and Popayán, regions where slave labor still seemed an economic necessity and where one would expect the greatest opposition to total emancipation. Scant attention has been given the abolitionist movement in New Granada and the extent to which economic, political, juridical, ideological, philosophical, and moral principles were operative and influential. In 1825 Joaquín Mosquera, analyzing the results of the manumission law of 1821, proclaimed that it would bring economic depression because the freed slaves would not work in the mines and that as mining production decreased the general economy would suffer.[48] A very recent study, on the other hand, tends to discount the economic factor as decisive in favor of political and ideological ones.[49] In his analysis of the debate over slavery in New Granada, Jaramillo Uribe has come to the conclusion that,

> In effect, apart from a few sentences and one or two poems, the theoretical arguments that were expounded [by the Romantic generation of 1850] either for or against the situation of the slave were the same as those which had sustained the fight of the Independence generation in favor of abolition. Slavery is contrary to reason and philosophy, civilization and the interests of humanity.[50]

It is his view that by 1851 the irrationality of slavery as an institution and its social and political incongruences were accepted and the heat of the struggle was centered on whether the slave owners could demand an indemnity when the nation declared the complete liberty of the remaining slaves.[51] By the law that came into effect on January 1, 1852, all slaves remaining in the territory of the Republic were freed, and, "in consequence, from that date [the freed slaves] will enjoy the same rights and have the same obligations which the Constitution and laws guarantee and impose upon all Granadine citizens."[52] With reference to the impact and reception of the law, the historian José Manuel Restrepo has written that, "Although the law

---

[48] Joaquín Mosquera, *Memoria sobre la necesidad de reformar la ley del Congreso Constituyente de Colombia, de 21 de julio de 1821, que sanciona la libertad de los partos, manumisión, y abolición del tráfico de esclavos: y bases que podrían adoptarse para la reforma* (Bogota: Tomás Antero, 1829), pp. 22–25, *passim*.

[49] Jaramillo Uribe, "Controversia en torno a la liberación de los esclavos," pp. 70–71.

[50] *Ibid.*, p. 81. Translated from the Spanish by Marie L. Rocca.

[51] *Ibid.*, p. 84.   [52] Act 1 of the law of 1851. Restrepo, II, 188.

was a direct attack against private property, the general opinion of the Granadines favored it because it was necessary to preserve public order and tranquillity." [53]

The next step in a historical study of the Negro in New Granada or Colombia should be an analysis of the role of the newly freed slaves in that society. But if scant attention has been paid the Negro slave in New Granada, less has been given the free Negro. While it may not be historically true to say that, "after final manumission these Negroes melted into the general population with scarcely a trace," [54] it is certainly true as a description of the current state of research on the subject. Nevertheless, we may try to give a general idea of what became of the freed slaves.

Population Migrations

Small numbers of freedmen, as well as runaways, began to migrate from the mining areas in the latter part of the eighteenth century. Throughout the first half of the nineteenth century some freed Negroes moved into the Pacific lowlands of Colombia and Ecuador, but most stayed in the mining areas as subsistence farmers or continued in the mining profession, usually working either as individual gold washers or free wage laborers in Spanish mines. [55] Some acquired ownership of small placers and one or two slaves. Efforts, too, were made by mine owners to persuade ex-slaves to continue to work in the mines. For example, Joaquín Mosquera, one of the largest agriculturalists in Popayán, rented all of his mines and equipment to freed slaves, calculating that he would at least realize about one-fifth his former income in this manner. [56] Other Negroes squatted on abandoned claims and worked only long enough to supply their needs. Thus, when general emancipation came in 1851, an occupational precedent had long been established, and most of the free Blacks continued as miners.

Migrations from mining areas to parts of the Pacific lowlands had increased during the period of gradual emancipation of slaves, from

[53] *Ibid.,* p. 189.
[54] Randall O. Hudson, "The Status of the Negro in Northern South America, 1820–1860," *Journal of Negro History* XLIX, No. 4 (October 1964), 229.
[55] West, *Colonial Placer Mining,* p. 89.
[56] Hudson, "The Status of the Negro in Northern South America," p. 233.

1821 to 1851. But the greatest exodus from the mining centers came in the years following final emancipation, 1850–1900. Large numbers of freed slaves migrated downstream, to settle better agricultural lands and become subsistence farmers and fishermen. In the Chocó, Negroes from Tadó, Condoto, and Nóvita in the upper San Juan River swarmed through the low divides across the Serranía de Baudó and occupied the rich natural levees along the Baudó River; others continued to the coast, where they settled along the better beaches and short coastal rivers, such as the Orpúa, Ijúa, Docampadó, and Virudó. Negroes from around Quibdó and the upper Atrato mining area settled as farmers in the upper Baudó and in fishing villages along the rocky coast north of the Cabo Corrientes. Many also traveled down the Atrato to settle the banks of its western tributaries, such as the Bojayá, Taguchí, and Buey. In the mining area between Buenaventura and Guapi, migrations were mainly downstream to better farm lands within and immediately landward from the fresh-water swamp zone of the coast; fishing villages and coconut plantations were established along the beaches.[57]

Negroes also formed the working and small merchant classes of the Pacific and Caribbean seaports. Here a sizeable class of small businessmen developed among the Negroes, involving mainly innkeeping and operating small general stores. The men who poled boats along the Magdalena were Negroes, organized and hired by Negro entrepreneurs who figured substantially in trade on the river. The free Negro's economic climb was negligible, however, limited undoubtedly by prejudice and fear on the part of whites. Generally speaking, we may note that, "There is no evidence that Negroes entered the professions to any appreciable extent."[58] Few became large landowners or important merchants. For the most part they formed a class of artisans and small merchants in the cities and day laborers and small landholders in the rural areas.

In the twentieth century, Negroes continued to form communities of gold miners in the coastal zone of the Pasto region.[59] In the area between Cartagena and Barranquilla used for sugar and cotton growing, as well as cattle grazing, the rural population is predominantly Negro. However, with the advance of modern technology in the placer mines of the Caribbean lowlands, there has been a migration of

[57] West, *Pacific Lowlands,* p. 104.
[58] Hudson, "The Status of the Negro in Northern South America," p. 234.
[59] James, p. 416.

Negro miners southward into the forests of the west coast south of the port of Buenaventura, where they have proved better able to maintain themselves than the Indian inhabitants of the forests.[60] In the port itself Negroes worked as stevedores and construction workers.[61] A monograph done in 1952 points out that the sprawling suburbs of the port "are made up of decrepit shacks, roofed with sheets of galvanized iron or flattened-out five-gallon gasoline cans, where live people of almost pure African blood." [62] Here some 95 per cent of the students of the local schools were of pure Negro or mulatto blood, while the teachers themselves were predominantly Negro. As pointed out in the opening lines of this paper, these conditions still exist in the port city. Negroes also made up the greater part of the population along the rivers that flow into the Pacific Ocean north of the Bay of Buenaventura. But this century has also seen the movement of Negroes from river settlements to various rapidly growing urban industrial centers, as well as to expanding agricultural sections of western Colombia, Ecuador, and Panama. Buenaventura has already been mentioned; we may add Cali, Cartagena, and Medellín. There were also migrations from the lowlands into the mild Cauca valley, where there was work on the sugar plantations.

Population Statistics in the Modern Period

Trying to trace the numerical extent of the Negro in Colombia in the late nineteenth and in the twentieth centuries remains difficult. The one set of figures encountered for the second half of the nineteenth century which includes an analysis of the racial composition of the population is that of Tomás Cipriano Mosquera, who served as military leader and, later, president of Colombia. Reportedly based on an 1851 census, his figures are as follows: whites constituted 19.04 per cent of the total population; Indians, 17.81 per cent; mestizos, 42.27 per cent; quadroons, 1.27 per cent; Negroes, 3.38 per cent; mulattoes, 11.90 per cent; and zamboes, 4.23 per cent.[63] Censuses were taken in 1864 and 1870; the former, taken under an administrative system which transferred the function of census taking to the federal states, was published only as a count of the number of

[60] *Ibid.*, p. 419.   [61] West, *Pacific Lowlands*, p. 106.   [62] Crist, p. 54.

[63] T. C. Mosquera, *Memoir on the Physical and Political Geography of New Granada* (New York: T. Dwight, 1853), p. 97.

inhabitants, while in the latter information on age and occupation was published for the first time. The 1870 census was the last general census before the civil war of 1899 broke out.

In the twentieth century the censuses of 1912 and 1918, conducted by the distribution of individual questionnaires and counting by individual districts, contain the most comprehensive and basic data extant relative to the races and their distribution in Colombia, for beginning with the 1938 census the racial or color classification was eliminated altogether. Both the 1912 and 1918 censuses recognize racial categories of "Whites," "Blacks," and "Indians," but all those judged to be of mixed descent were placed in a single category. It is obvious from the statistics that the mixed groups form the largest segment of Colombian society, but it is impossible to determine what percentages are mestizos, mulattoes, zamboes, or other crosses. The 1912 and 1918 census results were published as individual district censuses, with no nation-wide totals as to racial composition of the population. The 1912 census includes data only for the male population (except for the *departamento* of Antioquia, for which there is information on both sexes). The censuses also suffer from the fact that the *departamento* of Magdalena, in which Negroid elements are highly important, withheld the returns on racial classification in both 1912 and 1918; and the *departamento* of Bolívar, another in which the percentages of Negroes and mulattoes are high, withheld such information in 1918. Using figures available for 1912 on racial divisions in thirteen *departamentos* and three *intendencias,* we may calculate that approximately 33.26 per cent of the population was classified as white, 11.03 per cent as black, 7.87 per cent as Indian, and 47.81 per cent as mixed.[64] Using the same *departamentos* (except for Bolívar, which submitted no racial information in 1918) and *intendencias* as a base, the census of 1918 shows approximately 30.52 per cent of the population as white, 8.02 per cent as black, 5.90 per cent as Indian, 48.48 per cent as mixed, and 7.06 per cent as unspecified.[65] (The map opposite gives a graphic representation of the racial distribution of the Colombian population in 1918.)

[64] Population statistics for the computation of these percentages were taken from the *Censo general de la República de Colombia . . . de 1912* (Bogota: Imprenta Nacional, 1912), pp. 60–300, *passim.*

[65] These percentages are derived from statistics in the *Censo de población de la República de Colombia . . . de 1918* (Bogota: Imprenta Nacional, 1924), pp. 148–395, *passim.*

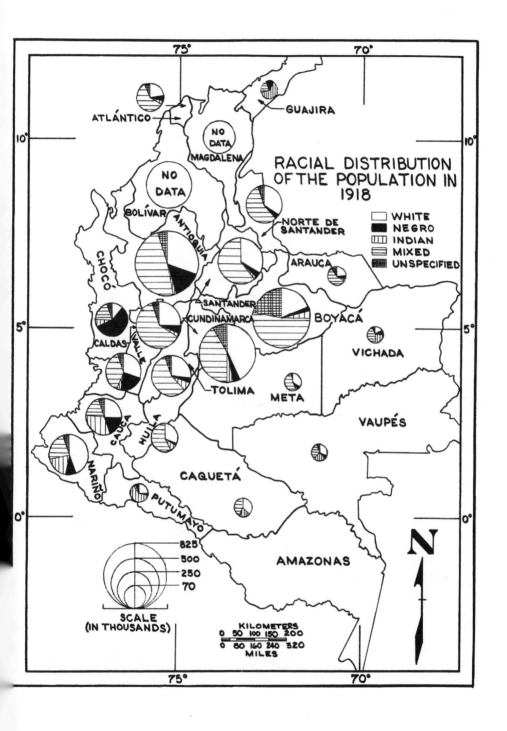

RACIAL DISTRIBUTION
OF THE POPULATION IN
1918

WHITE
NEGRO
INDIAN
MIXED
UNSPECIFIED

GUAJIRA

ATLÁNTICO

NO DATA
MAGDALENA

NO DATA
BOLÍVAR

ANTIOQUIA

CHOCÓ

NORTE DE SANTANDER

ARAUCA

SANTANDER

CUNDINAMARCA

BOYÁCA

CALDAS

VALLE

VICHADA

TOLIMA

META

CAUCA

HUILA

VAUPÉS

NARIÑO

CAQUETÁ

PUTUMAYO

AMAZONAS

N

825
500
250
70

SCALE
(IN THOUSANDS)

KILOMETERS
0 50 100 150 200
0 80 160 240 320
MILES

Because censuses after 1938 take no note of racial categories, it is difficult to establish the numerical strength and distribution of the Negro and Negroid element in the Colombian population in subsequent years of the twentieth century. Yet, it appears that it is those areas where the Negro was concentrated in earlier Colombian history that are the areas of present-day Negro and mulatto population concentrations and cultural influences. Sociologist T. Lynn Smith has noted that:

One who observes personally the fact that there is a large racially white population scattered about in the rural districts of the highlands to the north of Bogotá and another in the uplands of Antioquia and Caldas has no comprehensive statistical information with which he may test his observations. Likewise one who interviews hundreds of families along the Cauca river in the southern part of the *departamento* of Valle del Cauca and the northern portion of the *departamento* of Cauca may note that Negroes and mulattoes form the bulk of the population; if he visits the sticky overcast Chocó, drops down into the Valley of the Patía in Nariño, ventures out on the plains of Bolívar or makes his way up the Sinú River he is certain to conclude that the Negroid element predominates in the population; and if he surveys the heavily populated Banana Zone in Magdalena or finds his way into the numerous, small, remote, backwards settlements on the opposite side of the Santa Marta Mountains he will know that the majority of the population in those parts are of Negroid descent. But in all these cases, and in dozens of other localities he may have occasion to visit during his travels through Colombia, he will have no over-all quantitative data in which to anchor his conclusions.[66]

A look at the preceding map will show that the areas of relatively heavy Negroid concentration in the twentieth century—the *departamentos* of Antioquia, Bolívar, Cauca, Magdalena, and the Chocó, and to a lesser extent Atlántico, Valle del Cauca and Nariño—are the same areas where the Negro was important in earlier times. These areas—the Caribbean coast and the old colonial mining areas where Negro labor predominated—are today among the major regions of black or mulatto population of Colombia, regions where Negro influence is strongest and has left imprints on Colombian society and culture.

[66] Smith, "The Racial Composition of the Population of Colombia," pp. 213–14. Reprinted by permission.

Conclusions

The historical path of the Colombian Negro from African tribesman to slave in the mines to freedman and citizen, and his geographical distribution in that country, have been presented here in relatively schematic form, determined essentially by the quantity and quality of materials available. First, to identify the racial elements that have contributed to the formation of the present population of Colombia is a much easier task than determining their relative numerical importance at a given historical moment. Much of the data relating to population statistics is unsatisfactory, incomplete, or not readily accessible to the average researcher. Yet, an important part of the study of one component of a multiracial society is the determination of the numerical extent of that component vis-à-vis the others, for relative size of the groups will be one of the factors reflected in social relations. Also, only a small portion of the material published on the Negro in America concerns his history and geographical distribution in Colombia, whether as slave or freedman or citizen.

Nonetheless, a clear, if not detailed, picture of the Negro in Colombia emerges from this study. We have established the relative numerical importance of the black population from colonial times to the present: except in certain mining regions, slaves never outnumbered the free population. At the most, Negroes (both slave and free) formed 7 to 8 per cent of the total population of either the Viceroyalty of New Granada or the Republic of Colombia. The extent and growth of the various Negro mixtures with Europeans and Indians, the mulattoes and zamboes, respectively, has been obscured for the most part by their inclusion in censuses and population analyses with other racially mixed groups.

It is possible to trace the geographical distribution and migration patterns of the Negroes in the colonial period from the main port of entry, Cartagena, through the Caribbean lowlands into the highland mines of Antioquia and Popayán and the lowlands of the Chocó, and in the modern period their migrations from the highlands westward into the Pacific lowlands and southward into the forests of the west coast south of the port of Buenaventura. The most recent trend has been the movement of Negroes from small settlements to rapidly growing urban centers, especially Buenaventura and Cali, and to expanding agricultural sections of western Colombia, Ecuador, and

Panama. Yet, all of these population movements have taken place within the western third of Colombia, and generally speaking, the areas of relatively heavy Negroid concentration in the twentieth century are the same areas where the Negro was important in earlier times. And it is in these regions of black and mulatto population that African influences have made an impact on the cultural landscape of Colombia. In the economic sphere, we know that the Negroes performed an important function in the sixteenth, seventeenth, and eighteenth centuries, providing the labor that helped develop the country's all-important mineral resources. The general lines of the economic roles of the free Negro in Colombian society during the period of slavery and after abolition have also been sketched.

Under the existing state of research, however, more questions regarding the Negro in Colombia are raised than are answered, questions that deserve to be answered, or at least the attempt made, in view of the fact that the Negro or African element has definitely made itself felt in areas of Colombia and Colombian life. Now that the many laments over the scant attention paid the Colombian Negro have been made, much basic work remains to be done.

The Soviet View of the
Egyptian Agrarian Reform:
1958—1963

NORMAN LOUIS CIGAR

Introduction

In 1952 the new Egyptian government enacted the first in a series of laws designed to change conditions in the countryside. The Soviet view of these agrarian reforms is instructive in a number of ways. The land question was recognized by the Russians as one of the "basic questions" facing the underdeveloped East in general, and Egypt in particular. In these largely agricultural nations, the arena of decisive struggle in the second, or "social," revolution was to be the countryside. Great care had to thus be taken in the analysis of the "classes, the different social strata of the agricultural population, their economic interests and class goals, the attitude of the working class and the national bourgeoisie to the agrarian question, their struggle for the leadership of the peasant movement: the strategic and tactical slogans of the different parties and their agrarian programs." [1]

This was an important criterion used in judging the Egyptian regime and the "national bourgeoisie" in the East in general. In turn, these ideologically-based conclusions on the question of land reform in that country were influenced to some extent by the Soviet view of

[1] N. Kulagin, "Vvedenie," in *Agrarnyi Vopros i Natsionalno-Osvoboditelnoe dvizhenie,* (Moscow, 1963), p. 5. Throughout this paper, references to the "Eastern countries" in general will be applicable to Egypt in particular when the latter is one of the countries specifically so labeled in any part of the book or article.

the nature of the "national bourgeoisie" itself in other fields, especially in that of foreign policy.

This paper will examine Soviet opinion of the agrarian reform carried out in Egypt from 1952 to 1961, as found in Russian writings of the period from 1958 to 1963. This particular period has been chosen because it saw the appearance of a great number of extensive ideological tracts dealing with Egypt in particular, and land reform in the East in general, in contrast to earlier years. By extending the period to 1963, enough of a time lag could be granted after the important 1961 Reform to also include all relevant ideological analyses of that last significant measure.

From 1952 to mid-1958, the stand taken by Soviet observers in relation to Egypt's land policies fluctuated considerably, including long periods of approval, usually in response to periods of cordial relations between Egypt and the USSR and the acceptance of the "national bourgeoisie" as a "progressive" force throughout the East.

After 1958 one is faced with a quite uniform period of Soviet hostility to Egypt's actions in trying to deal with its agrarian problems. This is understandable in light of worsening relations with the Nasser regime in 1958 and 1959, as well as of disillusionment with the "national bourgeoisie" in general. However, this negative attitude continued to prevail through 1963, hardly affected by improving interstate relations, which were, in any case, still far from the cordiality of the 1956–1958 period. In this one can see the effects of the ideological reinterpretation of the nature and role of the "national bourgeois" regimes at that time. Possibly, also, the extensive theoretical works appearing during those years dealing with such an important matter filled with ideological rather than immediate implications, were less subject to the pressures of short-term foreign policy requirements, and could continue in their criticism of the Nasser regime in this field during this whole period. In any case, Soviet opinion on this question of agrarian reform did not oscillate according to short-term considerations to the extent common before 1958.

Basic Features of the Reforms

Agrarian reform in Egypt can be divided into two main periods, the first from 1952 to 1961, and the second after 1961, with the reform decrees of 1952 and 1961 being the highlights of the two periods, respectively. In 1952 immediately after the July Revolution, the first of a series of measures affecting the agricultural system of Egypt was initiated by the new government. The basic provisions included the expropriation of privately-owned land in excess of 200 to 300 feddans (depending on the number of the owner's children), this area to be eventually distributed to landless tenant farmers in plots of 2 to 5 feddans. Landowners could (until October 31, 1953) either sell their surplus land on the open market or accept government compensation, consisting of ten times the rental value, the latter being equated to seven times the basic land tax, in thirty-year nonredeemable bonds bearing 3 per cent annual interest. In turn, the beneficiaries of this reform were to pay the full value of the land received, over a thirty-year period, in addition to 3 per cent yearly interest and a 15 per cent surcharge to cover administrative costs. Membership in a cooperative was made obligatory for these new proprietors. In addition, rents were reduced, agricultural wages raised, and tenants' security of contract increased.

A series of complementary decrees led to the confiscation of the ex-royal family's property without compensation (November 1953), the subjection of *waqf khayri* or public endowments set aside for a charitable or religious purpose, to the general provisions of the Agrarian Reform Law (1957), the reduction of rents paid by Agrarian Reform tenants (1958), the change in the method of compensation (1958), and various amendments seeking to prevent the evasion of the legal ceilings on landownership (1958, 1959).

On July 15, 1961, a new series of decrees designed to bring about further reform went into effect. Landowners were now to be limited to 100 feddans per person, rented land to 50 feddans per family. Compensation for land taken under the 1952 Law was to be in nontransferable forty-year bonds bearing 1.5 per cent interest, for newly-expropriated land in fifteen-year bonds bearing 4 per cent interest. Confiscated land was to be sold at one-half the value of the land as assessed for compensation, to be paid in forty yearly installments, with 1.5 per cent annual interest. This modification was also to be extended to the beneficiaries of the 1952–1961 period.

Differing estimates of the total area and number of individuals affected have been made by different authorities, the official total area distributed being 430,850 feddans, to 162,773 owners and tenants before 1961, with approximately 300,000 more feddans available for distribution after that date.[2] Not to be forgotten, also, are the impor-

[2] See Gabriel Saab, *The Egyptian Agrarian Reform 1952–1962,* (London: Oxford University Press, 1967), p. 28, and Patrick O'Brien, *The Revolution in Egypt's Economic System,* (London: Oxford University Press, 1966), p. 204.

tant steps taken by the government to reclaim or open new lands for cultivation, including those available from the project at Aswan.

The basic philosophy of the Egyptian agrarian question as a whole was officially summarized in the National Charter of 1962, when it was stated that in agriculture socialism would not consist of "the nationalization of land . . . . and its conversion into public domain," but rather, of "private ownership of land" and the "reinforcement of private ownership of land by agricultural cooperation extending to all levels of production." [3]

All considered, the amount of land involved and the number of peasants affected is only a small percentage of Egypt's total agricultural population and cultivated area. As Gabriel Saab has put it:

This Agrarian Reform is important not only for the changes it has brought about in Egyptian rural life, but also because it has decisively influenced land tenure policies in the Arab countries of the Middle East and North Africa. It will doubtless remain a landmark in their socio-economic history. [4]

The Soviet View

SCOPE OF THE REFORM

By 1958 ideological analyses of these measures had begun appearing in increasing numbers in the Soviet Union, taking the Egyptian reforms to task for their limited nature in general, as well as for specific defects, and equating them with other "bourgeois" reforms in the East. L. Vatolina, in her report at the Conference on Agrarian Reform in the Countries of the East, published in August 1959, referred to Egypt's "half-way" policy of reform, an accusation later repeated by M. Gataullin.[5] The Egyptian experience was seen as part of the general "nonsocialist" Eastern reform attempts. All these countries, including Egypt had at best only limited the large land-owning class, not eliminated it; rather, they had all stopped "half-way," leaving considerable areas in the hands of the "landowners." Only the "most hated," "most negative" aspects of this system were

[3] The National Charter, Ch. 7, as found in Amin al-Ghamrawi, *Min Falsafat ath-Thawra ila-lMithaq,* (Cairo, 1962), p. 263.

[4] Saab, p. vii

[5] See M. Gataullin, "Vstupitelnaya Statya" in Sh. ash-Shafii, *Razvitie Natsionalno-os-voboditelnogo dvizheniya v Egipte (1882–1956),* tr. by V. Soloviova, (Moscow, 1961), p. 15.

modified, as, for example, landownership by the former royal family in Egypt. The very basis of the reform's direction was questioned. Quoting Lenin, N. Kulagin remarked that, " '*the basic question* is: to keep landlord private property rights or not' ".[6] (Emphasis in the original.) Since the choice in Egypt was for private property, the most that one could say was that "large feudalist property is [being] limited, but not liquidated." [7] All the measures taken could only modify or "partially alleviate," not solve, the problems of the countryside. Claims by the Egyptian government that feudalism had been completely eliminated were, indeed, vigorously refuted. The landed "elite" retained its privileged position, although in an attenuated form, since the maximum amount of land allowed was quite high, thus enabling it to retain a certain amount of economic power. The area affected was, in general, not regarded as being very significant. Thanks to the first reform, according to A. Sultanov, only about 10 per cent of the cultivable area was involved, affecting in all about 150 to 200,000 families, and only 5 to 6 per cent of the peasantry had entered cooperatives.[8] Moreover, religious and charitable *waqf* lands were maintained for a time, whose income, as before, was paid to the representatives of the "clergy" (*dukhovenstvo*).

It was frequently stated that the reform "only in part" had changed the situation in the countryside. In 1962, in fact, the estimate of the size of the area affected had even decreased from that of previous years in Soviet writings.

In any case, both the area of the affected land and the number of beneficiaries were claimed to be relatively small. The partial nature

[6] Kulagin, p. 10.

[7] Khaled Bagdash, untitled article in Kulagin, *Agrarnyi Vopros . . .* , p. 29.

[8] See A. F. Sultanov, *Polozhenie Egipetskogo krestyanstva pered zemelnoi reformoi 1952 g.,* (Moscow, 1958) p. 77, V. Bodyanskii, article "OAR" in *Ekonomicheskoe Polozhenie Stran Azii i Afriki,* (Moscow, 1960), p. 346. Soviet estimates in this field fluctuated from year to year and even from writer to writer; frequently, different units of area or various categories of confiscated or distributed land were used, making comparisons difficult. For example, see "Egipet" in the *Yearbook* of the *Great Soviet Encyclopedia,* 1958; M. Danilevich, "Rassloenie krestyanstva v kolonialnykh i slaborazvitykh stranakh" in *Polozhenie selsko-khozyaistva i krestyanstva v koloniyakh i drugikh slaborazvitykh stranakh,* (Moscow, 1958), p. 142; I. Matyukhin, "Obedinyonnaya Arabskaya Respublika," in *Ekonomicheskoe Polozhenie Stran Azii i Afriki v 1957 g. i v pervoi polovine 1958 g.,* (Moscow, 1959); the yearly article "OAR" by V. Bodyanskii, 1960, 1961, and 1962. In any case, the highest figure I have been able to find of land distributed was 2,500,000 feddans, in the 1962 *Yearbook*.

of all these measures, and their inefficacy, were thus repeatedly stressed. These, in turn, were linked to the government's motivation for undertaking land reform. All in all, as expressed by Khaled Bagdash, this "so-called law of agrarian reform is, in reality, not a law of agrarian reform, but at best a law of a certain limitation of feudal ownership of the land." [9]

DEFECTS OF THE REFORM

There were many specific points pertaining to this topic which drew Soviet disapproval, fitting in with the generally negative view. Among such criticisms directed at the UAR's land reform by Soviet analysts was the large amount of money needed by the fellah to pay for the land received from the newly-available areas. It was noted with regret that payment was demanded by the government even for those lands taken from the royal family. The cost of purchasing land, it was claimed, was a "heavy burden on the peasantry. Moreover, the necessary water and land taxes added up to a yearly total of up to 37 per cent of the gross value of the fellah's harvest, making it difficult to take advantage of the confiscated lands. [10] It was also pointed out that each feddan would cost the peasant from 230 to 280 pounds, while the average yearly income of a peasant family was only 40 pounds. [11]

All in all, the costs to the peasantry were seen by Gataullin to be "burdensome not only for the poor, but even for the middle farm[ers], striving to buy more land." [12] Indeed, another scholar claimed that many peasants were forced to resort to usurers, "well-to-do peasants," and landowners in order to continue making their payments, and it was for this reason that "the land is gradually passing . . . . into the hands of the rich peasantry." [13] Even when the price

[9] "Dva napravleniya v arabskom natsionalnom dvizhenii," in *Problemy Mira i Sotsializma*, (Prague), November 1959, p. 35.

[10] M. Maksimov, A. Maslennikov, and V. Rastyannikov, "Agrarnyi vopros na Vostoke," in *Mirovaya Ekonomika i Mezhdunarodnye Otnosheniya*, May 1959, p. 37.

[11] See N. A. Dlin's article "Ekonomiko-geograficheskii ocherk" in section "Obedinyonnaya Arabskaya Respublika" in *Afrika: entsiklopedicheskii spravochnik,* vol. II, (Moscow, 1963), p. 117.

[12] *Ibid.,* p. 14.

[13] R. Ulyanovskii, "Agarnye Reformy v stranakh Blizhnego i Srednego Vostoka, Indii, i Yugo-Vostochnoi Azii," in *Problemy Vostokovedeniya,* March 1961, p. 17.

of the land was lowered in 1961, the motive attributed to the government was the latter's desire to aid this class, that is to increase the number of individual "landowners." F. Nassar, in a Russian article, demanded land for "the peasants" throughout the Arab East "without any payment." [14] Thus, it was repeatedly noted, due to the high costs involved only the "rich" peasants, or *kulaks,* a rural group highly distasteful to Communist ideologues, could benefit.

Furthermore, the compensation paid to the former landowners for their confiscated lands was also severely criticized. At first, the size of the compensation was singled out. Within a year or so, however, the very idea of any payment at all to former landowners was firmly attacked. G. Kotovskii, discussing the agrarian question in the East in general, maintained that "a radical change in the condition of the multimillion peasant masses . . . . is only possible by the full liquidation of feudal landlord property rights without payment." [15] It was also noted that the government through this compensation, which could be used for approved industrial investment, "by all means helps the former feudalist to embark on the capitalist path of development." [16] Thus, compensation was criticized as an unnecessary measure, since it made confiscation expensive, enabled the former landed aristocracy to retain a degree of economic power, and opened the possibility for the capitalist development of the UAR's industry (at least until 1961) by that very class.

Another aspect of these reforms which was criticized was that connected with land rents. On the one hand, it was claimed that the lowering of rents favored the strengthening "of the positions of the well-to-do elite (*zazhitochnaya verkhushka*)," [17] which was by this means able to extend the area under its control. On the other hand, it was said that the poorer tenants still paid unreasonably high rents, despite the legal maximum allowed by law, which was so frequently evaded as to be only a "formal act."

Of greater importance was Soviet criticism of the cooperative system, an integral element of agrarian reform in Egypt. All beneficiaries of the various reforms were required to participate in a government-

[14] F. Nassar (General-Secretary of the Jordanian Communist Party), "O natsionalno-osvoboditelnom dvizhenii na Arabskom Vostoke," in *Sovremennyi Vostok,* February 1961, p. 11.

[15] G. Kotovskii, "Agrarnyi vopros na sovremennom Vostoke", in *Sovremennyi Vostok,* May 1960, p. 24.

[16] *Mirovaya Ekonomika,* May 1959, p. 36.   [17] *Ibid.,* p. 37.

sponsored rural cooperative, whose role was quite important, as seen by the functions which Doreen Warriner attributes to it:

to provide loans to their members, and to organize the supply of seed, fertilizers, livestock, and agricultural machinery, and the storage and transport of crops . . . organizing the cultivation and exploitation of the land in the most efficient manner, including seed selection, varieties of crops, pest control and drains. They are also able to sell the principal crops on behalf of the members. . . . They are required to render all agricultural and social services on behalf of their members.[18]

Actually, Soviet opinion in this area fluctuated somewhat during the period from 1958 to 1963. At first, the Egyptian cooperative system was generally viewed with favor. For example, L. Vatolina called it an "important result of the execution of the agrarian reform," [19] since peasants could now obtain credit on easy terms, seeds, fertilizers, equipment, and marketing facilities through them. It was even reported that in Hammada, a typical village, "the influence of the feudalist in the cooperative has come to naught, and this the peasants consider the most important change in the last [few] years," [20] implying similar conditions in the rest of the country. This same journalist, during 1959, however, took a decidedly different stand on this issue. No doubt reflecting the worsened USSR—UAR relations, in a typical analysis, he asked:

What is this Egyptian cooperative? It maintains private ownership of land and implements of production. Moreover, the cooperative is neither for production nor for distribution. . . . Therefore, the cooperative society is no more and no less than a distributor of loans. Through the encouragement of village cooperative societies we can perceive a policy which aims at strengthening the present regime of land ownership.[21]

This position was later modified, so that by 1962 cooperatives were once again in favor. K. Grishechkin, quoting *Al-Ahram*, noted that the peasants entered the cooperatives because they saw in them the

[18] *Land Reform and Development in the Middle East, A Study of Egypt, Syria, and Iraq,* 2nd edition. (London: Oxford University Press, 1962), p. 42.

[19] "Obedinyonnaya Arabskaya Respublika: Egipetskii raion" in *Agrarnye otnosheniya v stranakh Vostoka,* (Moscow, 1958), p. 620.

[20] S. Kondrashov, "U fellakhov Nilskoi delty," *Izvestiya,* August 27, 1958.

[21] S. Kondrashov, *Izvestiya's* Cairo correspondent in a Radio Moscow broadcast, "A Visit to Shibin al-Kum," August 12, 1959, as found in *Summary of World Broadcasts, part I, The USSR,* monitored by the BBC (hereafter cited as *SWB*).

means of delivering themselves from "the yoke and bondage of the money-lenders and exploiters," [22] that is, by benefiting from those functions of the cooperative which had been most severely criticized: its credit and loans activities. This trend continued for some time into 1963, when one could still read in the *Encyclopedia Yearbook* that "great importance" was attached to "cooperative agriculture" in the UAR.

However, by 1963 the Soviet mood was generally more hostile than before to this type of rural organization. During that year, fairly detailed studies of the cooperative principle appeared, the most instructive being that by M. Timur. According to Timur, little change had actually been brought about in the countryside by their existence. The agricultural cooperatives were said to be only a "capitalist institution, created in the interest of the minority, for the exploitation of the overwhelming majority of the Egyptian people." [23] The means of production, it was noted, were not pooled in these societies, and aid was extended directly to the landowners, not to their tenants. The "rich" peasantry was being given preferential treatment in the extension of credit, seeds, etc., thus promoting the more rapid development of this group in relation to the "poor" and "middle" peasantry. Moreover, the activities of these societies were closely connected with the "capitalist" banking system and with the Agricultural and Cooperative Credit Bank and the Egyptian Land Bank. In addition, as noted by another critic, control was not in the hands of the members, but rather "an administrator, appointed by the government directs all activities." [24]

These negative observations fit in with some other theoretical studies of "cooperation" in general which appeared at about this time, and which might help elucidate the motives for the Soviet appraisal of the Egyptian case. According to these studies, although "Communist and Workers' parties" supported "cooperation" in agriculture, the necessary conditions for this were seen as missing under a bour-

[22] K. Grishechkin, "Revolutsiya na beregakh Nila," *Za Rubezhom,* July 21, 1962, p. 15.

[23] M. Timur, "Selskokhozyaistvennaya kooperatsiya v OAR," in *Selsko-khozyaistvennaya kooperatsiya v usloviyakh kapitalizma,* (Moscow, 1963), p. 315. In fact, as the author further states, "the agricultural cooperatives of the UAR retain all the traits of capitalist enterprise." p. 336.

[24] A. Goldobin, chapter entitled "Arabskie strany: Egipet," in *Noveishaya Isotoriya Stran Zarubezhnoi Azii i Afriki,* (Leningrad, 1963), p. 555.

geois regime. It was maintained that "V. I. Lenin, in his works, showed the scientific unsoundness of the theory of cooperative evolution of agriculture under capitalism . . . . cooperatives under capitalism differ from capitalist enterprises only in form, not in substance." [25] Under these conditions, it was always the *kulaks* who benefited most from their activities, not the "poor" peasants.

In reply to those who might be inclined to see the cooperative movement as a path to the "socialist" restructuring of agriculture, particularly in Egypt, Timur answers: "These theories, independently of their subjective tendencies, sow illusions about the possibility of the fundamental transition to socialism by way of cooperatives (*kooperatsiya*)." [26] Nevertheless, these organizations were seen as useful in the fight against "imperialism" and the "internal reaction," since they could be used by the "progressive" forces. That is, the Communists might always hope to gain a foothold in them. In general, "Communist parties" were in favor of cooperatives. considering them as the material preparation for the future base of the "socialist reconstruction" of agriculture, but *not* when controlled "from above," to the exclusion of Communist influence.

Perhaps this, in addition to the fact that private property had been retained as an alternative to land nationalization explains in great part Soviet opposition to this system in the UAR—that is, the hindrance to possible Communist influence and agitation in the countryside. Timur, among others, specifically indicates as the goal of the Egyptian "national bourgeoisie" the "pacification (*umirotvorenie*) of the revolutionary peasantry." [27] As Afanasev further recognizes, "bourgeois authors" often maintain that the cooperative system under capitalism is a "stabilizing factor," a means of "pacification." Thus, not only is the "nonsocialist" path of development strengthened in

[25] Kulagin, pp. 17–18. L. Afanasev, "Vvedenie," in *Selskokhozyaistvennaya kooperatsiya,* also calling on Lenin for support, declared that in "capitalist society, cooperative societies (*kooperatsiya*) are subordinated to the interests of the bourgeoisie." p. 9.

[26] Timur, p. 323. He further remarks that "cooperative socialism" is, in many aspects, "petit bourgeois pseudosocialism", p. 323. Afanasev, p. 8, calls such theories "ideologies of opportunism", its holders "opportunists."

[27] *Ibid.,* p. 315. Similarly, Afanasev quotes Lenin as saying that "by this means [i.e., cooperation] the bourgeoisie attempts to attract the middle and even the poor peasants . . . away from union with the workers . . . to support the bourgeoisie in its struggle with the workers, with the proletariat." p. 5.

the agricultural sector, but also a significant part of the peasantry becomes "pacified," or satisfied, bringing about stability and support for the government, creating conditions less favorable for Communist agitation, and the second, or "social" revolution.

In any case, these reforms were supposedly carried out by the "ruling circles," from above. In fact, because of the government's complete control, its measures could only be labeled "state-capitalist," and the peasantry, it was claimed had "just been allotted the status of state tenants," [28] as a result. In a contemporary Soviet travelogue, two journalists, in describing the Pharanoic frescos in the Valley of the Kings, noted one depicting "the payment of the tax in nature to the all-powerful master of the land and the people," adding that the ancient Egyptians believed that everything in these pictures "would come to life, be transformed into reality in the next world," [29] perhaps another subtle criticism, comparing Pharaoh's central role with that of the modern Egyptian government. The state's role was decried probably because it pre-empted, and avoided involving, the local Communists in these rural changes. It was quite clear that these measures were being undertaken "without reliance (*opora*) on the democratic forces of the peasantry",[30] that is, on the Communists and potentially pro-Communist elements. The "national bourgeois" government of Nasser could thus reap all the political benefits and retain a high degree of control over the countryside to the detriment of Moscow's ideological protégés or potential power base.

In sum, as a result of all these deficiencies from the Soviet point of view, despite what Egypt's "official propaganda" maintained, this agrarian reform did not settle the "land question," as was so in all "nonsocialist" countries of the East.

[28] M. Maksimov and V. Rastyannikov, "Agrarnye reformy v stranakh Vostoka," in *Agrarnye reformy v stranakh Vostoka,* (Moscow, 1961), p. 31.

[29] I. Belyaev and E. Lebedev, "Kair-Luksor: putevye zametki," *Aziya i Afrika Sevodnya,* April 1961, p. 25. Kulagin, p. 11, presented as a basic criterion for judging such reforms the question whether the methods used were "democratic—with the participation of the peasants and Peasant Committees [i.e. Communist participation]—or bureaucratic—by pushing aside the peasants, in other words . . . from the top, that is by formal-bureaucratic (*kazyonno-biurokraticheskim*) means."

[30] R. A. Ulyanovskii, "Agrarnye reformy v stranakh Blizhnego i Srednego Vostoka, Indii, i Yugo-Vostochnoi Azii," in Kulagin, *Agrarnyi Vopros* . . . , p. 188. Also see Bagdash in *Ibid.,* p. 31.

MOTIVATION FOR THE REFORM

The USSR's view of the UAR's motivation in undertaking these numerous measures in the area of agrarian reform helps shed some further light on the reasons for Soviet criticism and apprehension. Besides the general ideological explanation that, as in all "non-socialist" Eastern countries, the "ruling circles were forced by the whole course of history to carry out agrarian reorganizations," [31] various other ideologically-based interpretations were proposed. Since the Egyptian regime was of the "national bourgeois" type, it was only natural that, "seeking to strengthen its political sway" and to "maintain its influence over the peasantry," it would carry out such reforms, which while not "liquidating fully the [large] landowning class, [would] substantially limit, and sometimes seriously undermine, its political and economic power in the countryside." [32] Thus, it was seen as a maneuver to weaken the regime's "chief competitor" in the struggle for power, that is, the large landowners, while at the same time supplanting the latter's control over the peasantry by its own.[33] The Egyptian rulers, it was claimed, relied especially on the "rich" peasants, or *kulaks,* as its particular base of power in the countryside, as well as on the "middle" peasantry which the bourgeoisie attempted to bring over to its side by letting it benefit in land reform. By these means, the upper classes had even tried to swing "the majority of the peasants to its side." [34]

These reforms were designed, more specifically, to "isolate the peasantry from the working class," [35] and from the traditional arena of Communist influence. This preoccupation of Communist activity, was seen as a great factor in encouraging the "ruling circles" to carry out some land reform in self-defense. As was pointed out by L. Vatolina, "it [the Egyptian national bourgeoisie] fears a social revolution," [36] and like all such groups, it attempted, according to Ulyanovskii, to "quiet" the peasantry's "revolutionary struggle" by these agrarian changes. This facet of the problem was forcefully un-

[31] Institut Narodov Azii A. N. SSSR, "Predislovie" in *Agrarnye reformy,* p. 4.

[32] Ulyanovskii, "Agrarnye reformy v stranakh Blizhnego i Srednego Vostoka, Indii, i Yugo-Vostochnoi Azii," *Narody Azii i Afriki,* May 1961, p. 27.

[33] See Ulyanovskii in Kulagin, *Agrarnyi Vopros . . . . ,* p. 223.

[34] Kulagin, p. 18.   [35] Ulyanovskii, *Narody Azii i Afriki,* p. 27.

[36] "Nekotorye itogi agrarnoi reformy v OAR," in *Kratkie Soobshcheniya Instituta Narodov Azii,* number 58, 1962, p. 13.

derlined when, in discussing it, Vatolina quoted Lenin as saying: "Reform is a concession, which is made by the ruling classes, *in order* to stem, weaken, or suppress the revolutionary struggle, in order to break the force and energy of the revolutionary classes." [37] (Emphasis in the original.)

In addition, the "ruling circles" of Egypt had intended to use land reform to encourage the development of industry, striving "by all means . . . . to accelerate the process of transition of the landowning class onto the path of capitalist enterprise," [38] as well as to raise the purchasing power of some categories of peasants, which would entail a widening of the internal market. Such economic results would, of course, most benefit the bourgeoisie.

Agrarian reform was thus viewed, first of all, as a maneuver by the Egyptian regime to break the power of its potential rival, the landed aristocracy, which was to be accomplished by limiting its rural-based economic power. Simultaneously, the measures undertaken were designed to create a rural base of power for the government, which sought to enlarge and strengthen the upper strata of the peasantry for that purpose. This would provide a measure of stability in the countryside, thus seriously hampering the rise of any revolutionary movement. Moreover, the economic goals of favoring investment in industry, at least until the nationalization of 1961, and the "capitalist" development of agriculture would have set the country on the "capitalist path," an event certainly unwelcome to Communist doctrine during this period.

Therefore, the Egyptian leaders were seen as being motivated mostly by political considerations, by a desire to strengthen their own class by "splitting" the peasantry. Economic motives were only secondary and after 1961 almost incidental factors, while humanitarian motives were never attributed to the executors of these reforms at all.

POLITICAL AND SOCIAL RESULTS OF THE REFORM

The results (economic, social, and political) of the agrarian reform as a whole were also viewed unfavorably by Soviet observers. Although land reform did play a "progressive" role by undermining feudalism, in general its consequences in Egypt were seen as being more negative than positive.

First of all, the betterment of the economic conditions of a certain

[37] Lenin quoted by Ulyanovskii in *Agrarnyi Vopros*, p. 188.
[38] Maksimov and Rastyannikov, p. 35.

number of peasants, to the exclusion of others, brought about by the "limited" reform measures, gave new impetus to the phenomenon of "class differentiation" in the countryside. Not all rural dwellers had been beneficiaries of the national reforms. One of the main criteria in judging this matter was proposed by N. Kulagin as: "above all, is the land passed on mainly to the very small (*malozemelnye*) peasants and agricultural workers or to the well-to-do (*sostoyatelnye*) peasants?" [39] In the Egyptian case, it was maintained, apart from those expropriated landowners who received compensation, it was this category of "well-to-do" peasants which profited most. Even after the 1961 decrees, "as before, land was distributed mainly among the well-to-do peasants," [40] since in addition to all the reasons studied above, which were seen as deficiencies by Soviet analysts, this category of peasants was able to use the largest part of the loans made available by the cooperative credit banks to purchase new lands. In fact, the substantial part of the peasantry was completely unaffected, and "substantial changes" did not occur in the "condition of the overwhelming mass of the fellahs." [41] The terrible conditions among the agricultural workers were also frequently described. Because of the distribution of the land, it was claimed by Khaled Bagdash that many agricultural workers and sharecroppers, including those who formerly worked on the confiscated land, became unemployed. As a result, Bagdash continues, the law dealing with minimum wages for rural laborers "has remained on paper." However, as it is later flatly concluded in the same essay, the ones to gain "least of all from the reform . . . [was] the peasantry." [42]

In sum, since those groups profiting most from the "partial" agrarian reform would become or were already supporters of the existing social order and government, the basic manual of Marxism-Leninism noted that, in non-Communist, Eastern countries, "it goes without saying, the biggest gainer from all the reforms carried out to this day has been the national bourgeoisie." [43]

This growing rural bourgeoisie was seen as quickly replacing the

[39] Kulagin, p. 11.

[40] Institut Narodov Azii of the A. N. SSSR, "Ekonomicheskoe polozhenie nekotorykh slaborazvitykh stran Azii i Severnoi Afriki v 1962g.," *Narody Azii i Afriki,* July 1963, p. 72.

[41] R. Avakov and G. Mirskii, "Desyat let antiimperialisticheskoi borby egipetskogo naroda (1952–1962)," *Narody Azii i Afriki,* June 1962, p. 43.

[42] *Agrarnyi Vopros,* p. 36.

[43] O. Kuusinen, ed. *Osnovy Marksizma-Leninizma: Uchebnoe posobie* (Moscow, 1959), p. 434.

ousted landed aristocracy, since by "taking part of the lands from the landowners for compensation and then selling it to the peasants, the state contributes to the strengthening and further development of private bourgeois ownership of the land." [44] Private property in the UAR was already the "dominant form" of land ownership, with the state intent on maintaining that situation. Thus, not only was the already-existing rural bourgeoisie being encouraged, but a new one was also being created, as a result of facilitated land purchases by which many former "rich" peasants were able to become "small landlords," renting out land. This process was seen as potentially even more dangerous since, "from among the petty bourgeoisie there will arise a middle [bourgeoisie], and then the large [bourgeoisie], that is those same elements against which war has now [1962] been declared in the UAR." [45] Of course, as a result of the retention of private property on such a scale, the transition to "capitalist" exploitation of land and hired labor was greatly facilitated, which is indeed one of the intentions of all "Eastern" governments. As was maintained in another study of land reform, in all non-Communist countries, "the ruling strata of the bourgeoisie. . . . cannot champion any other path, except the slow, gradual accommodation of landlord property rights to the demands of developing capitalism." [46]

Also, as a result of the growth of this new agricultural bourgeoisie, induced by land reform, class rivalry had actually increased. Quite a few Communist theoreticians at this time condemned this "sharpening of class contradictions between the peasants and the landowners"; [47] that is, the recent divergence of interests between the group profiting from land reform and the rest. In other words, those peasants (the "rich peasants", *kulaks,* or new *pomeshchiki*) who shared in the expropriation of the old landed aristocracy, thus becoming part of the bourgeoisie, no longer could or would be allies of the "landless," the "poor peasants," and the "agricultural proletariat" (those rural groups from which the Communist Party usually expects the greatest support), but would now rather hinder the "social" revo-

[44] *Mirovaya Ekonomika,* May 1959, p. 36, where all Eastern countries, including the UAR, are criticized for this.

[45] Grishechkin, p. 15.

[46] Maksimov and Rastyannikov, p. 74.

[47] *Mirovaya Ekonomika,* May 1959, p. 36. Also see Ulyanovskii, "Agrarnye reformy v stranakh Blizhnego i Srednego Vostoka, Indii, i Yugo-Vostochnoi Azii," *Problemy Vostokovedeniya,* March 1961, p. 18., Kotovskii, p. 24, and V. Pavlov, "Soyuz rabochego klassa i krestyanstva i sotsialnye preobrazovaniya na Vostoke," *Aziya i Afrika Sevodnya,* September 1961, p. 10.

lution demanded by Communist theory by siding with the "national bourgeois" government in such instances. According to Khaled Bagdash,[48] it was the latter class, thus, that now held the reins of power in the countryside. As Ulyanovskii observed, in all Eastern countries where land reform had occurred "there became clear the withdrawal of the well-to-do peasantry from participation in the peasant movement." [49] This was so, according to Kotovskii, where private property was retained, as in Egypt, because "the interests of the peasant elite diverge from the basic demand of the peasantry—the carrying out of further land distribution, since it fears that it might also affect its landownership." [50] This phenomenon, which ensued from the application of the agrarian reform measures, was seen by the Soviets as closely connected with the goals of the Egyptian government.

Thus, the results obtained from the agrarian reform were not welcomed by Soviet ideologues. The *kulaks* had benefited most, a new rural bourgeoisie had been created, and the principle of private "capitalist" property had been reinforced. A new political base was being built by the regime in the countryside. In effect, the portion of the peasantry which had been deradicalized, so to speak, was now more concerned with preserving the existing social order than with overturning it. Consequently, unity of goals or action among all categories of the agricultural population would now be impossible. All in all, the results were seen as insignificant for the majority of the peasantry and politically unfavorable to any of the USSR's long-range ideological goals in the UAR.

ECONOMIC RESULTS OF THE REFORM

Surprisingly, the purely economic implications of these measures received comparatively little attention from Soviet scholars during

[48] See *Problemy Mira i Sotsializma,* November 1959, p. 35. Kotovskii, p. 23, claims that in all Eastern countries, "the landowners were retained as a class." Of course, in some countries, their economic and political power was "considerably" weakened by land reform. In the list of such countries he does *not,* however, mention the UAR, indicating that he considered this class to have retained its economic and political power in that country.

[49] *Narody Azii i Afriki,* May 1961, p. 16. As was also noted by Kulagin, p. 14, (quoting Lenin): "as a private owner, the peasant gravitates toward the bourgeoisie, as a toiler and as an exploited [worker], toward the proletariat."

[50] *Sovremennyi Vostok,* May 1960, p. 24. Also see Maksimov and Rastyannikov, p. 40, for similar argumentation.

this period. The effects of the breakup of large estates into small private units on the total agricultural production and on output per acre or per worker were rarely discussed. More frequently, only quantitative data, unaccompanied by commentary, were presented.

In general, the level of production was viewed as still extremely low, especially that of foodstuffs destined for domestic consumption, whose quantity, it was claimed, had hardly increased from 1953. This fact was underlined by the publication in 1960 of the general index of Egypt's agricultural production, which clearly showed the very slow growth, and indeed retrogression in 1957/58, of output.[51] In view of these figures, it was obvious that the Soviets held the agrarian reform to have been of little economic significance.

Direct comments, indicative of either a rise or fall in the output per acre or per worker, because of changes in rural organization, were never ventured. However, it is possible to obtain an idea of the Soviet economists' evaluation of this aspect by analyzing the figures of the total product and acreage devoted to each crop appearing in various yearbooks throughout this period. As can be seen from the table that follows, their estimates of productivity per *hectare* of the chief crops shows that the latter had not been basically affected by the agrarian reform, even after 1961, either in a positive or in a negative manner. Only very rarely was there any reference to the fact that for some crops output per acre in Egypt was already among the highest in the world. Rather, Soviet writers emphasized the "extremely low" level of development which, when coupled with a rapidly expanding population, was seen as proof of the inability of the "limited" agrarian measures to solve Egypt's rural problems. As for the results on the output per worker, Khaled Bagdash noted that the cooperatives had not been able to raise the level of output per worker, "despite the fact that usually even under the conditions of capitalism, cooperation leads to higher productivity . . . in comparison to individual labor." [52]

One of the principal causes of this stagnation was, according to a

---

[51] *Mezhdunarodnyi politiko-ekonomicheskii ezhegodnik*, (Moscow, 1960), p. 548. See table:

Index of agricultural output

Egyptian region of the UAR. (1934–1938 = 100)	1946–7	1952–3	1954–5	1955–6	1956–7	1957–8	1958–9
	100	119	131	133	136	133	——

[52] *Agrarnyi Vopros*, p. 34.

Output per hectare *

tons/hectare	1934–38	1948–52	1953	1955–60	1961–62
corn	2.49	2.09	2.19	2.17	1.94
wheat	2.01	1.84	2.05	2.34	2.47
cotton	.536	.520	.552	.532	.496
rice	3.44	3.80	. . . .	5.17	4.80

* Computed by dividing total output by total acreage for each crop based on data appearing in the *Yearbook* of the *Great Soviet Encyclopedia* and *Ekonomicheskoe Polozhenie Stran Azii i Afriki,* yearly from 1958 to 1963. When varying results have been given for the same year by each source, the average of these has been used.

number of Soviet observers, the use of "primitive" tools and techniques. The "splintered" nature of the peasants' plots hindered the introduction of the necessary modern equipment. In 1961, however, it was claimed that due to the lowering of rents, some individuals were now able to begin using modern machinery, as a result of which the productivity (*urozhainost*) of some crops had risen somewhat. In fact, V. Bodyanskii praised the Egyptian government for introducing a number of new tractors in the countryside as part of its program to overcome the "backwardness" of the agricultural sector. Other writers, however, viewed the introduction of machinery from a different angle. M. Gataullin, for example, maintained that "the application of machines each year displaces a significant number of the working population from agricultural production," [53] which because of the already abundant urban labor supply was forced to remain in the countryside to swell the ranks of the unemployed. Since these divergent views both appeared during the same year, it would seem that a consensus among Soviet experts on the question of the role of mechanization on the cooperatives had not yet been reached. Members of one group (Bodyanskii, I. Belyaev) emphasized the positive results, such as the increased productivity, those of the other (Gataullin, Ulyanovskii) the negative aspects, such as the increased unemployment. This dilemma had by no means been solved even by the end of this period.

Finally, the effect of the reform on the size of the internal market was also noted. The purchasing power of the peasantry was seen as definitely on the rise, making possible the expansion of the domestic market for Egypt's industry, although at a modest pace.

[53] "Vstupitelnaya statya", p. 15.

In sum, according to the Soviet analysts, the effect of agrarian reform on Egypt's economy was minimal. While total production and productivity had not dropped, neither had they risen significantly, which in itself was seen as an indication of the failure of these reforms. The absence of any appreciable effect on the economy was, of course, in agreement with the Soviet view of the "limited" nature of the reform in general. In any case, the economic aspects of the latter were not studied as extensively as were its political implications, on the basis of which, in the final analysis, the Soviet critics were to form their over-all judgment.

FAVORABLE ASPECTS

This is not to say, of course, that the Soviet view remained so constant as to never permit any favorable mention of the UAR's land policies. Although Soviet opinion remained remarkably stable on this topic throughout this period, several signs of the effect of relations with Nasser were in evidence. In an article commemorating the tenth anniversary of the Egyptain Revolution, I. Belyaev commented that, "now, after the new [July 1961] decree by the President, a new step forward has been taken, additional groups of fellahs will receive land." [54] At about the same time, a journal article announced that the new reform had "not a small importance" and called it "another step in limiting large landownership." [55] L. Vatolina's book, *Ekonomika OAR*, generally favorable to the Nasser regime, and the *Yearbook* of the *Great Soviet Encyclopedia,* both published in 1962, avoided all criticism of agrarian reform. It seems that this was a series of exceptional instances of praise for Nasser in this field, no doubt as a political reward for improving relations, indicative of the rapprochement after the breakup of the UAR in 1961 and Soviet disenchantment with Qasim's regime in Iraq.

Similarly, in 1963, there were also a few such cases. It was again I. Belyaev who, in another *Pravda* article, noted: "it is characteristic that for the confiscated land in the UAR not one landowner has received a single millieme [1/1000 of an Egyptian pound] to this time," and "large landownership . . . is undergoing considerable change." [56] Perhaps here too, a timid hint of further accommodation

[54] "Na novom puti: K desyatiletyu egipteskoi revolyutsii," *Pravda,* July 23, 1962.
[55] Avakov and Mirskii, p. 49.
[56] "OAR: strana v dvizhenii," November 26, 1963.

with Nasser's regime was in evidence, since he was then one of the few not anti-Soviet Arab leaders, especially after the Baath takeovers in Baghdad and Damascus during that year.

However, these positive statements were very infrequent and not very important. Many of them appeared in the press, and probably were meant to have a passing, limited political effect—that is, during the rapprochement with Cairo. In any case, this trend was not followed up in more extensive studies and had little influence on the general opinion of Soviet experts in this area during the period dealt with here.

SOVIET CONCLUSIONS AND LONG-RANGE GOALS

Despite these fleeting favorable interludes, Soviet analysts, in general, had concluded that the Egyptian government, as all other Eastern "national bourgeois" regimes, not only would not, but could not, solve the agrarian problem. During this period there were frequent discussions of this question, the authors all deciding that this type of government could only choose this "moderate" solution, which could not bring about the improvements needed in the countryside.

Apart from these negative observations on Egypt's land reform, the Soviets also put forward positive suggestions, indicating what should be attempted, as well as the Soviet view of the "final stage" in the Egyptian countryside. The "reformist, reactionary" path was contrasted to the "revolutionary" path, which alone could really solve the agrarian problem. As Ulyanovskii put it, "the working masses of the city and of the countryside demand more radical domestic reforms, able to really improve their situation." [57] Most important of all the prerequisites for such an improvement was the abolition of private property, which was seen as favoring only the interests of "capitalist development." This was sometimes called the elimination of "landowner property rights," which, however, included most of the landowning peasantry. Sharp criticism was voiced at the "American" path, or small private landownership, and Lenin elsewhere was quoted as saying, "it is incorrect to suppose that the capitalist stage of development is unavoidable for the backward peoples." [58]

The best possible organization of the rural sector, as well as of so-

[57] *Agrarnyi Vopros,* p. 219. Also see A. Gromov, "Rost gosudarstvennogo sektora v OAR," *Aziya i Afrika Sevodnya,* May 1962, p. 23.

[58] Kulagin, pp. 4, 12–13. Also see Ulyanovskii, *Agrarnyi Vopros,* p. 225.

ciety in general, was of course, claimed to be the "Socialist" way. A. Polyak, indeed, talked of "the peasant way of solving the agrarian question, that is the nationalization of land." [59] This was seen as a basic necessity for the achievement of a "Socialist" society. As A. Yumashev, quoting Lenin, explains, "so long as in our countryside [that is, Russia] small [private] landownership will prevail. . . . a more solid base for capitalism than for socialism will be preserved." [60] In fact, this solution was frequently suggested to the UAR. For example, in a Moscow Radio broadcast, the head of a UAR agricultural delegation visiting Soviet collectives and state farms was said to have been favorably impressed, also noting that "it is known that nearly 80 per cent of agriculture in Uzbekistan is connected with the cultivation of cotton," [61] an obvious allusion to similar conditions in Egypt. Or also, the USSR's gift of farm machinery in 1959 was announced to be for a "machine-tractor station" in the UAR, again a reference to the means desired for that country's future development.

This "peasant way," the only complete solution, could come about only if "the determining influence on the social and economic life of the non-Socialist countries of the East will be exercised by the working class and the peasantry," [62] that is, by the Communist Party and its allies. This "next phase" of the national liberation movement would place the peasantry under the leadership of "the working class," leading it to the formation of a "national democratic state." It was stressed that only "the working class" could lead the peasantry from "capitalist slavery" to the building of a "socialist society." This process will entail the "neutralization of the national bourgeoisie," accompanied by the "rising of the democratic movement." [63] Only through such a "popular-democratic revolution" can this be accomplished, as the "national bourgeoisie" is committed to the " 'sacred' principle of private property," [64] and as it is certainly not likely to

[59] Report in "Agrarnye reformy v stranakh Zarubezhnogo Vostoka," the proceedings of a conference organized by the Institute of Oriental Studies and by the Institute of International Economics and International Relations of the A. N. SSSR in *Problemy Vostokovedeniya,* August 1959, p. 216.

[60] A. I. Yumashev, *Sotsialisticheskoe preobrazovanie selskogo khozyaistva v SSSR i stranakh Narodnoi Demokratii,* (Moscow, 1962), p. 20.

[61] *SWB,* Moscow in Arabic, April 24, 1959.

[62] Maksimov and Rastyannikov, p. 76.   [63] See Kulagin, p. 12–14.

[64] Kia-Nuri, "O roli burzhuazii v natsionalno-osvoboditelnom dvizhenii," *Problemy Mira i Sotsializma,* August 1959, p. 67.

carry out such radical measures "on its own initiative, without a shove from below." [65]

Of course, such plans for change in the agricultural sector and in society as a whole, which would require the overthrow of the "national bourgeoisie" in a "social revolution," are at best seen as only long-range goals in the East in general, and in the UAR in particular, even by the Soviets themselves. First of all, note is made of the "insufficient consciousness" of the peasantry, the weak influence of the "working class and its vanguard" on it. As is frankly admitted by Ulyanovskii, "the peasantry in these countries [that is, in the underdeveloped non-Communist East, including the UAR] is still not in a position to liquidate the class of landowners," or again, "the influence of the working class on the peasantry is still not [strong] enough to, by joint efforts, eliminate the ruling stratum of the country or to compel the ruling circles to embark on radical reforms in the interest of the 'bottom' peasant [layers] (*krestyanskih 'nizov'*)." [66] In other words, the Communist movement now, or in the near future, lacks the strength to undertake this "social revolution" in the face of bourgeois opposition, especially in the countryside. Thus, this is put off of necessity for the distant future.

Moreover, if the "national bourgeoisie" was "reactionary" in domestic matters, such as in its agrarian policies, its role in foreign policy was still "progressive." This, of course, was true of the Egyptian government during much of the period under consideration, especially after 1961. Since this regime was still useful for the USSR's national and short-range goals, it deserved the latter's help, as evidenced by the massive Soviet aid granted, including the financing of the Aswan Dam, which the Soviets frequently vaunted as an important element in solving the UAR's agrarian problems, but which in effect would contribute to the strengthening of the existing agrarian structure.

Conclusion

Therefore, the Agrarian Reform was attacked not so much for its economic failure or success (although it was maintained that it did

[65] L. Stepanov and G. Mirskii, *Aziya i Afrika: kontinenty v dvizhenii,* (Moscow, 1963), p. 121.

[66] Respectively, in *Problemy Vostokovedeniya,* March 1961, p. 34, and in *Agrarnyi Vopros,* p. 223.

not solve Egypt's rural problems) as for its political implications. Since Communist influence in the countryside was, as admitted, very weak, it does not seem that the Soviet Union expected to be faced by any concrete instance of a Communist-led revolt, where it woulld have to decide between actively supporting the local C.P. or the Egyptian regime.

Since direct Soviet involvement in the UAR's agricultural question was, in any case, minimal, this problem could be treated with less restraint than, for example, that of the UAR's foreign policy. In the latter instance, much greater care would have to be taken to mold the ideology to short-range Soviet interests, which would have great influence even on a theoretical discussion. Neither was the agrarian question such a burning issue as, for example, the dilemma of the continued existence or voluntary dissolution of the local C.P., where the Soviets were faced with the necessity of making a decision likely to have immediate and far-reaching consequences.

Soviet goals for the distant future in the Egyptian countryside, naturally, are still connected with a "socialist restructuring," involving the elimination of private property. Since this can be done only by removing the "national bourgeoisie," a "social revolution" is necessary, led by the Communist Party. Most of the criticisms of the Egyptian experience in this area can best be understood in reference to these goals. The "splitting" of the peasant front, the "pacification" of the countryside, the creation of a "political base" supporting the "national bourgeois" regime—all are aspects having a bearing on ultimate much more than on immediate Soviet goals. It is the possibility of the "social" revolution which is affected by these measures, and the degree of local Communist influence, actual or potential.

However, this question, even for the Soviet theorists, could not be totally divorced from the reality of the UAR regime's presence, and the USSR's short-range goals in dealing with it. Thus, after a thorough ideological attack on its agrarian policies, the final conclusion drawn was that conditions were not yet favorable for the attempt of any Communist-led movement in the countryside. That is, when it came down to practical action (given the likelihood of the failure of such an endeavor, in any event), the USSR of course found it preferable to continue benefiting from its relations with the "national bourgeoisie," postponing the "social" revolution indefinitely. This did not mean, though, that its long-range ideological goals had to be compromised. Indeed, Soviet commitment to these remained in full force.

A Cybernetic Reform Model
for the Soviet Union

FELICE D. GAER

Introduction and Purpose

The Soviet Union has reached a plateau in its development as a political system. The basic task of revolutionary reconstruction has been accomplished, not without severe tolls on the populace, the economy, the social structure, and the political system itself. The leap from a semi-backward underdeveloped country to a major industrial country (and one of the two major political powers) has been made. Rigid centralization and control have directed this development, for better or for worse. However, the economic and political irrationalities of the past can no longer cope effectively with the realities of the present economy, and of scientific and technological innovation. If the system is to move ahead, it must deal with the *real* economic problems in agriculture and industry, and with the *real* social problems—in education, culture, science, agriculture, and industry—especially within the Party itself. It is widely felt that the Soviet leadership must commit itself to a definite reform program to achieve the goals of progress, economic and social development, and rationality in this increasingly scientific age. Otherwise, it is feared, the system will stand still—it may even fall increasingly behind relative to the United States and other industrial nations. Such immobilism, which has already manifested itself to some degree in the Soviet leadership and in parts of the economy, may very likely increase. Thus, the system which has been built at so great a cost might unintentionally be the cause of its own destruction.

What, then, should the Soviets do? There are many alternative models which might be prescribed as a curative for the system's problems. One solution, which has seemingly been advocated by more conservative elements as well as by younger, technologically oriented personnel in the USSR, invokes cybernetics, the science of communications and control. This paper will evaluate a truly cybernetic solution—or model—for reform in the Soviet Union, both in terms of its theoretical utility and its political feasibility. Theoretical cybernetics, as distinguished from automation, offers exciting possibilities for reform, rationalization, *and* decentralization of the Soviet system, contrary to the conservative, orthodox viewpoint which conceives of cybernetics as a synonym for automation and as a means of maintaining and increasing a kind of centralism which it calls "control." This basic definitional misunderstanding is the reason for much of the widespread support that cybernetics has received from disparate elements of contemporary Soviet society.

What cybernetics really is and what its application can offer to the development of the Soviet system must be made clear. Once this is understood we will be able to make more sense of the different statuses of cybernetics as a science and as a program for reform in the Soviet Union.

Background: History of Cybernetics
in the USSR: Ideological Problems

Cybernetics made its formal world debut in 1948, upon the publication of *Cybernetics* by Norbert Weiner. With the development of the computer as a tool able to handle huge quantities of information and of cybernetics as a science, the current technological revolution ("The Second Industrial Revolution") began. Because of cybernetics' interdisciplinary nature, speculations abounded about economic, social, and political applications. Unfortunately, automation and cybernetics were treated by the popular press as more or less synonymous, leading to much misunderstanding of cybernetics.

In the Soviet Union, cybernetics was officially ignored until 1953. The last years of Stalin, which were intensely hostile to Western ideas, successfully inhibited acceptance of cybernetics. In May, 1953, three months after the death of Stalin, an article, "Whom Does Cybernetics Serve?," appeared in *Voprosy Filosofii,* signed by "Materialist." It condemned cybernetics as pseudoscience, as mechanism transformed into idealism, and many other pejorative things. Cybernetics, claiming to be a general science of control which cuts across distinct scientific, economic, and social boundaries—potentially into all areas of nature and society—has frightened Soviet ideologues, who have seen it as a threat to dialectical materialism.

A recurrent problem throughout the transition of cybernetics from "reactionary pseudoscience" to savior of the system has been precisely this: Is it or is it not compatible with Marxism-Leninism? As the utility of cybernetics and the development of computers with which to make use of cybernetics became more and more apparent, a softening of Soviet hostility developed. By 1958 cybernetics was "recognized" as a separate science. The technical journal called *Problemy Kibernetiki* appeared in 1958, and the Scientific Council on Cybernetics of the Soviet Academy of Sciences was established in April, 1959. Cybernetics was hailed as the solution to Soviet economic (and, consequently, social) development. In 1961 the first of a series of prospective articles by leading cybernetics experts was published under the editorship of Academician A. I. Berg. This volume was entitled *Cybernetics in the Service of Communism* (quite a reversal from "Materialist's" opinion!). Also in 1961, at the 22nd Party Congess, cybernetics was given explicit support, and its utility in economic development was stressed. Such support was also forthcoming at the 23rd Party Congress.[1]

Ideological compatibility of cybernetics and Marxism-Leninism has been "explained" as follows: dialectical materialism lies at the base of cybernetics, as it does for all sciences, according to official dogma. While cybernetics may be the general science of control and communication in complex systems, Marxism-Leninism is infinitely more universal in its interpretations of nature and society. Thus, the two do not contradict each other.[2]

Nonetheless, the issue of compatibility often arises, and Soviet writers carefully emphasize the dialectical materialist base of cybernetics (especially with regard to societal applications of cybernetics), and that it is only under socialism that cybernetics can fully develop

[1] For a more elaborate explanation of the development of Soviet cybernetics and the ideological arguments which ran parallel, see: Roger Levien and M. E. Maron, "Cybernetics and Its Development in the Soviet Union," RAND Memorandum RM-4156-PR, (Santa Monica, California: RAND Corporation), July, 1964; Loren Graham, "Cybernetics," *Science and Ideology in Soviet Society*, ed. G. Fischer (New York: Atherton Press, 1967), pp. 83–106; and Maxim W. Mikulak, "Cybernetics and Marxism-Leninism, *"The Social Impact of Cybernetics*, ed. C. R. Dechert, (New York: Simon and Schuster, 1966), pp. 129–60.

[2] Graham, p. 98.

and thereby advance society. Typical of such ideological insistence are the following:

The development of the problems of cybernetics in the Soviet Union is based on the firm foundation of the methods of dialectical materialism which is revealing the value of cybernetics for the scientific world.[3]

. . . cybernetic analysis of the processes of control in society should be based on the methodology of dialectical materialism, which is essentially profound, and be amplified by relevant sociological analysis.[4]

Similar ideological arguments are common in the German Democratic Republic (GDR), where experimentation with technological innovation and economic reform using cybernetics has developed. In many ways, it seems that the GDR has taken the necessary first steps towards implementing a large-scale cybernetic model. At the same time, the Germans have been able to maintain a high level of ideological orthodoxy and social control. Whether this East German "model" is applicable to the Soviet Union will be discussed later. Here, we note the continuing presence of public ideological assertions that cybernetics is subordinate to dialectical materialism. Such ideological arguments are particularly relevant in the GDR because of the presence and writings of such "institutional revisionists" as Georg Heiser and Georg Klaus. They advocate a form of "cybernetic revisionism" which views society as a complex system which can be modeled rationally on a cybernetic basis.[5] Thus, the East German political leadership is seriously concerned that the line be drawn between cybernetics that is compatible with Marxism-Leninism and the revisionist claims that are made for cybernetics in society, which would seriously alter today's Marxism-Leninism.

Both in the Soviet Union and the GDR cybernetics is viewed as

[3] M. Lebedeva and Smirnova (eds.), "Kibernetika," *Kultura, Nauka, iskusstvo SSSR* (Moscow: Politicheskaya Literatura Publishing House, 1965), pp. 97–101. Translated in *Soviet Cybernetics/Recent News Items* (hereafter SC/RNI) III (May, 1969), RAND Memorandum RM-6000/5-PR, 20.

[4] V. G. Afanasyev, "Yesche raz o problemakh nauchnogo upravleniya obshchestvom," ("Once Again on the Problem of the Scientific Management of Society"), *Nauchnoe Upravleniya Obshchestvom III*, ed. V. Afanasyev (Moscow: Misl' Publishing House, 1969), p. 20.

[5] For an introductory discussion of Klaus's ideological views in English, see Otto Krengel, "The 'Cybernetic' Revisionism of Georg Klaus," unpublished paper on file at Russian Institute, Columbia University; prepared for Colloquium G8430, Fall, 1969.

acceptable—in its automational aspects—as long as it promises industrial growth (if not miracles!). However, it must not interfere with or contradict the ideological tenets of the *political* system. Hence, that "it does not contradict dialectical materialism" is essentially an argument by fiat—that is to say, no argument at all.

Cybernetics Explained

As stated before, cybernetics, essentially, is the science of communications and control. Control is exercised upon systems, which, most simply, are anything which consists of parts connected together by a series of relationships.[6] But not *all* systems are the subject of cybernetics control. Systems differ from one another in any number of ways. One extremely useful, albeit arbitrary, scheme of classification of systems is based upon degree of complexity: simple, complex, exceedingly complex. If we distinguish between deterministic and probabilistic systems, as well as degree of complexity of systems, we end up with the following classification grid:

	Simple	Complex	Exceedingly Complex
Deterministic	Window catch Billiards Machine-shop layout	Computer Automation Planetary system	
Probabilistic	Dice Game Statistical quality control	Conditioned reflexes Industrial profitability	Business Enterprise The Economy Human Brain Political System

Source: After Beer, *Cybernetics and Management,* p. 18.

The utility of this classification scheme is that it focuses our attention upon the kinds of control to which different systems can be subject,

[6] Stafford Beer, *Cybernetics and Management* (New York and London: John Wiley and Sons, 1959), p. 9. The bulk of the discussion of theoretical cybernetics found in this essay draws upon the brilliant and lucid description of cybernetics in both the book cited above and, more especially, in *Decision and Control,* also by Stafford Beer. (New York and London: John Wiley and Sons, 1966). Other extremely lucid introductory discussions and explanations of cybernetics may be found in Henryk Greniewski, *Cybernetics Without Mathematics,* trans. O. Wojtasiewicz (Warsaw: Pantswowe Wydawnictwo Naukowe and Oxford: Pergammon Press, 1960) and in Arthur Porter, *Cybernetics Simplified* (New York: Barnes and Noble, Inc., 1969).

and thus, upon the proper scientific methods to use in order to control them.[7]

Now, we ask, what kind of systems are the proper subject for the study of cybernetics? Only the category "exceedingly complex probabilistic" systems. Deterministic systems, by definition, have completely predictable behavior. Even the computer, or a completely automated (not cybernated) factory can have its behavior described completely. Thus, these are, at most, "complex deterministic systems." A computer does what it is told to do. An automated factory acts according to its design. Probabilistic systems, on the other hand, are unpredictable in any specific action, but their general behavior *can* be described—only, however, in terms of mathematical probability. The term "exceedingly complex" is used by Stafford Beer to categorize systems that are so complicated that they are virtually indescribable. Since any deterministic system, no matter how complex, can eventually be described (by definition), the category of "exceedingly complex deterministic systems" is therefore claimed to be empty. "Exceeding complex probabilistic systems," on the other hand, do exist and might include, for example, a business enterprise, a country's economy, or, on an even larger scale, an entire country (a "political system" in its broadest sense). It is this final category, "exceedingly complex probabilistic," that is the subject of the science of cybernetics.

Once we understand this classification schema we will be able to focus more clearly on the misunderstanding alluded to earlier regarding cybernetics and centralization. A completely *centralized* political (and economic) system approaches, but does not reach, the category of exceedingly complex deterministic; that is, everything is believed to be ultimately describable. Hence, everything can be precisely determined from above, or, in orthodox terminology, can be "controlled." This differs entirely, as will be shown, from cybernetic control. But first, we ask the very practical question: is it possible to gather and process all the information necessary for deterministic modeling? According to present-day technology of the most advanced sort, (that is, Western computer technology), a computer, or system of computers competent to ingest all the raw data that a deterministic approach necessitates would have to cover an area of approximately 100 square miles.[8] Given the absurdity of so large a

---

[7] Beer, *Cybernetics and Management* (hereafter *C & M*), pp. 9–19.

[8] *Ibid., Decision and Control* (hereafter *D & C*), p. 383.

computer system, the disastrous state of the Soviet computer industry today, and the chasm between Western and Soviet computer technology, one can understand how ridiculous speculation about such deterministic modeling is for the USSR today. Let us assume, however, that the Soviets would also develop some sophisticated tools (and/or rent them from the West?) and would make their centralist policy sensitive to the real world, and that a measure, albeit small, of feedback were introduced. That is, the centralized system would be seeking some measure of homeostasis with the real world: a dynamic kind of equilibrium or stability. If the system were swamped with input upon input reporting real world information without a break, this homeostatic mechanism would ultimately end up initiating policy which is totally and solely reflective of inputs. It would therefore appear to be chaotic, oscillating back and forth in random fashion according to the precise "bit" of information coming in at each moment.[9] However, to function successfully, the control mechanism must be able to cope with the complexity of the real world in an orderly fashion. And *this* is precisely what cybernetics is all about: coping with complexity to the degree that a system will even be capable of reacting to *unforeseen* future developments as they arise. Although deterministic modeling recognizes that a multitude of factors is at work within a system, it cannot cope with this complexity except by irrevocably destroying it. Furthermore, deterministic modeling is based solely upon *past* performance, and has difficulty acting in a predictive way. Yet, the ultracentralists have long believed and, by and large, still believe that advanced technology utilizing computers, information retrieval systems, and data storage systems holds the key to their secret dreams of total orthodox control. They have made the mistake of viewing the world situation through deterministic-colored glasses.

Cybernetics utilizes all of these forms of advanced technology, adopting a probabilistic perspective, and coping with complexity through the fundamental principle of cybernetic control, the Law of Requisite Variety. Most simply expressed, this law says that only variety can control variety. (This does not mean stifle it, but rather, just be able to manage it.) Whatever the actions of the real world system being studied, if sufficient variety is provided in the corresponding control subsystem and can be proliferated, then, and only then, the

[9] *Ibid.*, p. 384.

control system can cope effectively with the real world situation. The levels of variety in the two systems must be equivalent. If the control system cannot proliferate requisite variety, it will not be of any use in control of a "real" world viable system.[10] The Law of Requisite Variety means that "orthodox" conceptions of control (usually conceptualized as a more or less crude form of coercion) must be abandoned regarding complex systems.[11] In orthodox control, the "controller" investigates the status of the phenomena to be controlled and then forces them to react according to a predetermined pattern. In a command economy, for example, there is intense simplification of the real world system as it exists at a given point in time. Thus, complexity is handled by killing off variety. Later, this orthodox control model will attempt to amplify the remaining bits of information to a level approximating the original one. However, this attempted amplification does *not* increase variety which was *irrevocably* destroyed earlier.[12]

The resulting orthodox control model lacks requisite variety to cope with the behavior of the system. It cannot deal with new, unforeseen disturbances. Furthermore, there is no place for error (deviation, breakdown) in such a model. All that has been created is a "static, inadequate, unadaptive model of what the world situation used to be like" at some time in the past.[13] Any similarity that this description ("static, "inadequate," "unadaptive") may bear to "planning" in the Soviet economy is not unexpected in this context.

Such an orthodox model cannot control such exceedingly complex probabilistic systems as an enterprise, an economy, or a political system, in their entirety. These are exceedingly dynamic, viable systems. Orthodox control refuses to recognize the essence of their viability. In fact, if orthodox control is imposed upon them for any length of time, these systems will be deprived of the very characteristics which make them viable. As a result, not only will they begin to behave atypically, but there will also be a steady decline in their ability to function. Degeneration of the system will follow, and it will eventually cease to survive: it will no longer be viable.

Cybernetics, on the other hand, accepts the innate complexity of viable systems, the complexity of interactions of viable systems with

[10] *Ibid.,* p. 279. For a more complete discussion of a cyberneticist's approach to controlling complex systems and to the question of requisite variety, see pp. 275–82 in this book.

[11] Beer, *C & M,* p. 21.   [12] Beer, *D & C,* pp. 308–309.   [13] *Ibid.,* p. 310.

their environments, and the complexity of internal interconnectivity of viable systems.[14] Viable systems may be characterized as follows: They can *learn* from repeated experience what is the optimal response to a stimulus not provided for in the system's design. They grow, or are able to renew themselves. They are not prone to internal breakdown and error, and most importantly, they continuously adapt to a changing environment and by this means survive, perhaps under conditions not foreseen by their designer.[15] A control model for a viable system must allow for, and encourage, these characteristics. How, then, does a cybernetic model do all these things?

To begin with, the cybernetic approach must also build a model which greatly reduces the variety present in the real world, because there is no alternative to this. The discussion above about deterministic processing of *all* available information made it clear that it is impossible and unfeasible for a control model to imbibe *all* available information, process it, and end up with a working control system. However, the difference in the cybernetic approach to this initial variety reduction, compared to the orthodox approach, is that the cybernetic approach rejects conventional simplifications which permanently destroy variety in an attempt to categorize raw data. Instead, cybernetics seeks to accomplish the variety reduction so that the variety which was initially lost can be amplified and regenerated at a later point by the control model.[16] The details of this procedure are complex, and will be left, for the present, for cybernetics experts to develop and explain.

The cybernetic commentary on world situations is that controls for them cannot be designed in the sense in which most people would understand that term, because there is nowhere near sufficient understanding about the detailed structure of the organism itself, nor of the environment to which it has to adapt, nor of the interaction between these two. *But this is not to say that controls for viable systems cannot be designed at all.* Certainly we can design those error-regulating negative feedbacks that directly reduce the powers allowed to a wandering variable and indirectly force it back to its acknowledged best level. But it has also been shown that feedback must operate on the entire structure of whatever proliferates variety, on its organization, on the built-in subsystems that produce aberrant behavior. It is this deeper level control that can be designed: a "meta-control" mechanism capable of amplifying such control power as is built into its design to cope with the unexpected.

This is what is meant by "implicit control".[17]

---

[14] *Ibid.*, p. 257.   [15] *Ibid.*, p. 256.   [16] *Ibid.*, p. 313.
[17] *Ibid.*, pp. 301–302.

Among the principles which are inherent in viable systems, and which cybernetics utilizes in a control system are self-organization, self-regulation, homeostasis, and learning. Brief remarks about their nature and relevance follow in Appendix A.

In the following pages, some cybernetic models are discussed. They focus especially upon the economic subsystem, which in the Soviet and East German cases is felt to be of primary significance in any and all total system schemas, and which has also been most prominent in theoretical discussions of societal cybernetic modeling.

Some Cybernetic Models

It is, of course, difficult for anyone to detail precisely what a cybernetic model for a political system might be like. While the following description will try to suggest the general type of model that cybernetics might yield, it leaves the rigorous modeling to the proper experts. The purpose of this description is to provide a little more insight into our general analysis of the rationale for, and the benefits of, a cybernetic reform model.

A rather simplistic kind of "cybernetic" model has been set forth by John Ford in his article, "Soviet Cybernetics and International Development." [18] It describes essential systemic functions in a single "loop" diagram, but is more a general information flow diagram than a cybernetic control model. (See Figure 1.) It allows only for partial feedback from the real world and there is very little homeostasis. Although there is much in this model that corresponds to the Soviet *leadership's* perception of a "cybernetic" system, it seems to be very close to an orthodox control model. In the Soviet political setting, this model might resemble Figure 2.

A much more complicated model which requires more explanation is shown in Figure 3. It is based on a model which Stafford Beer outlined for controlling enterprises in his book *Decision and Control,* and is adapted here to fit the more general case of a political system, showing the economic subsystem in some depth.

The left-hand side of this model reflects the economic subsystem and the right-hand side reflects every other subsystem in the environment in so far as it relates to the economic one. The rest of the environment (right-hand side) has been simplified visually into a single subsystem in order to make this model easier to understand. In real-

---

[18] In C. R. Dechert (ed.), pp. 161–92. (Diagram on p. 177.)

Figure 1: Block Diagram of a Cybernetic System

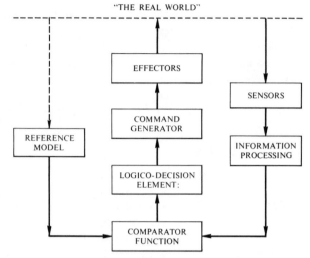

Source: after Ford, "Soviet Cybernetics and International Development," p. 177.

Figure 2: Adaptation of Figure 1 for Soviet Case

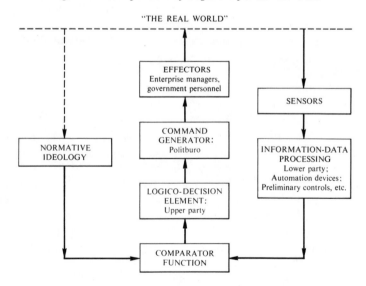

Figure 3: A Cybernetic Model for the USSR

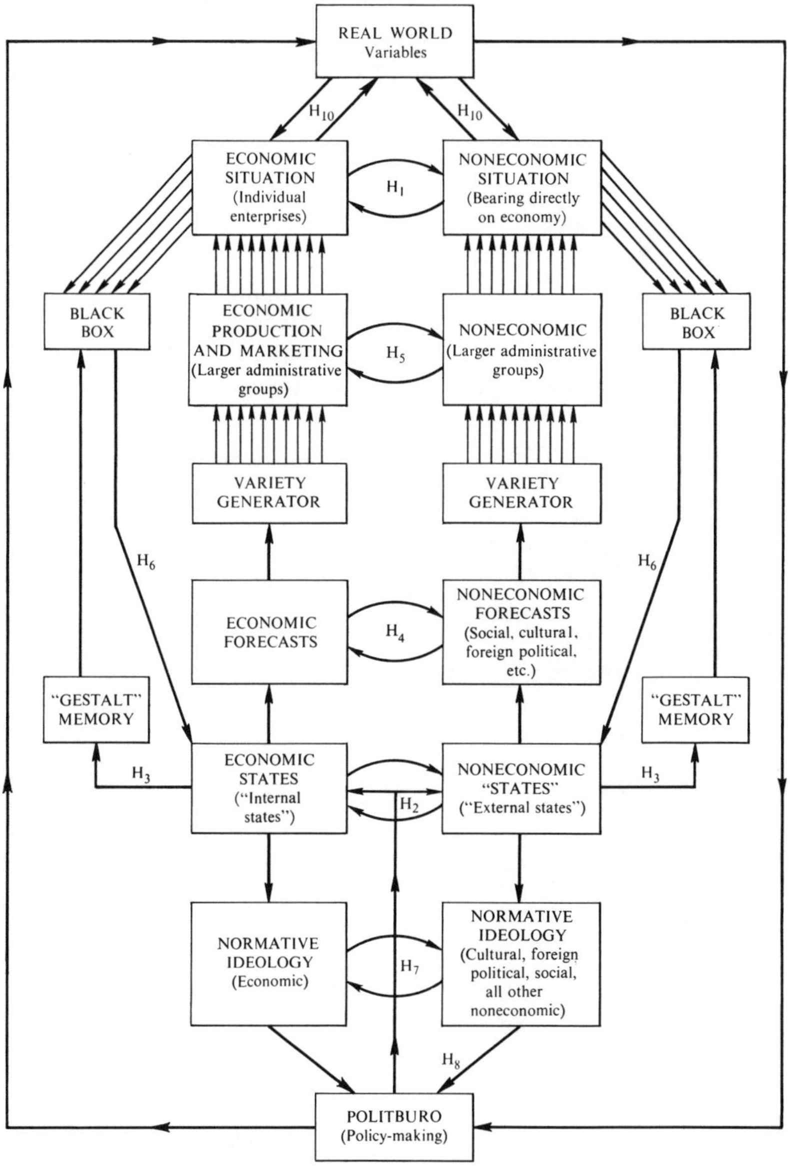

Source: after Beer, *Decision and Control*, p. 392. Adapted for Soviet case.

ity, there would be many interrelated subsystems on the right-hand side of the model, coupled in any number of complex ways to illustrate their influence upon one another and upon the economic subsystem. Even this greatly simplified model looks complex to the reader unfamiliar with cybernetic modeling. Its most obvious feature for the unaccustomed reader is the numerous homeostats (numbered H_1, H_2, . . . H_{10}) operating within the system. A clarification of the entire model follows.[19]

Let us assume, to begin, that a change in one or several factors has occurred in the "real world" situation at the top of the diagram. This affects both the "individual economic situations" which are analagous to individual enterprises, and the noneconomic situation, which includes cultural, political, educational, and other societal factors which have some interaction with the economic situation.[20] In each of these situations variety is abundant and amplified. As discussed earlier, the most important problem in cybernetic control is to become aware of, and be able to cope with, this variety.[21] It is at this point in the model that data processing and automation must be utilized. The incoming information is put into a "black box," and is processed. Lower variety output emerges, which is the vital information needed in management of the system. This information is fed into the crucial H_2 homeostat—which is a homorphic, homeostatic model of the "moment-to-moment state of affairs." [22] H_2 is a "highly structured and very stable" homeostat at the heart of the control system which does not change its state without good reason. It is not *simply* a reflection of the momentary state of affairs.[23] The information from H_2 is transmitted in several ways. In one of these, it goes to H_3, where the states of H_2 are recorded (in the "gestalt" memory boxes) and used to modify the first approximations and create second ones.

H_2 is used for short-range forecasting and control throughout the upper half of the model (H_6), and for long-range forecasting and control in the lower half (H_7 and H_8). In the lower half, where political decision-making is going on, there is a greater time lag. A notable

[19] This elaboration and explanation, as well as the model itself, follow Beer's detailing of a model for business enterprises in *Decision and Control,* insofar as technical details and explanations of component parts are concerned.
[20] Beer, *D & C,* p. 391.   [21] *Ibid.,* p. 392.   [22] *Ibid.,* p. 393.
[23] *Ibid.*

factor in the lower half is that the H_7 ideology homeostat—the long-term program—is determined at least *in part* by the output from H_2.[24] That is, while the ideology has some being of its own, it is affected by events in the real world—an observation of no great surprise to the student of Soviet politics who has seen the numerous changes in the "general line" of the ideology over the years. In the cybernetic system, the ideological component *must* react to real world phenomena. In fact, it *cannot* ignore real developments, lest the policy-makers (here, the Politburo) lose touch with the real world and drag the system into irrationality.

The importance of H_7 in the model is perhaps more obvious when one sees that its output largely determines the action of the politburo. This model can only be effective, then, when the ideology reflects reality.

The policy determined by the politburo is fed back to H_2. Thus, the "long range" intention of the top policy-makers largely influences and directs the way the real world will operate. This is shown in homeostat H_8, the interaction between what is happening now and what will be happening in the future.[25] As for the upper part of the model (H_6)—the policy execution half—H_2 transmits the necessary changes (or lack of changes) to H_4, which is the control system which prepares for immediate action in the real world. This could, for example, be performed by higher-level administrative apparatus (industrial or party). Automated computers and devices are utilized throughout the entire model, particularly in the H_2 and H_3 homeostats, and also in the H_4 homeostat and the variety generator. Before the "commands" from H_4 can be generated to the H_5 homeostat, there must be a proliferation of variety of the sort described earlier. This is shown diagrammatically by the numerous output "arrows" leaving the variety generator. The H_5 homeostat is the "planning" system which produces day-to-day decisions. Its output is a detailed program of action which impinges directly upon the "world situations"—or in this case, the economic situations (or enterprises), and the "noneconomic situation" (or economic environment). (The noneconomic situation refers, for example, to the local schools, to immediate political actions, and other varied societal facts.

If homeostats one to eight only were included, the system would probably be quite sluggish and slow to respond to initial changes, but

---

[24] *Ibid.*, p. 395.   [25] *Ibid.*

immensely stable. However, our system needs to be simultaneously *both* stable and highly responsive to events in the real world. Homeostats H_9 and H_{10} are intended to resolve this problem. Policy which is made by the "Politburo" or other top policy-making organ affects the real world directly through H_9, and the real world's reaction will, through H_9, have an immediate effect upon policy. One mechanism of H_9 might, for example, be announcements to the press (or in the USSR, to the Party) about certain policy intentions. The impact of such announcements can be measured quickly through H_9, in addition to the more lengthy and thorough means of H_6. H_9 adds some arbitrariness to the model and a measure of flexibility; however, this is more than compensated for by the rest of the model, which rigorously evaluates all incoming information,[26] removing it from the uncertainty of day-to-day decisions.

Homeostat H_{10} also increases the flexibility and responsiveness of the system. While changes are occurring in the real world and are directly affecting the individual enterprises and the noneconomic situation (H_{10}), the individual enterprises *and* the noneconomic situation are *also* directly affecting the real world and the variables therein. Hence, there is a dynamic equilibrium linking the smallest "parts" of the model with the "whole" on a moment-to-moment or day-to-day basis. This highly sensitive homeostat (H_{10}), however, is not meant to detract from the crucial significance of H_3 or of H_6, which are more complex and stable subdivisions of the total model. H_{10} merely supplements H_3 and H_6, thereby making the model more workable, and it also illustrates the fundamental interdependence of these elements in the total system.

There is quite a difference in a model of this nature as compared to the traditional Soviet command economy. In that irrational model, the lower portion of the cybernetic model was predominant (that is, the ideology and the policy-makers). Developments in the real world had little importance, relatively speaking, compared to the ideology and policy prescribed by the highest policy-makers. The output from the policy-makers was predominant in the system, and impinged on every level of activity. The opposite system would be akin to a laissez-faire one, in which the upper portion of the model was predominant—and where, in fact, only the most vague semblance of long-range forecasts and plans (ideology), and of general policy-making could ever be discerned.

[26] *Ibid.*, p. 396.

At this point, we must ask if a theoretical model similar to the one described in Figure 3 could be implemented in the Soviet Union: Is it economically and/or politically feasible?

Technical/Economic Feasibility of Cybernetic Modeling in USSR

One basic consideration in dealing with societal modeling is that societal systems and subsystems (for example, economic subsystem, educational subsystem, etc.) have so many different variables interacting in so many ways that it is impossible for conventional manual calculating devices to handle the variables and relate them in any coherent fashion. It is only with the advent of the computer that data from complex systems can be absorbed and analyzed. Computer hardware and software make possible collection and processing of the huge variety of necessary information which must be handled by a cybernetic system. Hence, the first prerequisite for cybernetic modeling is a high degree of automation; that is, a large number of sufficiently advanced computers, programs, and programmers.

If the Soviet Union is to maintain and advance its position among industrial countries, it must develop an advanced computer industry quickly. This is recognized in the USSR by both centralists (who see the computer per se as a means of greater control) and by decentralists (who recognize computers as a necessary technical base from which a decentralized, rationalized economy can be built). However, the computer industry has not developed as quickly nor helped improve the national economy as much as had been hoped. The industry has been beset by many problems, both technical and administrative. From time to time articles appear in the Soviet press which blame the various hardware and software problems in the computer industry upon the organization—or, rather, the lack of organization—of the industry.

The number of different ministries and committees which have jurisdiction over computer technology is astounding. Engineer V. Golovachev summed up this program as follows:

Each ministry has its own viewpoint and its own technical policies for its factories, scientific research institutes, and computer design bureau. . . .[27]

[27] V. Golovachev, "Rozhdaetsya Gerkules Chto Sderzhivaet Razvitie Elektronnoj Vychislitelnoj Tekhniki v Strane" ("A Hercules is Born that is Retarding the Development of Electronic Computer Technology in the Country"), *Trud,* (March 19, 1967), p. 3. Trans. in SC/RNI I (June, 1967), (RAND Memorandum P-3600/5-PR), p. 72.

Thus, this "patch-work" kingdom gives rise to what we term a "lack of centralized technical policy in the computer field." There is no primary center, no head scientific institute which might distribute task plans for various goals or for various types of machines to the different design bureaus, institutes, and laboratories; there are no scientific research institutes which might develop policy in this area.[28]

Engineer Golovachev's solution to this problem is to unite the entire industry under centralized control [29]—a rather conservative sounding statement, but one that is not far, in fact, from the view of most cyberneticians in the Soviet Union. This is not simply another question of centralization versus decentralization; it is asking for professional coordination, because the lack of coordination in the industry has resulted in overwhelming inefficiency and duplication of efforts. As noted, money and jurisdiction are spread out among many agencies who do not cooperate with one another, and who jealously guard their own jurisdictional prerogatives. Consequently, they not only duplicate each other's progress, but also often develop components and techniques which are not interchangeable from one ministry's computers to another's. What the computer industry in the Soviet Union needs is professionalism—creating, sharing information, learning from one another and improving upon each other's work while discussing together and working toward a similar goal. This is really what is sought by most technocrat advocates of a "centralized" computer industry: professionalism under central guidance.

Problems in software (programming and peripheral devices) have been, in essence, even more severe than those in hardware. Academician Berg, for example, has expressed grave concern about the paper shortage in the Soviet Union and its effect upon the computer industry.[30] Such absurdly simple and, one would think, trivial matters have caused severe setbacks in the pace and scope of the industry's progress in the USSR.

Recognition of and concern with the software problem in the Soviet Union are, in themselves, major "advances" for the Soviet computer industry. Only three years ago even the Academy of Sciences Computing Center was not particularly interested in software devel-

[28] *Ibid.,* p. 75.   [29] *Ibid.,* p. 72.

[30] A. I. Berg, "Problemy Informatsii," *Trud,* (Dec. 17, 1967), p. 2. Trans. in SC/RNI II (Dec., 1968), (RAND Memorandum P-3600/25), p. 37. For further discussion about the paper shortage and its effects upon industry, see also SC/RNI (Nov., 1968), (RAND Memorandum P-3600/24), p. 37, p. 57.

opment.[31] Nonetheless, the increased concern with and activity in software since 1967 [32] has not yielded real comparative advances in programming by the Soviet Union vis-à-vis the United States [33] (or the so-called world level).

In 1968, at the First All-Union Conference on Programming, Andrei P. Ershov, chairman of the Conference's Program Committee and one of the Soviet Union's top two or three programmers, revealed, that, on the whole, the Soviet Union is "on the 1963 level of world programming and this five-year gap is increasing." [34] Furthermore, he emphasized that

a consolidation of efforts in the development of high-quality, general-purpose software is of utmost importance.

Unfortunately, we cannot boast of significant achievements in this area. The majority of works are characterized by a lack of uniformity, by disparateness, by parallelism without competitiveness, and, so to speak, by an elementary state.[35]

The proliferation of ministries and authorities who have responsibilities in the computer industry creates a problem of political influence; namely, there is no ministry which speaks *solely* for the computer industry. This, indeed, may be one of the reasons that the repeated complaints about such industry problems as low level of utilization of machines, poor distribution of computers, shortage of highly trained programmers, low level of software and peripheral equipment, and impossible servicing conditions have not been met by any major changes of policy from "top" levels of command. The participants in the 1968 Kiev Conference on Large Scale Computing and Information Systems approved a resolution which asked the Academy of Sciences, the Ministries of Higher and Secondary Specialized Education, and the State Committee on Science and Technol-

[31] W. Holland, "Commentary" to V. Belyakov, "Mnogo li mashin nuzhno" ("How Much Does a Computer Need?"), *Izvestiya,* March 1, 1970, p. 3. Trans. in *Soviet Cybernetics Review* (hereafter SCR) IV (May, 1970), (RAND Memorandum RM-6200/5-PR), p. 22.

[32] W. Holland, "Soviet Computing, 1969: A Leap into the Third Generation?," SCR III (July, 1969), 1.

[33] See, for example, Belyakov, pp. 21, 22 and *passim.*

[34] A. P. Ershov, "Programmirovanie—68" ("Programming—68"), *Avtomatizatsiya Programmirovaniya* (Automation of Programming), (Kiev: no p., 1969), pp. 3–19. Trans. in SCR IV (June, 1970), (RAND Memorandum RM-6200/PR), p. 8.

[35] *Ibid.,* p. 6.

ogy of the Council of Ministers to establish a special ministry on computer technology and computing systems, which could take definitive action to resolve some of the difficulties.[36] However, we have heard nothing more of this resolution since it was made in May, 1968. Thus far, there has been no indication that this issue arose at the Second All-Union Conference on Programming, February, 1970. The problems still remain.

Just as much of the discussion of cybernetics has centered around the need for automation, so the discussion of the implementation of cybernetics throughout the country has often taken the form of a debate about the statewide network of computer centers. This network was originally conceived of as a geographically based unit, primarily responsible for information retrieval and processing and responsible ultimately to *one* agency. It was to cut across jurisdictional lines of ministries and agencies presently developing computers and computer systems of their own.[37] It was to be, in essence,

a "nervous system" tying together the system's sensors of internal and external environments at all organizational levels with the highest decision centers. These can then determine optimal courses of action and transmit information to the effector organs of the social system—ministries, production complexes, schools, defense installations, and so on.[38]

Such a gigantic system of information collection and transmission is, of course, necessary to a certain degree in any incipient cybernetic system. It is not, sufficient in itself, to create the kind of cybernetic system of organization and control proposed in this paper. Organizational, technological, educational, and other social changes must accompany such a computer network's development if a cybernetic system is to become a reality.

The problem surrounding the computer network is twofold: (1) Can Soviet technology produce such an advanced information network in a reasonable amount of time, and (2) how should the system be organized; centralized or decentralized; that is, hierarchically on a geographical basis, or jurisdictionally, by maintaining the current responsibilities of the existing agencies and subsequently uniting them?

[36] E. A. Bratalski and R. V. Tveritski, "Problemy sozdaniya bolshikh informatsionno-vychislitelnykh sistem i obrabotki informatsii na ETsVM," ("Problems of developing large-scale computing and information systems and computer processing data"), *Nauchno-tekhnicheskiya Informatsiya,* (*Scientific-technical Information*), Series 2, no. 9, 1968. Trans. in SC/RNI III (September, 1969), p. 53.

[37] Holland, p. 16.   [38] Ford, pp. 184–85.

As for technological capability, it is clear from the discussion above that significant changes must be made in the industry to enable it to advance computer production and utilization. Some sort of central guidelines are believed necessary. Serious problems still exist, however, in both hardware and most especially in software production. Another aspect of this problem relates to unresolved debates on the possibility of buying equipment abroad to meet the huge needs.[39]

Resolving the question about the organization of the industry is much more complex, involving many levels of economic and political debate. In some ways, it is a microcosm of the national debate on the economic questions of centralization, decentralization, technological change, and vested interests. Many conservatives see a geographically based system responsible to one agency as a means of control, in the orthodox sense, of the economy. They believe that obtaining all available information will give them this control.

On one level, the different agencies and ministries involved in computer development resent and fear the single geographically based system because they see themselves becoming dependent upon and subordinate to this super-agency for all information.[40] Both their funds and jurisdictional prerogatives would be threatened by a centralized system which cuts across jurisdictional boundaries. Furthermore, innovation might be significantly cut back as a by-product of centralization of the computer information system. On another level, a jurisdictionally based system might increase the tendency of specific agencies to give special preference to their own needs in the specific kinds of computers and systems that are produced, that is, a kind of "localism" is feared here, and the issue has not yet been clearly resolved in favor of one alternative or the other.[41]

This brings us to the question of modeling. In the Soviet Union,

---

[39] For more on this possibility, see V. Glushkov, A. Doroditsyn, and N. Fedorenko, "O Nekotorykh Problemakh Kibernetiki" ("Some Problems of Cybernetics"), *Izvestiya*, Sept. 6, 1964, p. 4. Trans. in SC/RNI I (July, 1967), (RAND Memorandum P-3600/6), pp. 37–47, and A. Doroditsyn, "Narodnoe Khozyaistvo Vychislitelnaya Tekhnika" ("National Economy and Computer Technology"), *Pravda*, February 24, 1966, p. 2. Trans. by JPRS in SC/RNI I (July, 1967), (RAND Memorandum P-3600/6), pp. 48–53.

[40] V. Przhiyalkovskij, "Chto Meshaet Mashin Dumat" (What Prevents a Machine from Thinking?"), *Pravda*, August 28, 1968, p. 2. Trans. in SC/RNI II (Oct. 1968), (RAND Memorandum P-3600/22), pp. 33–37, *passim*.

[41] See, for example, "The State Network of Computer Centers: 1) The Gosplan Approach, 2) The CSA Approach," SCR III (September 1969) (RAND Memorandum RM-6000/9-PR), pp. 59–75.

modeling has had considerable prominence in the crude form of the Five Year Plans since the 20s. However, in the modern technological age, modeling has gone beyond economics into the field of societal systems.

Administratively, a proliferation of agencies and ministries is engaged in the "scientific study" of social forecasting. These include, among others, such groups as the Science Research Committee on Forecasting under the Soviet Sociological Association, and subsections of the Academy of Sciences, Gosplan, and the State Committee on Science and Technology of the Council of Ministers.[42] They are studying the following main trends in social forecasting: (1) Forecasting prospects for the development of science and technology as social phenomena; (2) forecasting socioeconomic phenomena; (3) military and political forecasting; (4) social aspects of geographical and space forecasts; and (5) forecasting the social aspects of public health.[43]

Despite the specific recommendations of different spokesmen, there has been a great deal of acceptance in the USSR of the idea of modeling based upon modern science and technology. Such a viewpoint is, to a certain degree, a positive sign for advocates of a cybernetic model and, in any case, is an important prerequisite to any serious efforts in that direction. While cybernetic modeling is, indeed, based upon methods developed in mathematical modeling, linear programming, and heuristic programming, it differs from them especially in its approach to control: cybernetic as opposed to orthodox control.

Nonetheless, forecasting (*prognozirovanie*) is seen by most Soviets as necessary for economic and social advancement. Modern mathematical techniques seem to be able to cope, in the future, with the complexity of the world, and, with the complexity of social problems of the Soviet Union. Along these lines, Dr. of Historical Sciences I. V. Bestuzhev-Lada emphasized that "socioeconomic planning is now required, in addition to economic planning. Consequently forecasting is required not only for economic processes, but also for social processes in the broadest sense of the word." [44] Yet, this same author takes special care to remind readers that social forecasting is defi-

---

[42] I. V. Bestuzhev-Lada, "Obshchestvennoe Prognozirovanie," ("Social Forecasting"), *Prognozirovanie Nauchno-tekhnicheskogo Progressa* ("Forecasting Scientific-technical Progress"), (Moscow: Znanie Publishing House, 1968), pp. 6–12. Trans. in SC/RNI III (May, 1969), (RAND Memorandum RM-6000/5-PR), p. 57.

[43] *Ibid.*, p. 56.   [44] *Ibid.*, pp. 55–56.

nitely *not* an alternative to scientific communism, as some Western writers might suggest. Rather—and here the ideological argument discussed earlier reappears—research in social forecasting is based upon the theoretical propositions of dialectical and historical materialism.[45]

Thus, it is not clear to what extent the concept of orthodox control is present in the minds of those who speak about cybernetics in the USSR. For example, another Soviet, V. Afanasyev, who uses a good deal of cybernetic jargon about society, government, and so on has said that the essence of his view of "scientific management of society" is that "the problem of management of society and its separate sections is, first of all, economic, social, and ideological and not cybernetic, "natural" scientific, technical, or some other kind of problem." [46] He is also careful to reiterate the primacy of the Party in social management,[47] thus sounding rather orthodox.

Of course the various political issues which must be evaluated regarding modeling and cybernetics are quite complex and it is undeniably difficult to forecast the course of the "second industrial revolution" and the role of cybernetics in the Soviet Union in the *real* political environment. It will, however, come as no surprise that the Soviet leadership would like to have its cake and to eat it as well. It would like to garner all the benefits and rationality that cybernetics and modeling have to offer it *and* to maintain "orthodox" control over the system. Political realities being what they are, the Soviets have been increasingly interested in East Germany since the New Economic System was implemented there in 1963. The East Germans have examined the present technological era and have recognized the need to modernize and rationalize the economy on a technologically advanced level. At the same time, ideological strictness has been maintained; the social and cultural spheres have not loosened up.

The East German Case

There is much talk in the GDR about cybernetics and modeling. The economy has been restructured in a way which combines a mea-

[45] *Ibid.*, pp. 58–59.
[46] V. G. Afanasyev, "Once Again . . . ," p. 15. Cf. this to V. Afanasyev, *Nauchnoe Upravleniya Obshchestvom* (Moscow: Politizdat, 1968), p. 367 and *passim.*
[47] *Ibid., passim.*

sure of centralism with a great deal of decentralization, with much independent initiative and responsibility for the individual enterprises. Automation and systems planning are the most immediate objectives in the rationalization and modernization of the system. To this end efforts have been made to improve technical training. The Third University Reform has also tied the universities closer to industry and the needs of production.[48] The Party has experienced considerable changes, with a tendency toward inclusion of younger members who are more technically advanced and, in general, toward the inclusion of specialists.[49] Yet, the ideological and cultural rigidity of the regime has not loosened up. To the Soviets the GDR's path looks, in many ways, like the best of both worlds. Whether it is, and, if so, what the chances are in the USSR for this kind of change poses crucial questions before groups looking for reform in the system. To gain a better insight into this question, we had best look closer at the setup in the GDR.

In the GDR, the primary emphasis of reform has been upon the economic subsystem, which is, naturally, the most important subsystem for immediate progress, and, concomitantly, upon science and technology as essential for the advancement of the economic subsystem.

The old centralized structure of the economy in the GDR has experienced a fundamental organizational realignment, which amounts to a form of decentralization. Over-all management of the national economy is the primary responsibility of the Council of Ministers. Long range economic planning, as distinct from the earlier, rigid Five Year Plans, is delegated to the State Planning Commission. In place of the National Economic Council, which was abolished at the December 1965 Plenum of the CC SED, there are eight new

---

[48] See, for example, David Childs, *East Germany* (New York: Frederick A. Praeger, 1969), pp. 124–35, for a general description of educational structure and the Third University Reform. See also "Society and the Intelligentsia: Views From the GDR: Socialist Cultural Revolution and the Intelligentsia," *World Marxist Review* XII (September 1969), pp. 75–81; and Willi Stoph, "The New Function of Science in Socialist Society," *Forum* (E. Berlin), Dec., 1969, Supplement, pp. 1–8. Trans. by JPRS 49654, Trans. on E. Europe: Political, Sociological and Military Affairs, no. 175 (January 21, 1970) regarding the effect of educational reform on the society and economy and its general importance for the system.

[49] For a summary of changes in and the current nature of the leadership, see Childs, pp. 173–99, and P. C. Ludz, "The Future of the GDR," *Die Zeit*, October 10, 1969, pp. 53, 55–58. Trans. by JPRS 49251. Trans. on E. Europe: Political, Sociological and Military Affairs, no. 156, (Nov. 14, 1969), pp. 119–33.

ministries responsible for major industrial divisions of the economy.[50] There are approximately eighty Associations of State Enterprises (VVBs) under the eight industrial ministries. To a large degree the VVBs are the crucial level in the economic system. They have been given responsibility which formerly belonged to central agencies, as well as some responsibility which was formerly left to the individual enterprises. Thus, they are close enough, yet far enough, from the day-to-day actions of the enterprises to coordinate their actions within the framework of the system's broad goals, using rational criteria for economic efficiency and development. The individual enterprises (VEBs) deal with the most immediate economic problems. By far, most of the enterprises are responsible to the VVBs, although a few "crucial" or "sensitive" areas are still directly responsible to the industrial ministries, and a few to local economic councils.[51] The hierarchic setup is not centralistic in the way one might imagine. Each VVB is, to a large extent, an independent economic being, or is intended to develop into one. It receives only a minimum of directives from the central authorities and, thus, is a form of semi-independent industrial concern.[52]

In 1966 changes were made limiting the power of the VVBs in the economy, which, until then, had been quite great. However, the present setup offers increased participation in economic planning decisions by banks, trade unions, and local councils. The system truly is developing toward a rationalized, modern, technologically advanced system. Yet, despite this tinkering with the price system, decision-making, market research, and the like, a considerable amount of central direction remains. Walter Ulbricht called the balancings of these tendencies of centralism and increased independence in the GDR's economy "democratic centralism in the economy" and praised their presence.[53]

---

[50] There are other ministries concerned with the economy, but their organization and responsibilities are not essential to an understanding of the basic economic novelty of the East German case.

[51] Childs, pp. 125–28. For other excellent summaries of the structure of the New Economic System in the GDR, see D. Miller and H. G. Trend, "Economic Reforms in East Germany," *Problems of Communism* (March-April, 1966), pp. 29–36, and M. Gamarnikow, *Economic Reforms in Eastern Europe* (Detroit, Michigan: Wayne State University Press, 1968).

[52] Gamarnikow, p. 53.

[53] Walter Ulbricht, Speech at International Scientific Session on Karl Marx's 150th Birthday, *Neues Deutschland*, May 4, 1968, pp. 3–8. Trans. by FBIS Supplement, E. Europe, no. 103, supp. 24, (May 24, 1968), p. 20.

However, the term democratic centralism, as we know it today, hardly seems appropriate to describe the structure of the economy, which is far more subtle and complicated than traditional "democratic centralism."

Many writers have suggested that the GDR has, or is implementing, some kind of cybernetic model. This impression may be related to several factors: (1) the implementation of automation, which, as discussed earlier, is often confused with cybernetics; (2) the overt and sophisticated concern in the GDR with cybernetics, societal modeling, theoretical operations research, and so forth; (3) the presence of institutional revisionists such as Georg Klaus, who try to use cybernetic theory as a rational method for planning the system, and to develop a modern "revision" of dialectical and historical materialism based upon such cybernetic insights; and (4) the organizational changes in the economic structure of the country. In examining the organizational setup of the GDR economy, it seems that the apparatus does exist in which a cybernetic model could possibly take root. Of course, the automational and theoretical ability to handle such a model does not yet exist and seems rather far off. Nonetheless, the organizational decentralization of the economy, rejuvenation and specialization of the Party, and the reformed university system are the kind of prerequisites necessary in the GDR (or in the USSR) for the imposition of a cybernetic model. However, they need not necessarily lead to that end; rather, they are also the kind of changes needed simply for rationalization of the economic system. Whether or not they develop toward a cybernetically viable system depends upon the willingness of the leadership to relinquish its insistence on orthodox control in the social, political, and cultural spheres, as well as in the economic sphere, for these are all intimately interrelated in an ongoing societal system.

If we think back upon the theoretical cybernetic "model" which was proposed in Figure 3 and compare the East German system, we will note some structural similarities, and some real differences. Crudely, the East German system is pictured in Figure 4. The larger, striped arrows indicate those areas where a certain component part of the homeostat is much more dominant and influential for the course of development of the other component part. As can be seen, feedback from the politburo and/or Council of Ministers exerts greater direct influence upon the "real world" than the "real world" exerts upon the politburo (H_9). Furthermore, the politburo influences

Figure 4: Model of East Germany

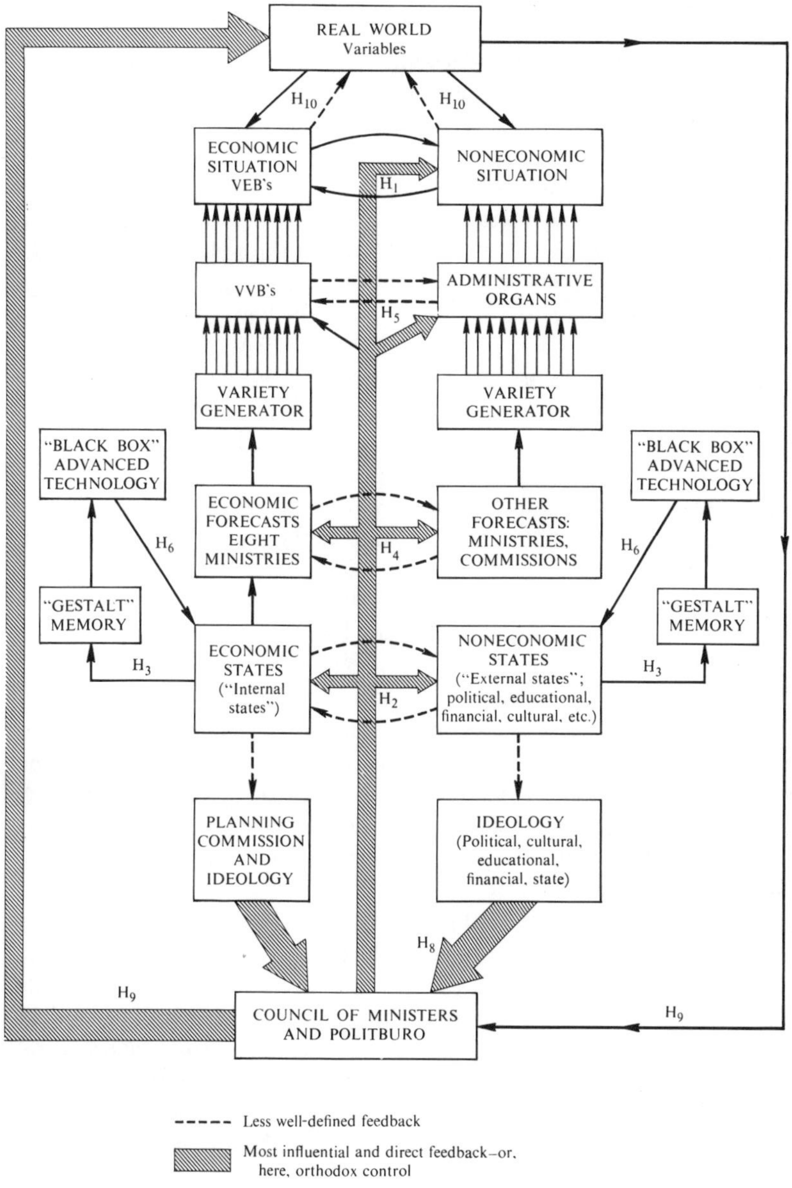

H_2 very significantly, at the present stage of development, probably because H_3 and steps between H_1 and H_2 are not yet well developed technically. The politburo also influences H_4 *directly*. The politburo's direct influence upon the noneconomic portion of the model is considerably greater than it is on the economic portion—which corresponds to the real situation in the social, cultural, and political spheres, and to the concept of orthodox control more closely than to any cybernetic phenomena. Note also that information flows directly from the politburo to these middle areas but does not flow back to the politburo, except indirectly and weakly through feedback in H_9, and by influencing H_2, also weakly. The politburo's "direction" is predominant in this area, yielding disequilibrium to the model. Thus, homeostats, H_2, H_4, H_5 will become even more greatly dependent upon directions from the politburo and even less dependent upon the rational model which is derived from the "real world" through H_3. While the politburo must have some influence upon H_2 if the system is not to degenerate into a laissez faire model, this influence cannot be disproportionate, nor can it extend directly to the other organizational components of the noneconomic subsystem if the model shall be capable of surviving. As long as such orthodox control is present within the model and remains predominant, the system's ability to learn, to grow, to be invulnerable to breakdown and error, and to adapt to a changing environment is severely threatened. The system begins to lose its viability.

The prognosis which this brief analysis engenders from the insights of cybernetics is simply this: Although the GDR appears to be developing successfully on its way to rationality while maintaining orthodox control, the East German regime must relax its orthodox control, indeed, must restructure controls, over the social, political, and cultural spheres if the system is to be cybernetically viable. Whether the political system could, at present, withstand the impact of such a "loosening up," given its history and the proximity of the West German alternative state, is another question. It is probable that East Germany would *not* be able to become politically viable at precisely this time in history if such a relaxation of political control came suddenly and totally. However, in the long run, this political/cultural "loosening up" is the direction the leadership must take if it is ever to develop both an economically *and* a politically viable system.

Prospects for Adoption of a Cybernetic
or East German Model in the USSR

The Soviets have been discussing the need for and problems involved in significant economic reform for years. To date, the Brezh-
nev-Kosygin collective leadership has sought the least disruptive
changes they could find. Reform has been piecemeal, totally administrative, cautious, and unsuccessful in the sixties. Most importantly,
reform thus far has not fundamentally altered the political status quo.
In seeking additional, more comprehensive—and optimistically,
more effective—reforms, the leadership (especially the party leadership) will undoubtedly also try to seek a solution which will neither
change the power configuration in the country nor greatly alter the
role of the party. The undeniable fact remains that East German economic development since 1963 has certainly been quite remarkable
compared to that of the USSR. Indeed, the East German "model"
has become increasingly attractive to the Soviets when compared to
the course of reform in Czechoslovakia. East Germany's reform program seems to be just what the Soviets are looking for: economic reform and development based upon scientific-technical progress which
does not presuppose political liberalization or the loss of orthodox
control.

This paper has argued for a different reform alternative: the adoption of a truly cybernetic model which is the only solution that offers
sustained viability and controlled progress (cybernetically controlled,
of course). The remainder of this discussion will be devoted to the
actual political prospects for adoption of either of these two models
in the Soviet Union.

There are many factors peculiar to the East German situation
which make any wholesale adoption of this model to the Soviet scene
unlikely, not to say difficult. Foremost among these is the basic factor of size. Both physically and in degree of complexity (geography,
climate, nationality differences) the GDR is much smaller and sim-
pler than the USSR. In the GDR, compared to the Soviet Union,
there is relative homogeneity in these factors.

Indeed, the complexity factor is also highlighted when one distin-
guishes between the GDR and the USSR in levels of industrial development. The GDR has attained a relatively even level of industrial

development throughout the country, whereas the Soviet Union has not.[54]

Since World War II, East Germany has made remarkable progress in economic recovery and development. Faced with Soviet pillaging of East Germany after World War II ("reparations"), a natural lack of raw materials, and a chronic shortage of labor, East Germany was, nonetheless, able to develop industrially to the point where, today, it ranks as one of the top ten industrial nations in the world. On a per capita basis, its development is even more extraordinary.[55]

This may, indeed, be related to the intangible factor of "national character," which is said to play so significant a role in Germany (for example, the tradition of strong labor discipline). Russian "national character" involves very different kinds of things.

The size of the labor force in East Germany and its industrial capacity are two of the most crucial factors regarding the future success or failure of the GDR's reforms because they are the fundamental growth factors. The labor force has been increasingly limited, particularly because of the mass refugee movement which existed until 1961, a relatively low birth rate, and an increasing percentage of elderly, retired persons. Only slight growth, if any, in the labor pool is expected in the decade to come.[56] Consequently, "intensive" industrial development is contingent upon increasing the productivity of labor and upon scientific and technological progress.[57] There is really no alternative to this. Furthermore, when the New Economic System was adopted the GDR's industrial growth rate had slowed to the lowest in the East European "socialist community." [58] Hence, in many ways, the East German reform program has been essentially one of necessity and not of "scientific" or "enlightened" thinking. In the USSR, on the other hand, there is a large labor pool whose resources are barely tapped, and thus considerable room for "extensive" development of the economy, although intensive development and increased labor productivity are highly desirable. Before the So-

---

[54] Childs, *passim.* For a more complete discussion of the disparities in economic development in the administrative divisions of the USSR, see H. J. Wagener, "The RSFSR and the Non-Russian Republics: An Economic Comparison," Radio Liberty Research Bulletin, CRD 399/68, Oct. 25, 1968, *passim.*

[55] Childs, pp. 136 ff.   [56] Ludz, p. 127.   [57] *Ibid.,* p. 131.

[58] J. F. Brown, *The New Eastern Europe: The Khrushchev Era and After* (New York: Frederick A. Praeger, 1966), p. 100.

viets attempt to adopt the East German model, they undoubtedly feel that they must have the time to see whether the East Germans can indeed overcome these two fundamental problems of growth in the next decade and accomplish the requisite changes in research and training facilities without fundamentally altering the political status quo. In many ways, perception of these immediate needs by the East Germans has probably speeded the reforms and their extensiveness. Despite the obvious needs of the USSR, it seems difficult to imagine the Soviet political leadership agreeing to jump decisively into such a complete reorganization of the administrative structure of the economy, even if it does appear to promise political and social control.

Two other factors which highlight the urgency of the East German reform program are the position of East Germany as half of a divided nation and the desire of the East German leadership to present the GDR as an economically attractive state both to their indigenous population and the the West Germans as well. The West does not provide an ever-present and immediately attractive alternative to the vast majority of the Soviet population to the extent that it does in East Germany, nor does Western radio have as great legitimacy and impact in the USSR as in the GDR. There is no alternative Russian/Soviet state which commands the loyalty of its citizens, although some of the nationalities do have alternative national groupings living in adjacent countries. Although the Soviet Union seeks to appear economically attractive to the world in general, and to the developing nations in particular, it has done this by emphasizing heavy industrial goods such as iron and steel, and the "glamour" industry represented by the space race, to the detriment of other industries and without rationalization of the economy.

While all of the factors mentioned above mitigate against the applicability and transferability of the East German "model" to the Soviet Union, none of them is so crucial that it would necessarily keep the Soviets from adopting the East German reform program, although it might keep the reform program from being as successful. What is far more influential in this respect is the nature and mode of operation of the Communist Party, the political leadership, and the Party apparat in each of these countries.

In East Germany the SED has been revitalized by the extensive inclusion of younger, technically trained personnel. Such specialists have not been mere technocrats; on the contrary, they are, by and large, also politically reliable people. (This characteristic is of crucial importance to the "directors" of the reform program.) The influx of technologically trained personnel into the Party does not stop simply at the level of the general apparat, and has had enormous impact in the Politburo, the Central Committee, and the Secretariat.[59] Furthermore, "the SED tries to keep ahead of the extensive modernization process it proclaimed." [60] Whatever political or tactical differences have existed in the revitalized party, the leadership has been able to control sharply, although not necessarily to suppress internally as completely as they might wish. As a result, however, the SED has maintained an extraordinary degree of public solidarity; indeed, East Germany has not had the kind of public debates preceding reform which are so typical—and important—in the Soviet Union and the rest of Eastern Europe. On ideological matters, in particular, the SED "has shown little tolerance for dissent within its ranks. It is probably the most authoritarian—or disciplined—of all the bloc parties. This characteristic helps to explain the relative lack of opposition to the economic model and hence, the rapidity with which the party has been able to get the reform program under way." [61]

A major factor—not *the* major factor—which has influenced the SED's solidarity and strictness is, clearly, the presence of a single strong leader: Walter Ulbricht. His willingness to submit to the needs of both the system and the modern age has been crucial to the circumspect, yet definite way the reforms have been initiated and executed in the GDR. The importance of a strong leader cannot be overestimated when comparing East Germany's movements toward reform to the action—or lack of action—of the Soviet Union.

Factors such as these differentiate the climate for a specific reform program in East Germany from that in Russia. There are, to be sure, other factors which have not been discussed here. But the point is that there *are* large differences which might inhibit adoption and success of a reform program applied from one to the other without discrimination. Furthermore, as was suggested above regarding the GDR "model," even *more* significant changes must be made in the noneconomic subsystems if the GDR's model is to be successful, or viable in long-range terms. To avoid adoption of a model predestined to failure, the Soviet Union should opt for a true cybernetic model of the sort described in Figure 3. Such a model, adopted in this entirety, offers decentralization, rationalization, technological progress, reli-

[59] Ludz, p. 123; see also Childs, pp. 45–79.
[60] *Ibid.,* p. 124.   [61] Miller and Trend, p. 31.

ance upon a truly scientific doctrine, cybernetic control, and—most importantly—viability.

The chance of the Soviets adopting as heretical a model as described in Figure 3 are, admittedly, rather remote. Half measures, at best, along the lines of the East German program are more the Soviet's preference, and even this is very doubtful. The Soviet Party leadership, not to mention the state and military leadership, are far from agreed about what kind of reform is needed. Having no strong unified central leadership is bound to continue to inhibit movement toward bold and meaningful reform. Problems in execution and implementation of the reform will undoubtedly result at lower administrative levels. The Party leadership as well as the apparat, are, in particular, likely to resist the infusion of technological specialists into the Party (an infusion which even the East German reform has required for its success), for this would undermine and eventually thoroughly change their ideologically derived position of supremacy in the system.

Vested interests are too great throughout the administrative bureaucracy for the managers and party hacks to favor, or even passively accept, a series of reforms that would make them obsolete. Extensive modernization of the system would involve technological retraining of those old managers and Party men who *could* be retrained at all. The old style manager—third-rate personnel in the system—would be replaced en masse by first-rate people resembling modern business executives. [62]

The "second industrial revolution" would require great changes and upheavals among the workers too. This is recognized even by those who argue for cautious automation of the system. Gvishiani has cited the "familiar psychological opposition of the workers" and of administrative personnel to the "rational use of machines," especially computers. [63] Chief Engineer of the Design Bureau of the Ordzhonikidze Plant, V. Przhiyalkovskij, expressed concern for educating decision-makers about the implications of modern technology, and for

[62] Gamarnikow, pp. 114–15.

[63] D. Gvishiani, "Sovremennye problemy organizatsii upravleniya," ("Contemporary Problems in the Organization of Management,") *Primenenie Elektonno-vychislitelnykh Mashin v Upravleniya Proizvodstvom* ("Application of Electronic Computers in Production Control"), (Moscow: Ekonomika, 1966), pp. 3–16. Trans. in SC/RNI I (June, 1967), (RAND Memorandum P-3600/5), p. 43.

the need to overcome the resultant psychological problems among the workers. Furthermore, he stressed that

far from all Party, council, and economic workers thoroughly understand the significance of computer technology in the future development of the national economy and science. Therefore, it is difficult to overestimate the significance of the project started by the Central Committee of the Belorussian Communist Party to teach the fundamentals of computer technology to the Republic's leading personnel, who will in many ways be responsible for the efficiency of its utilization.[64]

All of these problems are coterminous with the modern computer-automation process and, of course, with the implications of the East German model. The extent and impact of these problems would be multiplied many times over were the cybernetic model (Figure 3) adopted.

Furthermore, the implications of a cybernetic model, with its concomitant emphasis on computer technology and rationalization, pose a fundamental threat—qualitatively and quantitatively—to the very nature of the Party. The traditional Leninist concept of the Party would be altered: the Party would no longer be the agent of orthodox political control, but would be the prime mover in a system of cybernetic control and progress. The Party would not simply become a group of technocrats; rather, Party members would be societal planners, technocrats, and "business executives" all in one. They would comprise the topmost elite of the societal system in the computer age, coordinating the entire system on a rational, creative, and viable basis. This suggests, and even necessitates, that the Party would have to incorporate representatives of the various professional groups into its ranks on a wide scale, thereby developing a more instrumental relationship with society.

Inasmuch as the implications of technologization of the system and the implications of a cybernetic model are so disruptive to the "natural"—or past—order of the system, one expects this kind of reform program to meet with little positive reaction in the vast political bureaucracy known as the Soviet Union. However, viewed as a good and promising program, it prompts the question as to where and how preliminary tactical efforts to gain support for a cybernetic model must be directed.

Efforts to gain support and political influence among what Andrei

[64] V. Przhiyalkovskij, p. 36.

Amalrik describes as the developing "Democratic Movement" who represent the "embryo of a political opposition [65] and whose programmatic aims are far more comprehensive than those of the "systemic improvers" or the "liberalizers" would probably be totally unsuccessful and, very likely, counterproductive. The aims of this highly amorphous group have been centered primarily around liberal, democratic ideals and the rule of law. While they advocate decentralization of the economy, they seem to do this more on humanitarian grounds than because of any deep-seated belief or confidence in economic and scientific rationalization and progress. In fact, they are very likely reacting to the over-emphasis which the Party leadership has placed upon the "scientific-technical revolution," "cybernetics," and "scientific" doctrine by refusing to recognize or by de-emphasizing the impact or utility of these modern developments. After all, the result of the Party's emphasis on such rationality appears to be the elimination of freedom, creativity, and much of the "irrationality" of man's activities. Thus, to a certain extent supporters of the Democratic Movement are reacting properly to the meaning of the bulk of the orthodox control advocates' comments about the scientific-technical revolution and cybernetics. However, as we have tried to show above, science and cybernetics do not necessitate orthodox control; indeed, they fundamentally oppose and contradict such notions. The political opposition must recognize this fact and work covertly—through the system—to bring about a creative rational system by using the rhetoric of science and technology as a "cover" for their own ends. However, the chances that these highly idealistic supporters of the Democratic Movement will recognize this distinction, be willing to work *through* the system in a covert way, and risk the chance that their efforts will be co-opted by the conservative "orthodox control" people are extremely slight. These chances are reduced even more by the fact that these people seem to be committed to expressing their ideas in a straightforward fashion, with a minimum of concern for devious in-system rationalization.

Furthermore, the amorphous nature of this so-called movement, its lack of organization and of mass support, tends to restrict clear-cut action in any single direction by them. In the unlikely event such action were ever agreed upon it would, in addition, be extremely difficult for these advocates to find any friendly ears among the politi-

[65] Andrei Amalrik, "Will the Soviet Union Survive Until 1984?", *Survey* (January, 1970), p. 172 and *passim*.

cally significant groups. First of all, they have no formal direct access to any policy group at present. The Democratic Movement consists largely of intelligentsia, often elite intelligentsia, it is true, but it also includes open "dissenters" and opponents of the system. Persons committed more or less to the current order of the system, even the "liberalizers" (a broad term for middle policy groups), are likely to view their actions with open suspicion and hostility. Unless supporters of the Democratic Movement were to act covertly, their advocacy of a program would be a signal to more conservative forces to oppose that program. Thus, their open support of a specific program might end up being counterproductive, producing stricter controls over the society and the economy as well.

It is undoubtedly clear by now that "right-wing" elements of society do not provide the desired access channel for reformers either. The old-time party apparat, old-style managers, as well as the Army, the KGB, and advocates of heavy industry, are all relatively strong advocates of politcal status quo—or, what is worse, of a relapse into a so-called Stalinist system. They seek to maintain their own positions and political control over society. Any hints of modern, scientific enlightenment among them can usually be shown to have orthodox control notions just below the surface.

Thus, it would appear that the only access channel left that may offer any hopes of success for a cybernetic model lies somewhere in the vast middle, and slightly left of center, among policy groups in the Soviet Union. This might include spokesmen for light industry, or even for consumer goods, along with economic reformers in the "decentralization-rationalization" tradition who are disgusted with half-hearted, piecemeal reform, scientists and technological specialists, and possibly certain members of the creative intelligentsia. The influence of youth—technologically reared in the emergent "technetronic age"—is difficult to assess at this point. Whether they will emerge as "liberalizers" seeking fundamental changes in the system, or as moderate conservatives, anxious to preserve a system which will bestow privileges upon them as the technological elite, is quite unpredictable, although we would hope to see the first of these patterns emerge.

Those persons who are "used" to advocate a cybernetic model must challenge many of the theoretical underpinnings of the system, yet believe in working *through* the system if their goals are to have any chance of realization. Furthermore, in the majority of cases these will be people who actually have bases of influence and access channels to policy-making open to them. Their specific tactics may be varied in their advocacy of a cybernetic model, but they will take on the mantle of "rationalizers," and in so doing can utilize the tools of the system in trying to change it. One example among the many tactical possibilities suggests that the rhetoric of democratic centralism can be used to support a cybernetic model and decentralization, although cybernetics is far more than just "democratic centralism" as it evolved in the Leninist tradition.[66] One Western specialist in cybernetics has written that

Cybernetic insights show . . . that the totality of the organization ought to be made up of building blocks that will be called quasi-independent domains. This is the compromise notion lying between actually independent domains (decentralization) and no domains at all (centralization). These domains have a certain local autonomy and may (in their own language) claim to be altogether autonomous. But they are not autonomous in the metalanguage of the whole system which monitors their activities according to the laws of cybernetics.[67]

Such insights as these lend themselves quite easily to the rhetoric of democratic centralism. However, this rhetoric might be used by conservatively oriented persons to refer to democratic centralism in the old Soviet tradition of democratic centralism which, as we know, is centralization in *fact*. It is not always easy to tell the centralizers from the democrats in this regard. For example, D. Gvishiani, Deputy Chairman of the State Committee on Science and Technology, an advocate of systems analysis and technological advancement—and also Premier Kosygin's son-in-law—has the following to say about the organization of management:

A dialectical combination of centralization and decentralization is absolutely necessary to solve the fundamental problem of management organi-

[66] Analogy to the central nervous system and the autonomic nervous system is very helpful in conceptualizing the way a cybernetic system might function. The central nervous system is not made aware—explicitly—of the moment-to-moment activities of every local event in the system, nor does it directly control each action and impulse. The autonomic nervous system takes care of these moment-to-moment processes which are vital to the organism's survival, yet the autonomic nervous system is infused with central purpose and direction by the central nervous system. Lest the reader fear organismic analogies, this is meant to be illustrative and no more. After all, the cybernetic system which has led to some of the most meaningful discoveries in cybernetics is the human body, and other living beings.

[67] Beer, *D & C*, p. 381.

zation. . . . In order to solve a given problem, one must be guided by Lenin's principle of democratic centralism, which requires clear-cut centralization in solving the principal problems of management when there is extensive decentralization of all functions, the execution of which can be successfully carried out on the basis of local initiative. . . . At present strict centralization is impossible without the corresponding differentiations, without breaking down areas of management into a whole series of branches and functions, without involving large numbers of people in the management process, without first assessing the capabilities and the sense of responsibility of the persons participating.[68]

Gvishiani seems to be a reformer in the "East German" tradition; he seeks rationality with no loss of central control. Unfortunately, such a position is probably the maximum that most of the leading decision makers in the USSR would opt for. Whatever chances still exist for cybernetic reform probably can be found with the "liberalizer" group described above. There is always, however, a danger that the tactical efforts of the liberalizers will be co-opted and twisted to the advantage of the conservatives. This is the risk that comes with "in-system" rationalization, but it is one that must be taken.

On the whole, though, we must admit that the prognosis for a cybernetic model's political chances is not good, especially in light of the current movement toward the right that we seem to be witnessing in the Soviet Union. As noted above, the Party rank and file, as well as the old-style managers, are certain to be unalterably opposed to reforms, such as the cybernetic model, which threaten their positions in the system. The Party leadership appears to be no more favorably inclined toward such changes. The chances for implementing a cybernetic reform program are, clearly, quite slim without exceedingly strong commitment from top leaders. In fact, it is difficult to force implementation at any time unless there is a single extremely powerful leader who can unite the leadership firmly behind his program, or unless the elite as a whole is faced by and able to recognize a serious crisis, such as their system's falling markedly behind that of the United States. If worker resistance also occurs, the reform program would have to be put through in a manner which might make the collectivization campaign look mild by comparison.

To a certain extent, Walter Ulbricht fulfilled the role of the single strong leader who had the power to insure the significant changes which computer technology and rationalization necessitate. In the So-

[68] Gvishiani, pp. 29, 30.

viet Union, the situation remains highly speculative. Whether such strong leadership will emerge is one major "if"; whether it can be used for positive rationalization and decentralization, no less for a cybernetic model, is even more speculative. At present it seems rather doubtful. Whether or not necessity will engender (or force Brezhenev to find) the will and strength to accomplish such "sweeping out of dead wood," training, and retraining is hard to say. One thing appears more certain, however: if no unity prevails among the top leadership there will be little or no significant chance for initiation —no less for success—of any important reforms because of oppositional elements and vested interests which are capable of thwarting what they do not like.

Appendix: Some Fundamental Cybernetic Concepts

All highly complex systems are, to a certain degree self-organizing, rather than organized by some external "director" or control.[69] Furthermore, they are somewhat self-regulating: that is, they can control themselves implicitly, making certain that the system can find —or learn to find—the answers to the problems which arise before it and within it.[70] Viable systems cannot be entirely regulated from the outside, just as they cannot be organized completely from the outside. Self-regulation is regulation from within,[71] and is intimately connected with the concept of homeostasis, which is the characteristic of a system in which certain variables are held at a desirable level (that is, within certain definite bounds).[72] The concept of feedback keeps all parts of a system in touch with one another, interreacting and regulating the given homeostats. Learning is the ability of a system to adapt to a situation or stimulus which it was not originally designed to handle. A viable system which looks to the future *must* possess the capacity for learning. As Karl Deutsch points out, "Learning capacity of a system is related to the amounts and kinds of uncommitted resources. The larger the proportion of uncommitted to committed resources within a system, the greater the set of new kinds of behavior it can learn." [73] It is interesting to consider this statement about learning capacity in terms, for example, of the Soviet economy, where this insight might be one of the many arguments

[69] Beer, *D & C*, pp. 350 ff.   [70] *Ibid.*, p. 302.
[71] Beer, *C & M*, p. 23.   [72] Beer, *D & C*, p. 263.
[73] *Nerves of Government* (New York: The Free Press, 1966), p. 164.

supporting a considerable amount of decentralization as essential for a viable system which can learn and adapt.

There is one more fundamental concept before one considers cybernetic models and the Soviet Union specifically: namely, the Black Box. The important operational consideration when we speak of requisite variety in a situation subsystem is *how* will we be able to proliferate variety in the control system? The answer is, simply, that we will use a black box. In cybernetic terminology, a black box refers to:

a box to which inputs lead and outputs are observed to emerge. Nothing at all is known about the way in which the inputs and outputs are interconnected inside the box—which is why it is called black. The reason why we contemplate a box having such odd properties is that the more familiar box in which something *is* known about the internal connectivity has its variety constrained. . . . But a black box is assumed to be able to take on any internal arrangement of input-output connectivity at all; it can therefore proliferate maximal variety.[74]

The black box becomes a measure of the interaction between the analytic model and the world situation. It is a practical device for maintaining touch between the two subsystems.[75] It is difficult for the noncyberneticist to understand the concept of a black box and why it works, but, surprisingly enough, designing such a system and seeing that it does indeed work is apparently rather simple.[76] Furthermore, black boxes are absolutely necessary in cybernetic control models.

[74] Beer, *D & C*, p. 293.   [75] *Ibid.*, p. 323.
[76] See Beer, *D & C, C & M*, for more on the black box concept.

The Breakdown of a Political System Experiencing Economic Development: Greece, 1950—1967

MICHAEL J. BUCUVALAS

On April 21, 1967, a bloodless, military coup suspended Greek parliamentary democracy. The coup was a result of the deterioration of the bases of the parliamentary system which had made the electoral system an anachronism in Greece. The military merely rendered the *coup' de grâce* to this already tottering system.

The factors which made the old political system irrelevant to the changing Greek nation were inherent in the very stability which that system had demonstrated during the fifties. During that decade the Greek nation had begun to experience economic development. Part of this experience was rapid urbanization and an expansion of the references of the peasantry. These two factors combined to made the old politics—adapted to isolated peasant villages—increasingly dysfunctional. The old system had been built on a particularistic, dyadic structure for processing demands; during the fifties, changes in Greek society called for more general responses to the needs of the populace at the societal level. Mobility and urbanization had made many people aware of this problem by releasing them from the parochial loyalties of an earlier era in Greece.

The final and precipitating fact involved in the demise of the traditional Greek political system was the inability of the old leaders to adapt to the changed situation. The leaders who made up the *politikos kosmos* (literally, political world, a phrase referring to the journalists, lawyers, and politicians who made up the Greek political oligarchy) were firmly wedded to the old clientele system, and they could not free themselves from their old methods of operation. The combination of people looking for a new style of politics and politicians rooted in their old habits led to a period of crisis in Greece from 1965 to 1967, which was finally resolved by the intervention of the military.

The Greek electoral system was traditionally based on clientele networks. Within these networks, votes were traded for the particularistic services which deputies (legislators) could perform for their supporters. The deputy's function in this system was twofold. First, he furthered the interests of his clients to the exclusion of all others. Adamantia Pollis attributes this to there never being developed the concept of an institutional role: "The concept of an institutional role has been nonexistent, and the person occupying an institutional position has been viewed as serving his own interest and the interest of those he represents, which are never the interests of the nation." [1] The second duty of the deputy is a necessary concomitant of his first role; he protects his clients from the central government and its agents. Keith Legg attributes this to the distrust of the central authorities which is part of the political culture. It is in expressing this second role that one deputy described his function to Legg: "The deputy's main task is to survey the legislative work, and to defend the needs of the people and prevent injustices that are caused by the bureaucracy." [2]

One of the backbones of this system was the traditional, parochial orientation of the Greek villagers.

The peasantry's reference group . . . has been coterminous with the individual's membership groups; the cultural pattern imposes primary and personalized loyalties and obligations within a particular kinship system and deference towards the authority of the village elder and the village priest. The legitimate authority is the head of the family and the local notables—not some conception of the nation and nationality.[3]

Due to the limitations on travel which had been common in Greece before the fifties, the peasant was unlikely to have any connections with anyone outside of the neighborhood of his village. And the

[1] Adamantia Pollis, "Social Change and Nationhood," *Massachusetts Review,* vol. 9, winter 1968, p. 124.

[2] Keith Legg, *Politics in Modern Greece,* Stanford University Press, (Stanford, 1969), p. 178.

[3] Pollis, p. 124.

heavy emphasis placed on the family made this his primary reference group.

Any connection to the outside world was usually mediated for the peasant by the local village notables—civil servants in the larger villages and towns, priests and school teachers in the smaller. Either through these intermediaries or directly, the villager would ally himself to a local notable of enough status to be a candidate for the *Voulis* (the Greek parliament). Because of the strength of family bonds, there would often be an attempt to formalize this relationship through somehow forming a family tie to the local notable. By far the most common form this took was to have the local notable baptize one of his client's children. In the Greek Orthodox religion this makes the godfather a member of his godchild's family, and thereby forms a kinship bond between the peasant and the notable. The extent to which this occurred is demonstrated by the case of George Rallis, who was a deputy from Central Greece and was said to be the godfather of over one thousand children in his constituency. [4]

When these deputies reached the *Voulis,* they arrived with independent bases of power. They had been elected because of the strength of their own network of dyadic relationships and had no debt to any party apparatus. Since the government was formed in parliamentary style, it was important to the deputy to be in the ruling coalition; only from there would he be able to perform the services expected of him by his clients.

The only basis of political parties in Greece, therefore, was the "spoils" which parties could make available for the deputies to distribute to their clients. Thus, the deputy joined a group which constituted itself a party in order to be part of the government of the day. These parties were primarily electoral coalitions and "elections create parliamentary majorities, which invest certain leaders with ministerial office; in return, the political resources at the disposal of the ministers flow through clientage networks to the deputies, and eventually to the individual Greeks." [5]

The parties which were formed had no programmatic base and were mere coalitions of notables, each seeking his own personal advantage. Because of this, Greek parties tended to be very loose con-

[4] Kenneth Young, *The Greek Passion: A Study in People and Politics,* J. M. Dent & Sons, Ltd. (London, 1969), p. 166.

[5] Legg, p. 162.

federations made up of various factions. Each of these factions followed its own leader within the context of the *Voulis,* and he provided them with the resources to dispense to their clients, whenever he could get a ministerial appointment.

Each potential leader had his own group of followers. Thus, Spiros Markezinis formed the Progressive Party in 1955 when he led his followers out of the Greek Rally. In 1966 he and his party were the four key votes holding another coalition government in power. Even more to the point is the case of George Papandreou, a former prime minister at that time, who formed a party which contested the elections in 1950 and 1951 as the George Papandreou Party.

The major parties of the system—the Greek Rally, the ERE (*Ethniki Razospastiki Enosis,* National Radical Union), and the EK (*Enosis Kendrou,* Center Union)—were coalitions made up of these smaller groups in order to contest elections and select ministers. These parties were not unified by any internal policy agreement, nor were they divided by any issues (except at their respective fringes). Furthermore, the whole *politikos kosmos* was united in its view of politics as a way in which to further each notable's own and his clients' interests.

The instability of these coalitions and their nonprogrammatic base would have been more important if policy—social programs—had been made in the *Voulis.* But the *Voulis* was merely the base from which resources flowed into the clientele networks. Policy grew out of the "bargaining between parliamentary leaders and other major political groups (which did) not take place in an institutional framework." [6] These groups worked through their personal connections with politicians to assure the protection of their interests in the legislative process. This was carried out by attaching "photographs" to legislation. These "photographs" were amendments to legislation which protected (or furthered) the interests of the particular groups which the politican proposing the amendment included within his clientele network. Thus, a "photograph" might exempt a particular village or group of villages from the effect of the legislation.

The net result of this process was that no Greek government was capable of producing any unified programs. For even when legislation was drafted which dealt with general societal problems, ministers would have to allow a certain number of "photographs" to be at-

[6] *Ibid.*

tached in order to have the bill passed. And these "photographs" would deflect the original intent of the measure.

In fact, it is unlikely that the members of the *politikos kosmos* had any desire to treat societal difficulties at the national level. "In a society characterized by ties of personal loyalty, there are few general interests and demands to be articulated and answered; there is only the reality of each personal demand." [7] And the structure of the Greek political system was built on personal loyalties; especially in the rural areas, but also in the towns which were no more than administrative centers until the mid-fifties.

During the decade from 1950 to 1960 forces appeared which struck at the foundations of the Greek political system. After the end of the Civil War in 1950, relative peace contributed to economic growth, widening opportunities, and urbanization. Along with these factors came a growing sense of community and nationalism. These new perceptions were alien to the Greek system and presented a threat to the parochial, particularistic basis of Greek politics.

The government of Premier Alexander Papagos and the Greek Rally, from 1951 to 1955, created the conditions necessary for Greece's recovery from a decade of war and political instability. Under the direction of the United States, there was a flurry of activity, especially in the building of economic infrastructure—roads, telecommunications, and electric power grids. This, in turn, produced "a novel atmosphere of resolution and purpose" [8] which began to infect the commercial elites of the nation. Furthermore, the Greek Rally proved to be a government that would hold together and, at least, attempt to govern the country. Finally, as Campbell and Sherrard say, "gradually, over the next two or three years, political stability was converted into economic confidence." [9] And when Constantine Karamanlis succeeded Papagos, who died in October of 1955, the problem of inflation was solved by policies which placed a high premium on monetary stability. Karamanlis's new party, the ERE, was basically the old Greek Rally (except for two cliques which had dropped out), and as such picked up the credit for the accomplishments of Papagos and the loyalty of the civil servants who had been given jobs through the Rally's clientele networks. The ERE soon

[7] *Ibid.,* p. 166.

[8] John Campbell and Philip Sherrard, *Modern Greece,* Ernest Benn Ltd. (London, 1968), p. 252.

[9] Campbell and Sherrard, p. 252.

penetrated the government bureaucracy even more deeply and built for itself a permanent base of loyalty within it. These factors all contributed to the stability of Karamanlis's eight years in office (the longest term served by any Greek Prime Minister).

The increasing opportunities afforded by economic growth were reinforced by the growing availability of at least primary education throughout the country. This opened up the possibility of social mobility to much of the peasantry, since to the rural Greeks education had always been the path to social and economic betterment. Together the growing economy and the wider availability of education contributed to a climate of rising expectations throughout the society.

But probably the most significant aspect of the economic growth taking place was the rapid growth of Athens, the capital city, and to a lesser extent Salonika, the "capital of the North." During the decade from 1951 to 1961, Athens (and its suburbs, including Piraeus) grew by 34.4 per cent while the population of Greece as a whole grew by only 9.9 per cent. Thus, Greater Athens was growing at over three times the rate of the rest of the country. And Athens itself was growing still faster (40.4 per cent).[10] Not even Salonika—although growing twice as fast as the country as a whole—could keep up with Athens; it only grew 27.4 per cent.[11] The result was the ever greater concentration of population in Athens, which was the center of industry and government.

These new Athenians came from the countryside, the traditional stronghold of the clientele system. Approximately 62.4 per cent of the migrants to Athens came from the Peloponessos, Central Greece and Euboea, and the Aegean Islands. Of these new migrants about two-thirds came from villages of less than ten thousand inhabitants.[12] The population of the Peloponessos, one of the areas of Greece in which the traditional, conservative parties (like the ERE and the Greek Rally were strongest),[13] actually declined during this period by 2.4 per cent.[14] This was also true of Central Greece and Euboea [15] although the Aegean Islands had been competitive districts for reasons which will be developed below.[16] Salonika, too, drew from its hinterland in Macedonia those people who had been attached to the traditional, clientele systems in their rural villages.

[10] National Statistical Service of Greece, *Statistical Yearbook of Greece, 1969* (Athens, 1969), p. 27.

[11] *Ibid.*, p. 24.   [12] Campbell and Sherrard, p. 365.

[13] Legg, pp. 324–27.   [14] *Statistical Yearbook*, p. 27.

[15] Legg, pp. 324–27.   [16] *Ibid.*, pp. 324–27.

Their move to the urban areas removed the migrants from the political clientele networks of which they had formerly been members, although many of them used old dyadic relationships with relatives and friends in the city to secure jobs or residences. But they no longer had their votes to offer as *quid pro quo* for favors provided by their former political agents.

Even more important were the changes in the very nature of their demands which took place when they migrated to the cities. The urban areas were basically less personal, and therefore less amenable to the dyadic relationships which form the basis for clientele patterns. This was especially true in the Greek setting, where the traditional parties had no formal organization, only networks of relationships; in the cities, the newcomers were not part of the networks extant. Furthermore, apart from jobs and residences, the demands made by the new urbanites were not the kind that could be settled by particularistic intervention on the part of the deputies. These people were asking for services which were general demands. They wanted better transportation, better sewerage systems, more electricity.

The very act of moving to the urban areas also struck a fatal blow to one of the cornerstones of the Greek clientele system: the local orientation of rural Greeks. This has been made even easier due to the fact that Greece is essentially a unitary society with little in the way of ethnic, tribal, or religious differences. And while the migrants may not have lost their distrust of authority, they became dependent upon the government for many services which might have been community projects in their villages. In Greece, this means dependence on the national government due to the weakness of local governments. Permission must be granted by the appropriate ministry in order to undertake almost any project.

In sum, the effect of the mass migration from the rural areas to the cities has been to release a substantial portion of the Greek population (over one-fifth of the Greek population lives in Greater Athens [17]) from their clientele networks and to set them loose as free agents in the maelstrom of Greek politics. There was only one group active in Greek politics which was capable of harnessing this new force—the EDA (*Enosis Demokratiki Aristera,* United Democratic Left).

The EDA is the exception to every rule about Greek political parties: it has a disciplined, democratic organization at the local levels;

[17] *Statistical Yearbook,* p. 27.

it is urban-based; and, it eschews all forms of personalism. In addition it actually has a program: including an anti-Western foreign policy and a socialist orientation to economics. The EDA had been at a severe disadvantage in Greece because of the stigma of Communism attached to it. Although the veracity of this charge is of little importance in Greece, the charge is credible, and that is all that counts. The fear of Communism in Greece is very deeply ingrained, based on the misery caused by the Civil War and fear of the northern neighbors who all have Communist governments. This fear has been amplified for partisan, political reasons by the military, the monarchy, and the right-wing politicians. All of this has redounded to the disadvantage of the EDA.

However, the EDA managed to overcome this stigma with the newly arrived migrants in heavily urban areas—particularly in Greater Athens and Greater Salonika, the two most rapidly growing urban agglomerations. The explanation of this phenomenon has already been given. These people had been removed from their old clientele networks and had new types of demands. The important role that the EDA played in this process, however, is that it acted as a stimulating and reinforcing factor in the process of changing the perceptions of politics which the new urban dwellers held. Whether or not the EDA deliberately set out to overthrow the Greek political system, it did contribute to the feelings in the urban areas which made that system an anachronism.

The emphasis laid by the EDA on extracting Greece from its ties with NATO and the United States contributed to the growing feelings of nationalism among those in urban areas. Once they had renounced the parochial views of the village they were free to develop a national framework for their views and aspirations. This framework was reinforced by the EDA's emphasis on Greek "independence." These demands were even picked up by certain of the EK politicians (Elias Tsirimokis, who came to the EK from the EDA, and Andreas Papandreou, the son of the leader of the EK). These more traditional politicians lent respectability to some of the issues raised by the EDA.

The other basic policy of the EDA is advocacy of a socialist economy. This was, of course, in line with the demands made by some of the migrants. Since the EDA was the only group to represent general demands in the parliamentary system (despite the lip service paid by both the EK and the ERE), it was normal that the migrants should find the EDA attractive as their only avenue of expression and representation. Furthermore, the general demands made by the new migrants were reinforced by the party, which presented them as the only legitimate types of demands (again with some assistance from the groups around Tsirimokis and Andreas Papandreou).

Finally, despite the economic growth which Greece had sustained, the rewards were not evenly distributed.

"We must create the wealth first before we tackle the problem of distributing it more fairly," (Karamanlis) told a rally in Salonika. It was cold comfort for a land of "rising expectations," an electorate accustomed to disbelieve promises for the future from any government, and daily witnessing the lavish displays of wealth of a minority against the background of poverty and unemployment.[18]

This disparity in incomes did not lead to the Greek city-dwellers' becoming Communists or revolutionaries, but it did lead them to make demands on the government for greater social welfare measures. It became accepted that the government had a responsibility to assure the welfare of its citizens. This was a most revolutionary assumption in the context of Greek society, where one of the chief functions that the majority of deputies saw for themselves was protecting their constituents from the central government.

The changes which were taking place in the perceptions of politics held by the urban dwellers were being transmitted to the rural areas, which were at the same time undergoing a transformation themselves as they entered the market economy and achieved higher standards of living. Many of the villagers were posted at various points in Greece during their military duty—Greece has a system of universal conscription for service to the state—and when these men returned, they brought with them many of the ideas that had been forming in the cities. These changing perceptions were important, for the villages were the foundations upon which the clientele system had functioned (over one-half the Greek population was employed in agriculture in 1961).[19] As the Greek peasants became less parochial and turned to the government for services (such as education and agricultural credits), they were removing the support of the largest bloc of voters from the old politicians.

But, it was the very kinship system which had supported parochialism which most served to penetrate the rural villages with the influ-

[18] Young, p. 284.   [19] *Statistical Yearbook,* p. 123.

ences of the city. This kinship structure is very strong and withstood the impact of family-members' leaving for the cities. They regularly return to the villages from which they came (at least twice a year), and with them they bring the influence of the city. Even those who have gone to West Germany for jobs return to the villages on vacations and bring with them the attitudes they have acquired in the cities and factories of Germany.

This continuing personal contact has been assisted by the network of roads built in Greece after the Civil War with American aid. These roads were originally intended to afford the Army access to the villages for counterinsurgency operations, but they have subsequently served to allow the continued contact of the migrants and their families. And due to the importance of personal contact— especially between family members—in the Greek culture, these roads have made it easier for the Greek villagers to assimilate the ideas of the urban areas.

Furthermore, those who have moved to the city are often held in great respect in the villages, as they are usually more materially successful. But in describing the effects of this continued contact, Ernestine Friedl gives even more importance to the desire of the peasant to prove to his neighbors that he is more worldly-wise than they.

The line of urban influence, then, runs something like this: New ideas and attitudes, and changes in style of life, are brought to the notice of a village family by its urban relatives. However, if a village household adopts at least some of the new traits, it is only partly because of the respect which it pays to its urban kin. A more powerful influence is often the strong sense of competition which the rural household feels towards other village families, on which it hopes to score a point by showing superior sophistication.[20]

Since one of the most important indicators is the ability to discuss politics in the *taverna,* the villagers would be expected to adopt certain of their urban relatives' political viewpoints. They would thus increase their status by showing their greater political sophistication.[21] In a society where political discussion is of such importance, this should be one of the first areas to feel the effect of the urban migrants on village attitudes.

[20] Ernestine Friedl, "The Role of Kinship in the Transmission of National Culture to Rural Villages in Mainland Greece," *American Anthropologist,* vol. 61, February 1959, p. 35.

[21] J. Mayone Stycos, "Patterns of Communication in a Rural Greek Village," *Public Opinion Quarterly,* spring 1952, pp. 59–70 *passim.*

This may explain the fact that one of the few rural areas where the EDA has any influence is the Aegean Islands.[22] These islands were among the heaviest contributors to the growth of Athens during the fifties. This is especially true in terms of their own population, which declined by 9.7 per cent during this period.[23] The strength of the EDA in these areas may, thus, be attributed to the reciprocal influence of the migrants to Athens, who constitute a large proportion of the native population of the islands.

Other influences, such as the communications media, have also been operative in integrating the villages into the national society— although they do not appear to be as important as kinship ties, simply because of the emphasis laid on the family in the Greek culture. The new roads built by the Americans also made it possible for buses to reach formerly inaccessible areas, and these busses carry the Athens and Salonika newspapers. Along with radios—which increased incomes have made available to the villagers—newspapers now serve to assure the villagers' awareness of the activities of the national government. In the past, the villagers followed the activities of the personalities of the national government, but the new attitudes brought to them by their urban relatives have made them aware of the implications for them of decisions made by the government in Athens.

Furthermore, the Greek peasants have entered the economy. Most villages began producing at least some products for the market in the fifties. They were therefore more concerned with their income from these sources and the uses to which that income could be put. Furthermore, in their efforts to introduce modern methods, many of the peasants became indebted to the government, and the disposal of these debts was an interest of intense concern.

The concern with these debts led to demonstrations by farmers in 1965 and 1966. They "had more than once marched on Salonika, and had demonstrated angrily in the Peloponessos. Police had been compelled to open fire over the heads of tractor-led columns." [24] The last time activity of this sort had occurred was during the Civil War, and even then there had not been mass uprisings but only isolated bands of guerillas.

The Greek villager was changing as a result of the influence brought upon him by his relatives who had moved to the cities, the

[22] Legg, pp. 324–27.   [23] *Statistical Yearbook*, p. 27.

[24] Bayard Stockton, *Phoenix With a Bayonet*, Georgetown Publications (Ann Arbor, 1971), p. 198.

mass media, and his involvement in the economy. The new orientation of the peasant was no longer the local, particularistic concern upon which the clientele system had been built. He had become interested in national issues, and he had learned that there were changes necessary which could benefit the entire community. He no longer thought of his relationship with the state as completely personal; he was beginning to press general demands on the system. When the politicians tried to respond to, and counter, these demands their actions led to the breakdown of both the political system and the economy.

By the time of the 1963 elections the *politikos kosmos* apparently had realized that they would at least have to pay lip service to these new general demands. Both the ERE and the EK promised more education and higher incomes. However, neither party had really changed.

This is best demonstrated by the response of George Papandreou —the leader of the EK—to the results of the election. He had formed a coalition with the EDA in order to form a government. He pressed through two of his campaign pledges, free education and pay raises to government employees with the help of the EDA. He then called new elections for February of 1964 in order to collect payment on the services he had performed. It worked; the EK received 173 of the 300 seats in the *Voulis*.

Papandreou's response to the new types of demands placed on the government was to become the patron of the whole country. He had made education free and raised wages; he then enlarged the civil service, raised the wheat subsidy, and cut the income tax. These measures made good patronage and increased his popularity; they were also very bad economics and contributed to inflation, disinvestment, and balance of payments problems.

In answering the demands of the civil servants who had conducted strikes for higher wages under Karamanlis, Papandreou acted as would be expected from his political background in the Greek system. He paid off groups and expected their support in return. However, he was not acting as a responsible political leader. Even *Eleftheria* (an Athens newspaper which was aligned with the EK Finance Minister, Costas Mitsotakis) criticized him for not acting responsibly.[25]

[25] Young, p. 305.

Finally, on April 30, 1965, Mitsotakis warned Papandreou publicly that the measures instituted by the EK government, of which Mitsotakis was a member, were producing an inflationary spiral leading to the devaluation of the drachma.[26] But Papandreou could not take the stringent measures necessary to tighten the money supply and slow down inflation. These measures would have been directly contrary to his policy of acting as a national patron.

In this situation, Campbell and Sherrard are probably correct in observing, "It is possible that Papandreou welcomed this crisis." [27] The crisis to which they refer involved the military. The Army was opposed to Papandreou's freeing of political prisoners and the EK's affiliations and cooperation with EDA. They felt that he was threatening the national security. This was complicated by the discovery of a group of officers calling themselves *Aspida* (shield) with leftist leanings and allegedly encouraged, and maybe led, by Andreas Papandreou—George's son and the Deputy Minister of Coordination. George Papandreou's response to this was to try to purge the Army of the officers not loyal to the EK.

However, in order to do this he would have had to remove the Defense Minister, Petros Garoufalias, who staunchly supported the Army. Garoufalias refused to resign, and Papandreou took the matter to the King—proposing that he, Papandreou, be the new Defense Minister. King Constantine II refused to sanction this, suggesting that Papandreou propose another replacement to avoid charges of conflict of interest related to his son's involvement in the *Aspida* case. Papandreou refused this agreement and resigned. He felt that he could win the election—which the King would be forced to call.

Constantine did not call an election. Instead, he tried to find someone who could form a new government. The third man to try— Stephanos Stephanopoulos—succeeded with the support of the ERE. Stephanopoulos had been one of those prominent men who had brought his group to the EK in 1961. He led them out again in 1965. He took forty-five deputies with him when he left the EK, and this was enough to form a majority with the votes of the ERE and Markezinis's Progressive Party. The men who left the EK did so under threat of their lives, but they were offered ministries and under-secretaryships.[28] In the situation described by Legg, these positions are the basis for the patronage which builds political power; the

---

[26] *Ibid.*, p. 307.   [27] Campbell and Sherrard, p. 275.   [28] *Ibid.*, p. 277.

Greek *politikos kosmos* had not changed its perceptions of politics.

Stephanopoulos's government lasted until December of 1966 but was unable to take any significant action in a *Voulis* where it commanded a two-vote majority built on a three-party coalition. Meanwhile, riots raged in the urban areas of Greece. The newly mobilized population took its grievances about inflation and wages to the streets. These complaints were compounded by Papandreou's charge that the King had exceeded his constitutional prerogatives by not calling an election. The question of nationalism and political rights received a great deal of support in the new groups, and Papandreou had always been capable of exciting a crowd. He now had an issue and a populace which was dissatisfied with both the economy and the government.

One indicator of the extent of this dissatisfaction is the rate of emigration from Greece depicted in Table I. Here it becomes obvious that the climate of confidence referred to above had contributed to keeping the emigration rate down during the mid-fifties. However, as the rising expectations of the populace were frustrated and opportunities became attractive abroad, the number of emigrants—both permanent and temporary—rose to over two per cent of the population of the country, which is twice its rate of natural increase.[29]

The scale of emigration denotes a very high level of dissatisfaction with the opportunities available within Greece compared to other areas. In addition, the fact that two-thirds of those emigrating were leaving permanently shows that many people were willing to take a very drastic step to change their lot in life.

The *politikos kosmos* was not willing to take drastic measures. Even in the politically motivated riots of 1965 and 1966, the overtones of the old political machinations remained in the interpretations of the *politikos kosmos*. When the Stephanopoulos government lost its majority in the *Voulis* (December, 1966), it was due to an agreement between the ERE and the EK to hold elections in the spring, which would avoid the whole constitutional question of the role of the King—the issue over which the EK had been calling demonstrations for two years.

Various pictures have been painted describing the motivation of the *coup d'état* led by Colonel George Papadopoulos. He and his compatriots point to the Communist menace.[30] Others have voiced

---

[29] *Statistical Yearbook*, p. 26.

[30] George Anastoplo, "Retreat from Politics," *Massachusetts Review*, vol. 9, winter 1968, p. 94.

Table I. Emigrants from Greece (in thousands), 1955–1967

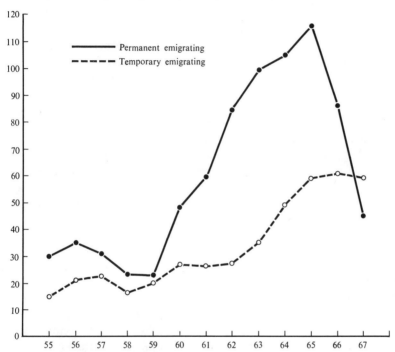

Source: National Statistical Service of Greece, *Statistical Yearbook of Greece, 1969* (Athens, 1969), p. 39.

opinions more or less the same; they admit that the Communists may not have been ready for a revolution but claim that they would have seized the opportunity presented by anarchy in Greece.[31] The argument has also been made that the colonels were the agents of the *politikos kosmos* which was protecting itself from social change.[32] Others accuse the United States of complicity,[33] if not of actually having engineered the take-over.

Despite the fact that each of these positions rests on some truth, none of· them is completely satisfactory. Despite the threats of Andreas Papandreou that the populace would rise against any military government,[34] there was no resistance to the colonels and apparently no organization on the Left capable of capturing the state. On the other hand, if the *politikos kosmos* had intended to use the military (which Andreas Papandreou—among others—claimed), they would certainly have preferred the *coup* which was planned by the general staff and scheduled for the end of May.[35] And the evidence of United States complicity is purely conjecture.

What seems to have happened is that the Greek political system was altered by economic development during the period from 1951 to 1965 to such an extent that the traditional political oligarchy was no longer able to cope with the situation. The clientele system upon which the Greek *politikos kosmos* rested was disrupted, and the country's political leadership was unable to replace it with another viable structure. The colonels through their control of the Army had a power base through which they could govern the country. And the people submitted to their superior force.

In fact, there is evidence that many people welcomed the stability which the colonels brought to Greece. *The London Times* observed, "There can be no denying that Mr. Papadopoulos's Government has popular if not enthusiastic backing. It is disliked by intellectuals, by politicians, and by politically conscious townspeople. The stability it has shown through nearly two years is welcomed in the suburbs and the countryside." [36] However, the colonels were only "welcomed" be-

---

[31] This is the thesis of Young (and, in part, Stockton).

[32] This position was taken by Pollis in the article quoted above.

[33] In the same volume of *Massachusetts Review,* Roy C. Macridis proposed this thesis in "Greek Political Freedom and United States Foreign Policy."

[34] Anastoplo, p. 106.

[35] Robert McDonald, "Greece: April 21, 1967," *Massachusetts Review,* vol. 9, winter 1968, p. 59.

[36] Editorial, *The London Times,* January 29, 1969.

cause the parliamentary system had ceased to function. It was no longer capable of dealing with the demands placed upon it by the newly mobilized groups.

In this sense, Greece became an example of what Samuel Huntington would call a "praetorian polity" where political participation exceeded institutionalization.[37] But the Huntington thesis must be altered somewhat in order to fit the Greek case. This alteration may also serve a valid purpose in other instances. The Greek people cannot be said to have participated "more" in politics during the 1960s than during the 1950s. Rather, they changed the form of their participation, and the level of their involvement in things political. This qualification is important; in very few countries today does the population not participate to some extent in politics. However, this participation is often channeled through traditional social institutions —like the clientele system in Greece. It is hard to say that they participate "more" if they are outside of these institutions, but it can be seen that the form of their participation has changed. It is this change in the nature of participation which can lead to the established system's not being able to process demands.

The example of Greece demonstrates how this process may be related to economic development. During the scattered periods of parliamentary government in Greek history, the populace voted and petitioned its deputies for services. In short, the people participated in government. However, the changing economic structure of Greece brought many people to the cities where they were severed from their traditional clientele networks and exposed to new influences. They developed new sorts of demands and new ways of pressing these demands on the government. Furthermore, the kinship structure transmitted these new ideas to the villages which were changing in response to their participation in the market economy.

These new demands represented a new form of participation; people were concerned with government at the national level, not just their personal relationship with it. This represents a major change in the political system; it is a change in the form which participation takes; but, it is not just "more" participation. Political systems have proven themselves capable of adapting to quantitative increases in participation when they have extended the right to vote. Greece admitted half its electorate, women, after the Civil War with no disas-

[37] Samuel P. Huntington, *Political Order in Changing Societies,* Yale University Press (New Haven, 1968), p. 79.

trous consequences. A system can deal with more participants; it has trouble when the behavior of the participants becomes erratic or does not follow established patterns. This is what brought down the Greek system: economic development and migration to the cities had led to a different form of political behavior by a large part of the population. This type of change requires system change, and system change is revolutionary. The *politikos kosmos* could not be expected to renounce the structure which had created them. In a way, the politicians were the clients of the clientele networks, in that they depended on these networks for their support. When clientelism no longer functioned as the principal means of channeling demands to the government, the whole system had to be changed.

Japanese Foreign Policy Decisionmaking in the Middle Taishō Period: An Institutional Case Study of the *Gaikō Chōsa Kai*

MICHAEL K. BLAKER

Japanese scholars sometimes refer to the Taishō period as Meiji to Shōwa no tanima (the valley between Meiji and Shōwa). Not only does the phrase describe quite accurately the low level of our knowledge about Japan during the 1912–1926 period but it also expresses how sharply these years can be contrasted historically with what went before and what was to follow. Taishō Japan was in many ways a time of transition when traditional power relationships among the elites were changing considerably. By the middle of the period the aging *genrō* (elder statesmen) had become less willing to participate directly in policy making, party pressures for truly representative government had heightened as never before, and the army and navy cliques had already demonstrated the depth of their institutional and personal power. In international affairs, Japan had turned brashly assertive, involving itself in the First World War, in the scramble for colonies, and in the political conflict after the war that was to influence so decisively the future of Asia. As a natural result of these changes, the institutional structure of the Japanese government came to be perceived as inadequate for dealing effectively with radically new internal and external circumstances.

In this time of continuing crisis, Japan's political leaders engaged in some institutional tinkering in an effort to adjust. A number of special government councils were created: for example, the *Bōmu*

Kaigi (Military Affairs Council), the *Rinji Sangyō Chōsa Kai* (Temporary Production Council), the *Rinji Kyōku Gyōsei Chōsa Kai* (Temporary Educational Administration Council), and the *Takushoku I'in Kai* (Colonization Council). Home Minister Gotō Shimpei even proposed during the war the creation of a *dai chōsa kikan* which, if established, was to study problems relating to foreign trade, science, and industry and to recommend long-range programs in these areas.[1] Gotō's organization was to function independently, outside party disputes in the Cabinet or Diet. Perhaps the best known of these experimental government bodies, and without doubt the most important both in terms of level of function and quality of membership, was a council established in June 1917 that was to play a critical role in the formulation of Japanese foreign policy until 1922. This was the *Rinji Gaikō Chōse I'in Kai* or Temporary Deliberative Council on Foreign Relations. This paper is concerned with the origins, development, structure, and function of the *Gaikō Chōsa Kai* during this period.

Origins of the Council

It is generally agreed that the idea for a *Gaikō Chōsa Kai* grew out of a desire to remove foreign policymaking from the arena of party politics.[2] Miura Gorō first suggested such a council to be composed of *genrō* who would formulate and guide national policy in the delicate and crucial areas of military expenditures, financial administration, and diplomacy. The elder statesmen, however, were unimpressed. While Matsukata did not entirely reject the notion, Inoue begged off because of illness, and Yamagata refused to consider the plan at all.[3]

Despite this rebuff from the *genrō*, Miura did not give up on the plan. During May and June 1916 he arranged for a series of meetings in Kyoto with leaders of the three political parties, Hara Kei (Seiyūkai), Inukai Ki (Kokumintō), and Katō Kōmei (Dōshikai). Feeling it essential to present a united front in any peace negotiations after the war, these party leaders agreed to place problems relating

[1] Sawada Ken, *Gotō Shimpei Den* (Tokyo: Dai Nihon Kōza Kai, 1943), p. 273.

[2] See, for example, Kobayashi Tatsuo, "Rinji Gaikō Chōsa I'in Kai no Setchi," *Kokusai Seiji,* no. 2 (1964), pp. 57–58.

[3] Itō Masanori, *Katō Kōmei* (Tokyo, 1929), Vol. II, pp. 64–65.

to diplomacy, national defense, and financial administration outside partisan politics. For Katō, who had consistently worked for Foreign Ministry control over foreign policy, this was a substantial concession.

When Ōkma resigned as Prime Minister on October 4, 1916, Yamagata named his aging disciple, Terauchi Masatake, then Governor-General of Korea, to head the government. The day after Terauchi took office on October 9, the Chūsai Kai and the Kōyū Club joined with the Doshikai to form the Kenseikai, giving the new party a majority of seats in the Diet (197 of 381). Although the Terauchi Cabinet was transcendental, the new Prime Minister wanted Sieyūkai support and a majority in the Diet. It would have been ill-advised for him to have sought Seiyūkai support without at the same time protecting himself from the Kokumintō. Therefore, he sought Inukai's assistance as well.[4] He also brought a major ex-Dōshikai figure into the government as Home Minister—Gotō Shimpei. Terauchi's forthright tactics proved successful. In the general election of April 1917 the Kenseikai majority was broken and firmly pro-government party alliance achieved control of the Diet.

While Terauchi was working for party support, governmental leaders were accelerating their efforts to reach unity on foreign policy questions through the creation of a council that would deal specifically with these matters. Concrete, detailed plains for a foreign policy council were discussed by Gotō and Viscount Itō Miyoji in January 1917. Itō had been the disciple of Itō Hirobumi, a participant in the drafting of the Meiji Constitution, and was the foremost living authority on the legal aspects of government. Together wtih Gotō, Itō drafted an ordinance for the establishment of the *Gaikō Chōsa Kai*.[5] Now the original conception of a supraparty foreign policy council had become a specific plan of action. Miura's idea of a *genrō* dominated group operating independently of the Cabinet had been discarded because of Yamagata's opposition, and, in its place, a council outside the Cabinet without direct *genrō* representation was created.

Following several months of informal discussion on the proposal among various officials, Terauchi invited Hara, Inukai, and Katō to a meeting to consider matters "relating to affairs of state." Both Inukai and Hara accepted immediately but Katō was suspicious and asked

4 Kobayashi, "Rinji Gaikō . . . ," p. 60.
5 *Hakushaku Itō Miyoji* (Tokyo, 1938), Vol. II, p. 68.

the precise meaning of the vague phrase "affairs of state." Terauchi responded that this meant "foreign policy." Reluctantly, Katō agreed to attend.[6]

At the meeting (June 2, 1917) Terauchi emphasized the urgent need to establish national unity (kyokoku itchi) and asked the support of the three party leaders for the proposed *Gaikō Chōsa Kai*. In addition, he invited them all to join the group. Hara and Inukai readily consented but Katō would not succumb even to the temptation of an immediate share in decisionmaking power. He wanted to think it over. On June 4 Katō made his position clear in a memorandum to Terauchi in which he repudiated the idea of the council as a blatant infringement of the constitutionally guaranteed rights of the Cabinet and the Foreign Ministry to conduct foreign affairs. For this reason, Katō declared, he would not join the group.[7] There may have been reasons other than those of principle for Katō's demurrer. As Itō Masanori notes in his biography of Katō, his refusal may have been due in part to Terauchi's half-hearted appeals for his support. Terauchi, Itō observes, did not even visit Katō personally to win his endorsement.[8]

Despite Katō's personal boycott, plans for the Council moved swiftly ahead. On June 4 Yamagata, Saionji, and Matsukata discussed the group with the Emperor,[9] and with his approval the *Gaikō Chōsa Kai* was officially established. The text of the ordinance creating the organization is as follows: [10]

Imperial Ordinance Establishing the Rinji Gaikō Chōsa I'in Kai
Dated June 5, 1917 and Promulgated June 6, 1917

In view of developments in the general situation and in consideration of our permanent interests, we recognize the need to establish a temporary council in the Imperial Court which shall have as its function the discussion and exploration of internal and external matters. To that end, we hereby approve and proclaim the creation of the Temporary Deliberative Council on Foreign Relations.

Article 1: The Temporary Deliberative Council on Foreign Relations

[6] Itō Masanori, *Katō Kōmei*, p. 263.   [7] *Ibid.*, pp. 263–64.   [8] *Ibid.*
[9] *Tokyo Asahi Shimbun*, June 5, 1917, cited in Takeuchi Tatsuji, *War and Diplomacy in the Japanese Empire* (New York: Doubleday, 1935), p. 45.
[10] Japan, Gaimushō, *Nihon Gaikō Nenpyō narabi ni Shuyō Bunsho* (Tokyo: Hara Shobo, 1965), p. 434.

shall be established in the Imperial Court and shall discuss and deliberate directly under the Emperor matters relating to the general situation.

Article 2: The Temporary Deliberative Council on Foreign Relations shall be composed of a president and a number of members.

Article 3: The presiding officer of the Council shall be the Prime Minister. Members shall be selected from among Ministers of State, former Prime Ministers and Ministers of State, those who are accorded treatment on the Minister of State level, and those officials personally appointed by the Emperor.

Article 4: The President of the Council shall have responsibility for supervising the membership and he shall report on the proceedings of the conference.

Article 5: One member of the Temporary Deliberative Council on Foreign Relations shall be designated Chief Secretary and several others shall serve as secretaries. The Chief Secretary shall regulate the official business of the Council while serving concurrently as a member.

Article 6: In particularly urgent cases, temporary members shall be appointed to the Council by the Emperor from among those with special expertise or experience, irrespective of the stipulations set forth in Article 3 above.

Article 7: For those members holding positions in the Government, treatment shall be made according to their official ranks. Special provisions shall be made for others.

Initial Opposition to the Council

As soon as the formation of the *Gaikō Chōsa Kai* was announced, a great hue and cry arose against it. Leading the opposition were Katō, Kenseikai members in the Diet, intellectuals, and most major newspapers.[11] Objections to the Council centered mainly upon its relationship and other governmental units such as the Cabinet and the Privy Council, its ties with the Emperor, its constitutionality, and its anticipated functions in the conduct of Japanese foreign policy.

The Council was considered by its critics [12] to be an obvious usurpation of the Cabinet's control over foreign affairs, which was guar-

[11] Kobayashi, "Rinji Gaikō . . . ," p. 69, lists the Tokyo *Asahi, Mainichi, Nichi Nichi,* and *Hōchi* and the Osaka *Asahi* and *Mainichi* as against the Council.

[12] See the Sasaki Sōichi statements in the Tokyo *Asahi Shimbun* beginning on June 14, 1917, as compiled in Kobayashi Tatsuo (ed.), *Suiuso Nikki: Itō Ke Bunsho,* (Tokyo: Hara Shobō, 1966), pp. 223–37. Katō Kōmei's objections are summarized in Itō Masanori, *Katō Kōmei,* pp. 64–70 and 260–80.

anteed by Article 55 of the Meiji Constitution. According to that article, "affairs of state" (*kokumu*) where to be decided by the Minister of State. Foreign relations, the critics charged, fell wtihin the category of affairs of state and ought properly to be handled by the Foreign Minister through the Cabinet.

Another key constitutional question concerned the Council's relationship to the Emperor. Here the language of the ordinance was ambiguous. In Article 1 it was announced that the group would be set up "in the Imperial Court" and would function "directly under the Emperor." Moreover, the word "report" (*fusō*) used in Article 4 seemed to indicate that the organization would report and be responsible to the Emperor. Finally, the word *sokkin ni* (alternatively read *sobachikaku ni*) in the preamble, translated here as "in the Imperial Court," strongly suggests a relation to the Emperor. On the basis of the language used in the ordinance, critics concluded that the Council was designed to advise the Emperor independently of the Ministers of State and was, therefore, a direct violation of the Constitution. As Kyoto University Professor of Constitutional law, Sasaki Sōichi concluded in the Tokyo *Asahi:* "As long as the Constitution does not specifically provide for advisors other than the Ministers of State, creating such an organization to advise the Emperor is not permissible." [13] Sasaki elaborated on this point, noting that advising the Emperor was not unconstitutional unless such advice came from an organization outside the Ministers of State and if that advice related to "affairs of state." He stressed the essential difference between the *Gaikō Chōsa Kai* and the *Bōmu Kaigi* and other *Chōsa Kai* formed since 1914; namely, that these other groups, unlike the *Gaikō Chōsa Kai,* were responsible to the Cabinet and did not directly advise the Emperor.[14]

Critics denied any practical need for the Council to be set up at all. Sasaki pointedly observed that if the function of the Council was to be merely information gathering, then there was no sense in altering the existing institutional structure of the government because this task could be managed adequately either by revamping the Foreign Ministry or by seeking out more effective personnel.[15] If it were essential to solicit opinions on foreign policy outside the Cabinet, he asked, why not just debate these issues in the Diet? Moreover, if the Council was, in fact, merely an advisory body, then Ministers of

[13] Sasaki statement cited in Kobayashi, *Suiusō Nikki*, p. 229.
[14] *Ibid.*, p. 236.   [15] *Ibid.*, p. 225.

State should be included formally as members. Finally, Sasaki acknowledged the fact that Hara and Inukai had been included in the group but he wanted a guarantee that party leaders would be officially represented at all times.[16]

At bottom, opposition to the new Council reflected the intense dissatisfaction felt in many quarters with continued authoritarian control over the making of national policy. The *Gaikō Chōsa Kai* seemed to its critics just another example of the use, or misuse, or arbitrary *hanbatsu* power. It was feared that the Council would wield decisive authority over foreign policy-making and that the Cabinet, the Diet, and popular opinion would be effectively ignored.

Itō Miyoji to the Defense

Terauchi answered his opposition through the conservative Itō Miyoji, who was eminently qualified to launch the counterattack when the disputed subject was his specialty—the Meiji Constitution. Itō drafted a rebuttal entitled *Rinji Gaikō Chōsa I'in Kai Yogi* (Commentary on the Temporary Council on Foreign Relations) which was distributed with Terauchi's approval.[17]

Itō prefaced his reply with the general point that the international situation required national unity. He stressed the importance of preparing adequately for peace, observing that placing the resolution of issues relating to national defense and diplomacy outside partisan politics would enable Japan to present a strong and united front to the Powers.[18]

Next, Itō pointed to the limitations of the Council. He referred to the historical development of the *genrō,* noting that no one had criticized that group as a violation of either the letter or spirit of the Constitution. He emphasized two major differences bewteen the Council and the *genrō,* however: namely, that while any one of the *genrō* could individually advise the Emperor on any subject, the *Gaikō Chōsa Kai* would advise only as a collective body (*gōgitai*) and was limited in its area of competence to matters relating to foreign affairs. Itō also stressed the temporary (*rinji*) nature of the Council.

To the charge that the Council would infringe upon the right of

---

[16] *Ibid.,* pp. 227–31.   [17] Kobayashi, *Kokusai Seiji,* pp. 69–70.

[18] This paragraph and much of the following text is derived from the complete Itō statement as contained in Kobayashi, *Suiusō Nikki,* pp. 238–65.

Ministers of State to handle matters relating to *kokumu,* Itō promised that the group would not execute but merely investigate problems of policy in this area. He maintained that having the Prime Minister preside over the Council and the Foreign Minister as Chief Secretary would insure full communication between the Cabinet and the Council. Itō recalled, moreover, that the Privy Council, the *Bōmu Kai,* and the various other *Chōsa Kai* had not violated the *kokumu* prerogative of the Ministers of State.

Itō evaded the issue of whether the Council would prove to be a "cabinet on top of a cabinet" by emphasizing that Article 55 of the Meiji Constitution included no provision whatsoever as to *how* the cabinet system might evolve. The existing cabinet arrangement, he pointed out, was based upon Article 10 of the Constitution, giving the Emperor the right to determine the organization of different administrative branches of government. The *Gaikō Chōsa Kai* was created under this supreme Imperial prerogative (*shison taiken*) and could not, therefore, be unconstitutional.[19] Besides, Itō continued, the Constitution nowhere stated that an advisory organization could not be established outside the Ministers of State.

Itō then addressed himself to the role of the *Gaikō Chōsa Kai* in foreign policy-making, differentiating its function from that of the Privy Council. The *Gaikō Chōsa Kai* would not invade the competence of the Privy Council, he felt, because the latter was a permanent body whose function was to discuss *kokumu* and to advise the Emperor on it. It could not initiate action. The *Gaikō Chōsa Kai,* on the other hand, would be concerned with diplomacy, not *kokumu* and, moreover, would be capable of formulating drafts on foreign policy problems. It could discuss these issues even after they had been brought before the Cabinet. To Itō, then, the Council was to be more than an advisory body; it was to have the power to initiate independent discussion while the Privy Council could only debate "treaties and agreements" or specific proposals from the Cabinet. Itō envisaged an organization which, more or less in tandem with the Cabinet, would have substantial authority over foreign policy formation at the highest level.

Despite Itō's energetic defense of the Council, opposition continued, wih the scene shifting to the Diet. During the stormy 39th Spe-

---

[19] Sasaki had written that this was beside the point, which was the usurpation of Cabinet authority.

cial Diet session beginning in June, Ozaki Yukio, perennial government critic and noted political theorist, sponsored a no-confidence
motion on the grounds that Terauchi lacked a base in the Diet and
that his government was, therefore, a violation of the previous election.[20] Through the united opposition of the Kokumintō, Seiyūkai,
and Ishinkai, however, the motion was soundly defeated, 124 to 23.[21]
On July 12 Diet member Morita Shigeru moved to abolish the Council, claiming it violated the Constitution. This proposal, too, was
overwhelmingly rejected.[22]

If Katō's tactic in refusing to join the Council had been to use the
opposition to it as a device to increase his power in the Diet, it had
proven ineffective. As both Hara and Inukai had sided with the government from the outset, any possible united party effort to destroy
the fledgling organization was doomed. With the exception of Katō,
the other party heads seemed to recognize that to sit in the councils
of power it was necessary to compromise principle and to work with
the holders of real authority in the political system—the oligarchy
and the bureaucracy.

Membership in the Gaikō Chōsa Kai

According to the terms of the original ordinance establishing the
Council, the Prime Minister was to preside over the meetings while
the procedural business was to be handled by a Chief Secretary and a
number of assistants. Members were to be drawn from the highest
level of government service. Those prospective members who did not
or had not in the past held the rank of Minister of State were to be
named *shinnin* officials.[23] Secretaries were to be simply "high officials" (*kōtōkan*) chosen from among the officials in the Foreign Ministry, the Cabinet, or high-ranking officers in the army or navy.

The original members appointed to the *Gaikō Chōsa Kai* were: [24]

[20] Kobayashi, *Kokusai Seiji.* p. 70.
[21] Kobayashi, *Suiusō Nikki,* pp. 244–45.   [22] *Ibid.*

[23] Shinnin officials represented the highest level of the classified civil service, including cabinet ministers and ambassadors and corresponding to
generals and admirals. Robert M. Spaulding, Jr., *Imperial Japan's Higher
Civil Service Examinations* (Princeton: Princeton University Press, 1967), p.
328.

[24] See the membership chart for the entire group. The chart was compiled
from *Hara Kei Nikki,* Vols. 6–9; Kobayashi, *Suiusō Nikki;* the Tokyo *Asahi
Shimbun,* 1921–1922; and Miwa Kai and Philip Yampolsky, *Political Chro-*

1. Terauchi Masatake (President)	Prime Minister
2. Montono Ichirō	Foreign Minister
3. Gotō Shimpei	Home Minister
4. Katō Tomosaburō	Navy Minister
5. Ōshima Ken'ichi	Army Minister
6. Makino Shinken	Privy Councilor
7. Hirata Tōsuke	Privy Councilor
8. Itō Miyoji	Privy Councilor
9. Hara Kei	Seiyūkai
10. Inukai Ki	Kokumintō
Montono Ichirō (Chief Sec'y)	Foreign Minister
Suzuki Kantarō (Sec'y)	Vice Admiral
Shidehara Kijūrō (Sec'y)	Vice Minister of Foreign Affairs
Yamada Ryūichi (Sec'y)	Army Lieutenant General
Komaka Hideo (Sec'y)	Cabinet Secretary

James Morley quite effectively assesses the initial composition of the Council as follows: [25]

In terms of official organs of the government the advisory council is seen to have represented the premier, the two military bureaucracies (the army and the navy); the two most important civilian bureaucracies (the Foreign and Home ministries); the Privy Council, whose approval was needed for all treaties and any other important measures the Emperor cared to refer to it; and the two houses of the Diet, which together exercised legislative, including budgetary control. An analysis in terms of the unofficial cliques and groups represented is even more enlightening. Except for Motono, who was relatively isolated, and Itō, who was inclined toward independence although he often cooperated with the Choshu leadership, the members of the advisory council fell neatly into three powerful groups: the Choshu clique (Tehauchi, Gotō, Ōshima, and Hirata), the Satsuma clique (Makino and Katō) and the Seiyūkai and Kokumintō political parties (Hara and Inukai).

Another informal cross-elite coalition, in addition to the clan groupings mentioned by Morley, was the so-called three-cornered alliance (*sankaku dōmei*) composed of Itō, Inukai, and Gotō. It is difficult to measure the significance of this coalition, although a reading of the Council records and Hara's Diary leaves the impression that

---

nology of Japan 1885–1957 (New York: Columbia University, East Asian Institute, 1957).

[25] James W. Morley, *The Japanese Thrust into Siberia, 1918* (New York: Columbia University Press, 1957), p. 26.

these three leaders did, in fact, support each other on most issues. Sawada Ken, in his biography of Gotō, believes that the *sankaku dōmei* was the key political factor at the time.[26] The important point is that the Council is not easily divisible into subgroupings that acted as units because of these very complex, and often conflicting, personal and institutional patterns of loyalty.

When the Hara Cabinet was formed in October 1918, Terauchi and Gotō were both invited to remain on the Council. Several years later, Prime Minister Takahashi was asked and decided to stay in the group even after his term of office had ended. One reason for this practice may have been a desire to maintain continuity of policy. There was some concern whether or not the ailing Terauchi would be physically able to continue to serve on the Council, but as he had Yamagata's strong support, it was decided that he should continue even though he would have to miss some of the meetings.[27]

General Tanaka Gi'ichi was named to the Council to replace Ōshima, who had been appointed Governor-General of Taiwan. Yamagata had not specifically nominated Tanaka for the Army ministership (and concurrently a seat on the Council) but did include his name in a list of three generals he favored.[28] Once on the Council, Tanaka worked very closely with Hara and with the bureaucracy.[29] Incoming Foreign Minister Uchida Yasuya assumed the Chief Secretaryship of the Council and continued to occupy this post until the Council was finally dissolved in September 1922.

There were no formal provisions for the resignation or replacement of members. Moreover, unlike the National Security Council in the United States, there was no official document indicating the composition of the organization; that is, the allocation of seats on the Council among the various elements holding authority in the political system.

On the basis of scattered evidence, however, it is possible to suggest how the process of informal recruitment into the organization developed. First, as is clear from the following chart, in addition to the Prime Minister and Foreign Minister, who occupied official posts on the Council, both the Army and Navy were continuously represented

---

[26] Sawada Ken, *Gotō Shimpei Den,* p. 162.

[27] Kobayashi, *Suiusō Nikki,* p. 37. As it turned out he did miss almost all subsequent meetings of the Council.

[28] Ishigami Ryōhei, *Hara Kei Botsugo* (Tokyo, 1960), p. 315.   [29] *Ibid.*

Council established June 6, 1917 *Council abolished September 18, 1922*

Cabinet:	*Terauchi*	*Hara*	*Takahashi*	*Katō*
Members:				
1. Chinda Sutemi		x————————————————————————		——x
2. Gotō Shimpei	x——————————————x (assassinated September, 1921)			x
3. Hara Kei	x————————————————————			x
4. Hirata Tōsuke	x————————————————————————————————			x
5. Inukai Ki	x————————————————————————————————			x
6. Itō Miyoji	x—— navy minister ———————————— / prime minister ————			x
7. Katō Tomosaburō	x—— / Versailles delegate / ——x July 5, 1920 resigned			x
8. Makino Shinken	app't Nov. 6, 1918			
9. Motoda Hajime	x——————x April 23, 1918 died			
10. Motono Ichirō		x——		
11. Ōka Ikuzō	x———————x September 29, 1918 reassignment			x
12. Ōshima Ken'ichi	x—— army minister ———————x prime minister / ——			x
13. Takahashi Korekiyo		x————————x		
14. Tanaka Giichi	x——————— June 9, 1921 ——x			
15. Terauchi Masatake				x
16. Uchidaa Yasuya				x
17. Yamanashi Hanzō				x

through the Army and Navy Ministers in the Cabinet.[30] Military representatives only served on the Council concurrently with their Cabinet posts. As far as the Privy Councilors were concerned, all continued through to the end, so there were no replacement problems regarding that group. Second, one seat on the Council created during the Hara administration and retained under the Takahashi and Katō Cabinets appears to have been specifically intended for a Seiyūkai leader possibly as a reward for loyal party service. In this connection, it is instructive to relate how Motoda Hakime was appointed to the *Gaikō Chōsa Kai.*

Prior to the formation of his Cabinet, Hara had discussed possible appointments to the Council with various government figures. Hara had recommended Mizuno Rentarō for membership to Itō Miyoji but Itō resisted, claiming that members of the Council had to be "first rank statesmen" *(ichiryū no seijika).*[31]

On October 8, 1918, Makino visited Hara to sound him out regarding the possibility of naming Admiral Yamamoto Gombei to the Council.[32] Hara, however, anticipated an unfavorable response to Yamamoto's nomination from Yamagata, and the matter was dropped.[33] Hara and Terauchi both wanted Motoda in the Council because of his party connections (Seiyūkai). Both had desired Mizuno's nomination as well but that had proven impossible because of Itō's firm opposition. Only Motoda was finally named to the Council, receiving approval by the Emperor at a *shinninshiki* (personal appointment ceremony) on November 6.

Motoda resigned from the Council on July 5, 1920, and was replaced immediately by Ōka Ikuzō, another elder Seiyūkai figure like Motoda. When Ōka, in turn, was considering resignation in 1922, two names were circulated in the press as likely candidates for his "seat" on the Council. These two men were Takahashi Korekiyo, President of the Seiyūkai (even though he was already on the Council), and Tokonami Takejirō, former Railways and Home Minister and a Seiyūkai leader.

---

[30] Katō served concurrently as Navy Minister and Prime Minister after June 1922.

[31] *Hara Kei Nikki,* Vol. 8, p. 41. See also Kobayashi, *Suiusō Nikki,* pp. 38 & 58. Itō's version uses the phrase *dai ichiryū no jimbutsu.* Itō records that he opposed Mizuno because of his previous connections and policies.

[32] Kobayashi, *Suiusō Nikki,* p. 38.

[33] *Hara Kei Nikki,* Vol. 8, p. 45; and Vol. 7, p. 206.

In sum, the basic alignments within the Council did not change particularly over time. Army-Navy representation in the group was accepted and an additional seat for a Seiyūkai leader was established. Total membership in the Council reached seventeen by the time it was abolished but membership at any given time was stabilized at between ten and twelve. There was the general requirement of "first rank statesmanship" for membership but this was to a great extent determined by the reactions of a few key people—Itō, Hara, Yamagata, and Terauchi—and was not based strictly on merit.

Still, this was an outstanding group of men. Although Katō Kōmei had criticized the original group, with the exception of Montono,[34] as "amateurs" in the making of foreign policy, this was an overstatement. Of the total membership, seven were either former or future Foreign Ministers, and, among the Privy Council group, all had served previously as Ministers of State in the Cabinet.[35] It was also a homogeneous group. All were "second generation" leaders and all were born between 1851 and 1865. Their average age on appointment was sixty years.

After the Versailles peace treaty had been ratified by the Privy Council in October 1919, certain Japanese leaders suggested that the group be dissolved. Inukai wanted to quit and expressed doubt concerning any future need for *Gaikō Chōsa Kai* since the peace issue had been settled.[36] According to one source, Itō and Gotō both expressed a desire to Hara to withdraw from the Council.[37] Makino also wanted to resign. Part of the reason for their not resigning at this time may have been, strangely, that Hara was not sure how a member should resign, as the procedure was not set forth clearly in the ordinance establishing the Council.[38] After the Washington Conference, Gotō, Ōka, and Inukai told Katō that they intended to resign.[39] Hirata also wanted to do so because of his appointment as

[34] Itō Masanori, *op. cit.,* p. 268.

[35] Makino, for exmaple, had served as Foreign Minister in the first Yamamoto Cabinet, Education Minister in the first Saionji Cabinet, and Education and Agriculture Minister in the second Saionji Cabinet. Hirata had been Agriculture and Commerce Minister in the first Katsura Cabinet and Home Minister in the second Katsura Cabinet. Itō had been Agriculture and Commerce Minister in the third Itō (Hirobumi) Cabinet.

[36] *Hara Kei Nikki,* Vol. 8, p. 357.   [37] Takeuchi, p. 48.
[38] *Hara Kei Nikki,* Vol. 9, p. 232.
[39] Osaka Mainichi Shimbun (ed.), *Mainichi Nenkan,* 1923, p. 122.

Lord Keeper of the Privy Seal.[40] Only Itō among those members outside the Cabinet expressed a desire to continue the Council, feeling that there were still a number of problems for the Council to discuss.[41] The position of the Katō Cabinet was to retain the organization.[42]

Without the support of the non-Cabinet leaders and without any vital foreign policy issues remaining after the conclusion of the Paris and Washington conferences, however, there was little real need for the Council to continue to function. Moreover, Yamagata, always a staunch supporter of the Council, had died in 1922. In any event, lacking essential backing by the top leadership, the *Gaikō Chōsa Kai* was rather summarily dissolved on September 18, 1922.

Procedural Rules for the Council

Shortly after the formation of the *Gaikō Chōsa Kai* a set of ground rules for the organization was settled upon. Motono, Gotō, and Itō discussed these rules at a meeting on the afternoon of June 8, 1917, after which their draft was submitted to Terauchi for his approval.[43] Most of the rules were procedural and can be summarized as follows: [44]

1. Meetings shall take place in the *san-no-ma* room of the Imperial palace.

2. All matters relating to Council meetings shall be absolutely secret.

3. Records relating to Council meetings shall not leave the meeting room except with the permission of the President.

4. Meetings shall take place on fixed days to be communicated in advance by the Chief Secretary.

5. Meetings shall be divided into two types: informational and discussion.

6. Subjects for discussion shall be approved by the President and shall be presented by the Chief Secretary at the meetings.

7. Decisions of the Council shall be considered as drafts and shall be presented to the Emperor.

[40] Tokyo *Asahi Shimbun,* September 15, 1922.
[41] Tokyo *Asahi Shimbun,* August 21, 1922.   [42] *Ibid.*
[43] Kobayashi, *Suiusō Nikki,* pp. 210–12.   [44] *Ibid.*

8. Reports of the Council shall be made to the Cabinet.

9. Documents containing information relating to diplomatic questions shall be distributed to members by the Chief Secretary.

10. Secretaries shall maintain records of the meetings.

An earlier draft of these rules had elaborated on point no. 5 above concerning types of Council meetings. It was stated that at informational or briefing meetings the Chief Secretary, who was the Foreign Minister, was to present the background of the particular problem under consideration, answer questions, and provide data and documents for examination. At discussion meetings (*hyōgikai*), on the other hand, debate was to take place on drafts distributed to members prior to the meeting, drafts presented at the meeting, or matters introduced orally by the Foreign Minister.[45] Decisions reached at these discussion meetings were to be written up by the Chief Secretary and, with the approval of the President, were to be distributed to each member. Results of the meetings were to be reported to the Emperor and, if there was a special request, a minority opinion could be included in this report.[46] The early draft also noted that at the meetings the Chief Secretary was to read documents containing any pertinent information as well as telegrams from representatives abroad. It was unofficially settled that the Council was to meet twice a month with the exact time to be set in advance by the Chief Secretary and communicated to the members, but the Chief Secretary was free to name any time for the meetings. Individual members of the Council were to be allowed to present draft proposals before the group as long as they presented them to the Chief Secretary in advance and secured the approval of the President. In those cases where the attendance of persons outside the Council was required on problems of national defense or diplomacy, provision was made for their participation with the permission of the President. The possibility of holding special meetings (*rinji kaidō*) was also noted.

Voting procedures for the *Gaikō Chōsa Kai* were not mentioned in these preliminary rules and later practice is not clear. Hara, Inukai, and Katō all felt that a majority vote taken at the Council should not be binding. Inukai thought the Council ought to adopt the procedure

[45] *Ibid.,* p. 210.

[46] There is no record in the documents examined for this study of a "minority" opinion having been formulated or having accompanied a decision of the Council when it was reported to the Emperor.

of unanimous decisions followed in the Cabinet,[47] and available records of Council meetings suggest that, in fact, all decisions on major foreign policy questions were reached unanimously. This does not mean that all decisions were unanimous or that debate at the Council lacked intensity or, occasionally, even hostility and rancor. The goal, however, was to achieve consensus on policy decisions and, to that end great efforts were made to accommodate through compromise the objections of individual members.

The Gaikō Chōsa Kai *in Practice*

Snyder, Bruch, and Sapin, in their pioneering work *Foreign Policy Decision Making,* draw a distinction between what they term the "explicitly prescribed" activities of an organizational unit and those patterns of action which are sanctioned or conventionalized by precedent and habit. Both sets of activities, they point out, comprise the "competence" of a unit, which is to say, "the totality of those of the activities of the decision-maker relevant and necessary to the achievement of the organizational objective." [48] In the case of the *Gaikō Chōsa Kai,* the original ordinance establishing the group indicated that its area of competence was to be discussion and exploration of "internal and external matters" or "matters relating to the general situation." The actual operation of the Council was to make more precise the meaning of this vague terminology. This section is concerned with the types of issues decided by the Council; in other words, with its area of competence.

Under the Terauchi Cabinet, Council business centered upon three major areas: China policy, the Siberian Intervention, and the Lansing-Ishii negotiations. During Hara's administration (October 1918—October 1921) the Council dealt mainly with policy and instructions for the Paris Peace Conference. A second key issue continued to be relations with the Soviet regime. After the peace treaty had been signed the Council focused on the return of Shantung to China, the Dairen Conference, withdrawal from Siberia, and the Washington Conference. Throughout its existence the Council took up, in addition, rather specific policy problems as they arose: for example,

[47] *Hara Kei Nikki,* Vol. 7, pp. 181–85.
[48] Richard C. Synder, H. W. Bruch, and Burton Sapin (eds.), *Foreign Policy Decision Making* (New York: Free Press of Glencoe, 1962), pp. 107–108.

whether to bring Japanese warships back from the Mediterranean immediately after the war; how to handle the Nikolaevsk Incident in 1920; whether to recognize Finland's independence; and what to do about Yap. While the dividing line seems to have been somewhat arbitrary, less critical problems such as tariff levels, fishing agreements, and minor important treaties were not discussed at the Council. Korea also was not discussed, perhaps because relations with it were not considered foreign!

Of more significance than the distinction between important and minor foreign policy problems was defining which segment of the total national policy spectrum was exclusively or primarily "diplomatic" in nature and thus within the scope of the Council's concern. Two major restrictions, it appears, were made upon its competence. First, although the ordinance creating the Council stated that it was to discuss "internal and external matters," this was quickly refined in practice to become complete noninterference in domestic affairs (*naidei fukanshō*). Both Itō and Inukai appeared to want an expansion of Council competence to include domestic issues, but Hara firmly maintained that the Council was to discuss foreign policy exclusively.[49] This continued to be a source of friction that raised the practical issue of Cabinet versus Council jurisdiction and, more broadly, revealed sharply a more fundamental dilemma—can the "foreign" aspect of national policy questions be isolated?

Sometimes hard choices had to be made whether to discuss or to dismiss a particular issue. These borderline problems were generally handled by referring them to the Cabinet for its decision. Another method followed was to make a decision either "in principle" (*shugi ni*) or "in general" (*daitai*) but to leave the draft proposal unsigned. A final approach was to allow briefing on a domestic issue or on the military aspects of an international problem but not to permit formal debate on the question in the Council.

A second general restriction upon the area of competence of the Council related to military affairs and national defense. Military representatives like Ōshima, Tanaka, Katō, and Yamamashi did not participate as actively as some other members, usually confining their remarks to the military implications of policy. Often they briefed the others on issues involving military matters prior to debate. This was the procedure followed when the Council considered the return of

[49] *Hara Kei Nikki*, Vol. 7, pp. 207, 211–13.

Japanese warships from the Mediterranean,[50] railroad conditions in Siberia,[51] the return of Tsingtao to China,[52] and military implications of the League Covenant.[53] While Hara, during his tenure as President of the Council, favored in principle the discussion of military affairs (*bōmu*) if they were "essential' to the handling of a diplomatic problem,[54] in general he felt that [55] "problems of national defense are not subjects for discussion at the Council. If, [however], there is information to be reported [on these questions] we should simply listen to the explanation without expressing our own opinions."

In sum, leaders of the Council sought to limit its area of competence to important policy matters relating exclusively to foreign policy. In order not to infringe upon the jurisdiction of the Cabinet or the military, they attempted consciously to exclude domestic affairs, national defense, and military matters except for occasional briefings by the Army and Navy representatives on the Council.

Relation of the Council to other Groups concerned with Foreign Policy

THE CABINET

It is evident from the membership chart persented on page 160 that at any given time roughly one-half of the Council was composed of Cabinet members. Moreover, they occupied the most prestigious posts—Army Foreign Minister, Navy Foreign Minister, and Prime Minister. Because of this high level of parallel representation, there was little need for formalized channels of communication between the two bodies; they did not function toward each other as separate closed units.

Some group identification did develop on the Council. Past Council decisions and methods of handling problems strongly affected subsequent action.[56] Moreover, the Council became another "shared experience" in the official careers of its members, which doubtless

[50] Council Meeting, May 17, 1919, in Kobayashi, *Suiusō Nikki*, p. 508.
[51] Council Meeting, April 30, 1918, *ibid.*, p. 484.
[52] Council Meeting, June 26, 1919, *ibid.*, p. 543.
[53] Council Meetings, February 19 and 22, 1919, *ibid.*, pp. 412–34.
[54] *Hara Kei Nikki*, Vol. 7, p. 204.   [55] *Ibid.*, p. 313.
[56] See, for example, Kobayashi, *Suiusō Nikki*, pp. 595–600.

had some effect on their later thinking and personal relationships. Finally, membership on the Council was in a sense an honor and conferred a special status. Itō was especially sensitive to the status given to Council members. As he noted in his *Diary,* if persons "on the second level or lower" were named to the Council, neither public opinion nor the *rōkei* (elders, but he may have meant *genrō*) would allow it.[57] Hara thought, and it seems likely, that Itō was trying to use his position on the *Gaikō Chōsa Kai* to gain for himself an advisory post on foreign relations or a promotion from viscount to count.[58] In fact, after the Paris Conference all members of the Council were promoted in rank except Hara, who alone declined the honor.

Although domestic affairs and national defense questions were not actively debated by the Council, foreign policy issues were considered in the Cabinet. The Cabinet met much more often than the Council, usually every few days. The Council generally met twice a month but quite frequently during such crisis periods as when policy was settled on the Siberian Intervention or the Paris Conference.

Judging from the Hara and Itō diaries, the Foreign Minister briefed both the Cabinet and the Council on foreign policy questions. Often, decisions were made first in the Cabinet,[59] whereupon these decisions and/or background information relating to them were reported to the Council for confirmation or revision.[60] If major revisions proved necessary (which was quite unlikely at this stage of the process), a draft proposal might be referred to the Foreign Ministry or a subcommittee within the Council might be appointed to study, amend, and resubmit the draft.

This process was often reversed; that is, a report of an incident in China, an urgent telegram from Versailles, or a policy proposal introduced by a member of the Council might first be discussed and a decision reached by the Council before the Cabinet was notified. When an immediate response was essential, as during the Paris Conference, the Cabinet was many times not informed of the Council's decision until after reply instructions had already been dispatched.[61] At one point during the negotiations Hara indicated that he wanted

[57] *Ibid.,* p. 38.   [58] For example *Hara Kei Nikki,* Vol. 8, p. 229.

[59] In the form of either a *kettei* (decision) or *naitei* (tentative decision).

[60] In at least one major case a Cabinet decision was rejected outright, the Cabinet then agreeing to the Council's decision. Morley, *The Japanese Thrust into Siberia,* p. 322.

[61] *Hara Kei Nikki,* Vol. 8, pp. 149–50.

to avoid convening the Council each time new reports arrived from Paris but desired instead to answer the telegrams at once and then inform the Council. Itō, Gotō, and Inukai (the three-cornered alliance), however, opposed such a move and expressed their willingness to meet at any time, day or night, to discuss urgent matters relating to the Conference.[62]

Much time at the meetings was devoted to reading telegrams from Versailles. Partly to avoid this procedure and also to eliminate the need to call Council meetings each time new telegrams arrived, Hara then suggested to Itō that they meet informally to discuss reply instructions. It appears that such an arrangement was made and that the two men did meet often outside the Council to talk over problems relating to the peace settlement.

On the surface, the arrangement whereby telegrams were read, reports made, and discussion held both in the Cabinet and in the Council appears to have been grossly inefficient. It was time-consuming and involved a tremendous duplication of effort without bringing many more individuals into the policy-making process. It does not appear that the Council in practice usurped Cabinet authority in foreign affairs as some critics, notably Katō Kōmei, had feared. Rather, what is striking is the close relationship that developed between the Cabinet and Council, particularly during the Hara administration.

THE FOREIGN MINISTRY

Attempting to determine which group or individual ultimately controlled the making of foreign policy during this period is a frustrating if not impossible task. Truman's "the buck stops here" aphorism has no equivalent in the Japanese system. In other words, in foreign policy-making the Japanese political system in the mid-Taishō period does not appear to have had a clearly defined institutional pattern for locating supreme authority. At least no group or individual seems to have had exclusive jurisdiction over foreign policy; rather, it was decided through a system of shared responsibility, with the degree of participation and authority varying over time according to fluctuations in the relative strength of key individuals and groups.

Despite Katō Kōmei's determined efforts to secure this responsibility for the Foreign Ministry, he never succeeded. He had made the prohibition of military interference in the conduct of diplomacy a

[62] Council Meeting, February 3, 1919, in Kobayashi, *Suiusō Nikki,* p. 400.

precondition for his joining the third Katsura Cabinet and he had rejected *genrō* intrusions as well, charging that their role in foreign affairs was "the cancer of constitutional government." [63] His well-known personal foray into international politics—the presentation of the 21 Demands—was a political miscalculation that incurred the wrath of the *genrō*. Yamagata was especially angry because Katō had failed to inform the oligarch of his decision in advance. That only half-hearted efforts by the *genrō* were made to bring Katō into the *Gaikō Chōsa Kai* may have represented an attempt to punish him for his unauthorized independence. Even later, just prior to the opening of the Paris Peace Conference, Yamagata rejected Katō outright as a possible Japanese delegate to the negotiations.[64] In any event, the Foreign Ministry had not decided policy even prior to the creation of the Council, and its formation appears merely to have formalized its subordinate position.

The biographers of two famous Japanese diplomats [65] attack the oligarchs for having seized from the Foreign Ministry the right to make foreign policy. They lament the fact that neither of the two foreign ministers under the Terauchi Cabinet (Motono and Gotō) was capable of speaking out against the "militarists." They credit the Council as being the formulator of top-level policy while relegating the *Gaimushō* to the role of executor of policy that it had no power to change.

This harsh criticism notwithstanding, most draft proposals submitted to the Council for its approval originated in the Foreign Ministry. Many *Gaimushō* drafts were approved without any revisions whatsoever. Also, the Foreign Ministry and its representatives abroad naturally played a significant role in influencing the flow of information to the Council. Although the Army representative normally provided background on the Siberian front, the Foreign Minister was the source of information on the situation in China and on diplomatic negotiations abroad. Finally, subcommittees were often formed by the Council to work with Foreign Ministry officials to hammer out an acceptable draft. Itō, who was the most energetic

[63] Shinobu Seizaburo, "Taisho Gaiko Shi no Kihon Mondai," *Kokusai Seiji,* no. 6 (1958), pp. 2–4.

[64] *Hara Kei Nikki,* Vol. 8, p. 86.

[65] *Obata Yūkichi Denki* (Tokyo, 1957), p. 194 ff.; and *Shidehara Kijūrō* (Tokyo, 1955), pp. 122–35.

figure on the Council and its prime mover, was most often selected for these tasks. He generally worked with Sjidehara Kijūrō, with whom he had an exceptionally good relationship.[66] Council discussion on the topic was normally postponed until an adequate draft had been produced.

Negotiation on the text of documents to be submitted to the Council often brought representatives of the Army and Navy as well as the *Gaimushō*. For example, the basic draft proposals regarding Japanese policy for the Versailles negotiations were prepared by an Army-Navy-Foreign Ministry committee of section chiefs.

THE GENRŌ

Throughout the period during which the *Gaikō Chōsa Kai* was in operation, the *genrō* continued to set the main lines of foreign policy. They had not performed daily policy-making tasks for some time prior to 1916 but had relied upon their followers to act in their place in accordance with their wishes. Of the *genrō,* Yamagata seems to have been the most active in foreign affairs. He was the dominant force behind the decision to conclude an alliance with Russia in 1916 [67] and, as Morley demonstrates, he was the individual most influential in the decision to intervene in Siberia. Hara was close to Yamagata and met frequently with him either in person or through a representative in order to sound out the aging statesman's views. Hara also consulted, although not as often, with Saionji and Matsukata.

The *Gaikō Chōsa Kai* was established with the explicit approval of the *genrō.* Yamagata even went so far as to endorse personally the characters (keiyoku, "explore"), the key term in settling the nature of the Council's anticipated function in foreign policy-making. This term appeared ultimately in the preamble of the official ordinance creating the group.[68] Itō had thought that these particular characters strongly implied that the Council was to stand on an equal level with the *genrō.* The mere fact that *genrō* approval was required reveals both their continuing political strength and their concern with even the most detailed matters relating to foreign policy. During the Hara

[66] *Ibid.,* p .122.

[67] Peter Berton, *The Secret Russo-Japanese Alliance of 1916* (Unpublished Ph.D. dissertation, Columbia University, 1956).

[68] *Hara Kei Nikki,* Vol. 7, p. 186.

administration, the *genrō* continued to meet periodically in *genrō kaigi*.

Shinobu Seizaburō, a noted Japanese authority on Taishō politics whose views are heavily influenced by Marxist inclinations, emphasizes with satisfaction a deterioration of *genrō* dominance around 1917. To support his view, he mentions the inability of Yamagata to unify *genrō* opinion on foreign policy and the Chōshū oligarch's failure to convince Hara on the intervention question. The fact that Hara dared to oppose Yamagata convinces Shinobu that the *genrō* were on the decline. Shinobu points to a Chōshū (Terauchi, Yamagata) "defeat" on the Siberian question which took place at the *Gaikō Chōsa Kai*. He observes: "The *Gaikō Chōsa Kai,* which was established in order to have the political parties cooperate with the bureaucracy . . . had now changed to the point where the parties were able to criticize Terauchi and the Cabinet. . . . and. . . . the Council thus lost its significance." [69] Shinobu properly underscores the fact that party influence was increasing during the Taishō period, but this increase was relatively minor. The *hanbatsu,* symbolized by the *genrō,* retained ultimate authority.[70] The Council did not replace the *genrō* [71] or the Cabinet in foreign policy-making; rather, it deferred to the *genrō* on most important issues. All members of the Council had to have *genrō* approval for appointment. On every major foreign policy question, the views of the elder statesmen were solicited regarding basic policy, draft instructions to diplomats abroad, and the selection of delegates to international conferences. This was more than deference to age and prestige; the *genrō* had shown that they could easily break a cabinet. Possibly it was to avoid such an eventuality that all Council members had originally favored having the elder statesmen either in attendance at meetings or at the head of the organization.[72]

[69] Shinobu Seizaburō, *Taishō Seiji Shi* (Tokyo; 1951–52), Vol. II, pp. 517–22. This quoted section appears on page 517.

[70] See Roger F. Hackett, "Political Modernization and the Meiji Genrō," in Robert E. Ward (ed.) *Political Development in Modern Japan* (Princeton: Princeton University Press, 1968), p. 86, 90–91, 94.

[71] For this view, see James B. Crowley, *Japan's Quest for Autonomy* (Princeton: Princeton University Press, 1966), p. 21.

[72] Kobayashi, "Rinji Gaikō . . . ," pp. 64–68, and *Hara Kei Nikki*, Vol. 7, p. 182.

Functional Aspects of
the Gaikō Chōsa Kai

This paper has been concerned with the origins, prescribed functions, and subsequent institutional development of the *Gaikō Chōsa Kai*. In this final section, the functions of the Council will be discussed.

For purposes of analysis it is useful to view the Japanese political system during the mid-Taishō period as essentially distributive or pluralistic; that is, comprised of several institutional elite groups competing for power. Strictly speaking, the system was not perfectly distributive if that means each elite (civil bureaucracy, military, parties) shared equal power or access to power, for the *dei ex machina,* the *genrō,* remained outside and above the arena of direct elite conflict. As Hackett observes, the *genrō* were the supreme coordinating body with the power to preserve political equilibrium.[73] Moreover, elite competition was not the total confrontation of closed and thus mutually exclusive groups. There were many interelite cliques or coalitions, based primarily upon personal ties, that cut through the formal elite structure.[74] Still, it is best to perceive the system as basically distributive while bearing in mind the influence of the *genrō* and other groups close to the Throne (for example, the Privy Council) as well as the web of complicated interelite connections within the system. The question to be discussed in this section is how the *Gaikō Chōsa Kai* functioned within and in turn affected this system.

INTEGRATION

In the political system at the time the *Gaikō Chōsa Kai* appears to have performed mainly an integrative or stabilizing function in several ways. First, the Council gave a role in the decision-making process on the highest level to persons representing the political parties and the Privy Council who might not have been included otherwise. While this did not necessarily mean the direct articulation of elite positions at the Council (Hara, for example, maintained that he was

[73] Hackett, "Political Modernization. . . ," pp. 94–95.

[74] John K. Fairbank, Edwin O. Reischauer, and Albert M. Craig, *East Asia: The Modern Transformation* (Boston: Houghton Mifflin, 1965), p. 557. This Citation is taken from a chapter written by Albert Craig.

a free agent and not a representative of the Seiyakai when attending sessions),[75] it did open up a potential channel for the communication of these interests. Even informal representation of the Council did indicate at least tacit recognition of increased party influence in the political system. Nomination of Privy Council members to the Council could be justified on the basis of personal ties (Hirata's relationship with Yamagata, for example) or by the need for legal and constitutional expertise (Itō). Another consideration may have been to have members of the Privy Council participate in actual policy-making so that they would be less likely to obstruct passage of the Peace Treaty when it came before the Privy Council for ratification. Although there were frequent and intense debates in the Council, they appear to have been less dysfunctional than organized party opposition to, or Privy Council delay in, the ratification of the Peace Treaty. The *Gaikō Chōsa Kai* thus broadened participation in foreign policy issues.

Second, the Council to some extent insulated the government (the Cabinet) from attack by blurring the lines of direct responsibility for action. As the primary organ in the formal structure of government handling foreign policy questions, the Council naturally became the target for criticism and dissent. The obvious ambiguity in the ordinance creating the Council may have been a conscious effort to obfuscate the ultimate source of policy-making authority in the system and, by so doing, to diffuse responsibility among the elites.

Third, the Council to some extent performed a liaison function between the military and the government. Unlike the Liaison Conferences held between 1937 and 1941 in Japan, the Council meetings did not include the Chiefs of Staff. The Army authorities through the Army Minister on the Council occasionally presented official position statements (*ikensho*). The military retained control over operations (*gunrei*), the right of supreme command (*tōsuidin*), and the right to appeal directly to the Emperor (*iaku jōsō*), all of which were outside the jurisdiction of the Council. After the Siberian misadventure Hara was able, however, to assert more Cabinet control over military affairs, and there was greater coordination between military and government policy through the Council.

Finally, the Council aided in maintaining continuity of policy. As mentioned above, Takahashi and Terauchi were invited to remain on

[75] *Hara Kei Nikki,* Vol. 7, p. 188.

the Council even after their terms of office had expired. Basic membership stayed essentially unchanged during the Council's existence of five years and four months. Moreover, elements of group identification did develop over time. It seems likely that continuity of membership despite Cabinet changes as well as strong feelings of group involvement reduced the chances of any abrupt shifts in policy.

On the other hand, the introduction of another decisionmaking unit into the political system to some extent decentralized policy formation and control. Once the Council was established and in operation, the very absence of clearly defined lines of authority caused confusion among members. Also, its position at the apex of the decisionmaking structure alarmed many groups outside the Council—the Kenseikai, the newspapers, liberal Diet members, and intellectuals. Ozaki Yukio, Sasaki Sōichi, and others maintained their contempt for the organization and heightened their criticism when they became convinced that the trend of the times (*sekai no taisei*) had changed toward the type of increased popular involvement in foreign policy-making outlined in President Wilson's diplomatic package.[76] The Council was to them merely one more example of oligarchic interference in state affairs which they felt should properly be handled through the parties.[77] It should be recognized, then, that the Council did not succeed in removing foreign policy issues from partisan politics, but, rather, itself became a source of political conflict.

LEGITIMIZATION

A second major function performed by the Council was the legitimization of decisions made outside the formal government structure and of decisions or tentative decisions reached in the Cabinet.

Japanese decisionmaking at this time appears to have involved two main types of bargaining. The first could be described as formal or institutionalized bargaining between elites within the traditional government structure. This process generally involved the circulation

---

[76] Ozaki even proposed reshuffling the Cabinet itself (*naikaku kaizō*) to bring about true "party"government and to abolish secrecy in policy-making. Itō Miyoji was quite pleased, by way of contrast, that strict secrecy had been maintained in the Council and that there had been no leaks from its records. *Hakushaku Itō Miyoji*, Vol. 1, p. 105.

[77] This is basically the position taken by some contemporary analysts. See, for example: Shinobu Seizaburō, *Taishō Seiji Shi* (Tokyo, 1954 and by the same author, *Taiskō Demokurashii Shi* (Tokyo, 1954).

of draft policy statements. Such drafts normally originated in the upper (*kachō and kyokuchō*) levels of the ministries and then were advanced to the Cabinet and *Gaikō Chōsa Kai* for discussion, approval, or referral back to the ministries for revision and resubmission. In this sphere, bargaining tended to be horizontal among the ministries and communication was mainly written, that is, through definite policy drafts and statements.

A second and equally critical bargaining area lay outside the formal structure. This sphere encompassed personal meetings between individual *genrō,* members of the Cabinet, *Gaikō Chōsa Kai,* Privy Council, Army and Navy officials, and ambassadors on home leave. On a lower level, there were middle-level officials in the ministries and their contacts outside the ministry. At social events [78] or private meetings, tentative agreements or arrangements (*uchiawase*) were often made of foreign policy questions, procedural matters, and personal alignments. This type of negotiation, of course, takes place in other political systems. One hardly needs to be reminded of covert agreements like the one made by certain Soviet leaders prior to a meeting of the Presidium to oust Khrushchev from power. Rather than ascribing any unique bargaining pattern to the Japanese political system, the point here is simply that informal noninstitutionalized bargaining dominated within that system. Communication in this sphere of action was mainly verbal, through telephone conversations, direct personal meetings, or indirect contact through a personally appointed representative. This process of informal communication may have acted to reduce individual commitment or responsibility.

Covert bargaining may have minimized problems of coordination within the formal governmental structure. Cabinet and Council meetings in large measure legitimized prearranged decisions and compromises. In fact, excessive debate or confrontation at Council meetings seems to have indicated that insufficient effort had been made before hand toward accommodation and reconciliation. Council meetings were quite long, it is true, but this was due more to the practice of reading telegrams and to Itō's verbosity than to any profound disagreement over policy.

[78] A good example of this type of meeting was a dinner held on June 25, 1920 and attended by the then Crown Prince Hirohito, Uchida, Hara, Katō, Tanaka, and others at Hara's residence, after which discussion was held on the Nikolaevsk Incident and the Siberian withdrawal. *Hara Kei Nikki,* Vol. 8, p. 576.

INITIATION

A third major function of the Council related to foreign policy formulation. The Council did perform basic research tasks and generated some policy proposals of its own that were designated *"Gaikō Chōso Kai no An"* (Council Drafts) and that were often considered along with a Foreign Ministry or Army draft. Council drafts were submitted to the Cabinet for its reaction.

Normally, policy initiation or innovation was not a major Council function; rather, it passed upon proposals from the ministries. The Council was not especially creative and rarely struck out boldly in new direction on foreign relations. General discussions regarding Japan's over-all policy and role in international relations rarely took place in the Council. This type of discussion took place outside the group. Once, when Itō suggested the Council debate general China policy, Hara refused on the ground that the subject was "too abstract." [79] Nevertheless, the Council did initiate and direct the preparation of draft instructions for later discussion and formal action by the Cabinet and Council.

Thus, the *Gaikō Chōsa Kai* represented an institutional response to severe internal and external stress on the Japanese political system. It failed to become permanently institutionalized partially because certain leaders came to believe that its functions could be performed adequately by the Cabinet. Although membership in the Council was extended to party representatives in a possible response to increased party power, the dominant members of the Council were those like Itō and Hirata whose strength was traditional and derived from their close ties with the bureaucracy and the oligarchy. When they withdrew their endorsement, the Council collapsed. Still, at a time when solid support for basic national policy was considered absolutely essential, the Council provided this foundation through the extensive personal connections and influence of its members. While it was unsuccessful in stifling dissent, the *Gaikō Chōsa Kai* did help to create a viable consensus on foreign policy during the difficult years 1917–1922.

[79] *Hara Kei Nikki,* Vol. 9, p. 322.

The Cuban Missile Crisis:
Strategic Theory in Practice

STEPHEN ADLER

This is an examination at the relationship between strategic theory and strategic practice in a particular case—the Cuban Missile Crisis. The focus is on deterrence relationships and why in this case they nearly broke down, and on the general motives of governments in such a situation. An attempt is made to draw conclusions concerning both the nature of the deterrence relationship and in particular certain of the dangers and pitfalls inherent in such a relationship.

Aspects of the crisis which have been touched on only in so far as they seemed relevant to the major theme include the decisionmaking processes of governments,[1] and their capacities for crisis management; or the problems which governments have in their perceptions of each other's intentions;[2] or the role of personality in decisionmaking.[3] The reader who wishes to pursue these other aspects further is referred to the relevant citations in the footnotes, and to the bibliography.

The *Theory of Nuclear Deterrence*

Deterrence in miltary theory differs from defense in one major respect. If the object is to resist so that the enemy cannot succeed even

[1] See, for example, Roger Hilsman, *To Move a Nation—the Politics of Foreign Policy in the Administration of John F. Kennedy,* Delta, New York, 1967.

[2] See, for example, Roberta Wohlstetter, "Cuba and Pearl Harbor," *Foreign Affairs,* July 1965.

[3] See, for example, Thomas M. Mongar, "Personality and Decision Making," *Canadian Journal of Political Science,* 1969.

if he tries—this is defense. If the object is to persuade him not to try by making the attempt so painful that even if he succeeds it is hardly worth it, then it becomes deterrence.[4] As such, it is not a new theory in military affairs. For example, in the fifteenth century the Swiss relied on their reputation for obstinate courage not so much in order to prevent invasion, but in order to make invasion extremely costly to a potential enemy.[5]

Nuclear deterrence, then, is the attempt to persuade a potential enemy by the threat of nuclear weapons to abandon a particular course of miltary or political action.[6]

In the early 1950s the deterrence posture of the United States was one of "massive retaliation"—a doctrine which had its origins in the days of the American atomic monopoly and which relied on the threat of an overwhelming nuclear response by the United States to any Soviet (or Chinese) miltary incursion.[7] The development in the later 1950s of a Soviet nuclear capability led to a nuclear stalemate, the essence of which was to keep the United States and the Soviet Union from launching a nuclear war, because each could force the other to pay an exorbitant price for victory.[8]

Under these conditions deterrence theory took on a new subtlety. When both sides were armed with a large number of nuclear weapons and sophisticated delivery systems, the concept of deterrence became mutual, since it is self-defeating to initiate a nuclear attack if the attacked power is able to strike back. Adequate deterrence therefore depended on one's ability to ride out a first strike by the enemy and have sufficient weapons remaining to launch a second strike against him that would cause him "unacceptable damage." Unacceptable damage is a proposition that can only be stated tautologically: there must be a good chance that enough of the attacker's society will be destroyed in retailiation to make him think that a first strike presents too great a risk of self-destruction.[9]

The knowledge that a first strike will lead to either side's own destruction undermines the idea of massive retaliation. Nuclear weap-

[4] Thomas C. Schelling, *Arms and Influence,* Yale University Press, New Haven, 1967, p. 78.

[5] Schelling, *Ibid.,* p. 78 n.

[6] Philip Green, *Deadly Logic—The Theory of Nuclear Deterrence,* Ohio State University Press, 1966, p. 3.

[7] Henry A. Kissinger, *Nuclear Weapons and Foreign Policy,* Norton, New York, 1969, ch. 2.

[8] *Ibid.,* p. 110.   [9] Green, *Deadly Logic,* p. 9.

ons become reserved for use in a retaliatory strike against a move by the other side which would lead to one's own destruction anyway. For lesser provocations and smaller miltary or political incursions or adventures, it would ensure catastrophe for oneself.

It was partly in response to this problem that the so-called McNamara Doctrine was espoused by the Kennedy Administration. Many analysts had pointed out the dangers, faults, and inadequacies of the massive retaliation approach.[10] Secretary of Defense McNamara replaced massive retaliation by the theory of "graduated response." Graduated response meant simply that the United States would seek a conventionl war capacity as well as a very large and flexible arsenal of nuclear weapons and delivery systems in order to be able to respond to any provocation on the particular level required, and hence deter it. This would prevent escalation to the extreme limit of violence implied by a massive retaliation and lessen the danger of war-by-misunderstanding because it would give policymakers more options, and raise the nuclear threshold.[11]

The mutuality of deterrence leads, in theoretical terms, to the hypothesis that strategic conflict is a "game" in the sense that in a game of strategy—as opposed to a game of chance—the best course of action depends on what the other player may or may not do.[12] International conflict resembles a variable-sum game rather than a zero-sum game because of the mutual interest of the players in avoiding an all-out nuclear war.[13] Thus, conflict is not irrevocable and absolute (zero-sum), but has large elements of co-operation as well (variable sum).[14] Variable-sum games are bargaining games, and the

[10] See, for example, Kissinger, *Nuclear Weapons and Foreign Policy,* ch. 5; and Thomas C. Schelling, *The Strategy of Conflict,* Oxford University Press, New York, 1969.

[11] Raymond Aron, *The Great Debate,* Doubleday Anchor, New York, 1965, pp. 67–68.

[12] Schelling, *The Strategy of Conflict,* p. 3.   [13] *Ibid.,* chs. 1, 2, 3.

[14] A zero-sum game is one in which the sum of all payoffs to all players equals zero; thus, anything that one player gains, another player must lose. In a zero-sum game between two players, whatever is good for one must be bad for the other. The pattern of the game is thus one of unmixed and unrelieved conflict. In contrast, a variable-sum game is one in which the payoffs do not necessarily add up to zero, but may be any positive (or negative) number. In such a game there is an element of cooperation, since both players may jointly gain or lose according to their ability to coordinate their moves. For a further discussion of the properties of zero-sum and variable-sum games see Karl W. Deutsch, *The Analysis of International Relations,* Prentice-Hall, Englewood Cliffs, New Jersey, 1968, ch. 11.

bargaining may be tacit or overt. The players may resort to threats or deception or precommitment (that is, committing themselves prior to their "move" to a particular course of action, thus altering the opponent's perceptions of the payoffs of his own move) in order to improve their relative positions. The threat of all-out war may be used on occasion, but the essence of successful threatening is not to have to carry out the threat. As Thomas Schelling wrote, "A theory of deterrence would be, in effect, a theory of the skillful *nonuse* of military forces." [15]

The theory of deterrence as it has been outlined is not, of course, without its difficulties. Ethically it raises all sorts of questions. For example, is it "right" to threaten, and if necessary carry out, a countercity strike against the Soviet Union or China? [16] Furthermore, one could question the stability of the deterrence model on its own terms. Is the arms race implied in a deterrence relationship destabilizing or not? The conventional wisdom among deterrence theorists is that the more missiles each side has the greater the stability. [17] This is because the larger the number of missiles on each side the less chance there is of one side carrying out a successful counterforce first strike, thus leaving more missiles for retaliation. Both sides, knowing this, refrain from first strikes. Also, the greater the number of missiles the greater must be the absolute and proportional increase in missiles that either side would have to achieve in order to ensure the destruction of the other side's countercity retaliatory capability. [18]

On the other hand, critics of deterrence theory have pointed out the strains imposed by an arms race. If, for whatever reason, one of the two competitors appears to be gaining a significant lead in the race, the other side may be tempted to strike first before it becomes

[15] Schelling, *The Strategy of Conflict*, p. 9.

[16] A countercity strike is a punitive strike against the opponent's cities. A counterforce strike is a strike against his military power—missile sites, army, air-force, industry, etc. A counterforce strike would tend to be a first strike attempting to pre-empt the enemy's striking back by blunting or removing his offensive capabilities. One of the novelties of the McNamara Doctrine was that a nuclear exchange could limit casualties by striking in the first instance at a counterforce level in the hope that the exchange could be halted before reaching the countercity level. In contrast there is an implicit suggestion in the massive retaliation doctrine of a countercity strike in the first instance. See Aron, *The Great Debate*, pp. 66–75.

[17] On this point see, for example, Schelling, *The Strategy of Conflict*, pp. 234–37.

[18] *Ibid.*, pp. 234–37.

unable to do so.[19] It will be one of the themes here that a primary motivation for the Soviet Union to place missiles in Cuba in the first place was the severe economic and political strain involved in trying to compete with the United States in the arms race.

The View from the Soviet Union: Why Put the Missiles In?

There are approximately three main explanations that have become current as to why the Soviet Union put missiles in Cuba in October 1962.

THE RUSSIAN EXPLANATION

The official Soviet explanation of why the Russians put missiles in Cuba in that the missiles were there for no reason other than to protect Cuba and the Castro revolution from being overthrown by the United States. Chairman Khrushchev told the Supreme Soviet in December 1962 that "we carried weapons there at the request of the Cuban government . . . . including the stationing of a score of Soviet IRBMs (intermediate range ballistic missiles) in Cuba. These weapons were to be in the hands of Soviet military men. . . . Our aim was only to defend Cuba." [20] In Khrushchev's recently published memoirs he tells substantially the same story.[21] He writes, "We wanted to keep the Americans from invading Cuba, and we wanted to make them think twice by confronting them with our missiles" [22] There is little doubt that this is at least in part what the Russians

---

[19] See Kenneth E. Boulding, *Conflict and Defense—A General Theory*, Harper Torchbooks, New York, 1963, ch. 2; and Green, *Deadly Logic*, ch. 3.

[20] Quoted in Arthur M. Schlesinger, *A Thousand Days—John F. Kennedy in the White House*, Fawcett, New York, 1967, p. 728.

[21] Nikita S. Khrushchev, "Khrushchev Remembers," in *Life*, Dec. 18, 1970.

[22] *Ibid.*, p. 48B. There is an interesting conflict between Khrushchev's statement to the Supreme Soviet in December 1962 in which he said that the missiles were placed in Cuba at the request of the Cuban government, and the account in *Khrushchev Remembers* in which he writes that the missiles were his own idea. "It was during my visit to Bulgaria (in May 1962) that I had the idea of installing missiles with nuclear warheads in Cuba without letting the United States find out until it was too late to do anything about them." *Life*, Dec. 18, 1970, p. 48. This conflict may be accounted for perhaps by the possibility that *Khrushchev Remembers* was not really written by Nikita S. Khrushchev—or at least not in the form in which it has appeared in the West. Nevertheless, most of the official Soviet explanation remains the same

hoped to achieve, and they certainly had justifiable worries on that score. After the Bay of Pigs invasion in April 1961 the Soviet government clearly felt that another attempt to overthrow Castro could not be far behind. There was a great deal of pressure on President Kennedy to mount another invasion of Cuba, this time using United States ground forces. A statement by Senator Everett McKinley Dirksen in September 1962 reminded Congress of the President's obligations: "As President Kennedy has already stated in his speech to the United States editors (April 20, 1961), 'If the nations of this hemisphere should fail to meet their commitments against outside Communist penetration,' then the United States must act on its own." [23] On September 7, 1962, before any missiles had been placed in Cuba, but after the decision to put them there had already been taken, President Kennedy requested Congress for authority to call up 150,000 reservists—an act that must have seemed ex post facto justification by the Soviet government for its missile decision.

However, there are several reasons for thinking that the Soviet government had more in mind than simply protecting Cuba.

First of all, if merely deterring the United States was the sole objective, then this objective was blatantly out of proportion to the means and the risks involved. The logistics of the operation were immense.

The Soviet plan was in two phases. [24] The first phase was the ringing of Cuba by defenses—SAM anti-aircraft missiles, MIG fighters, harbor defense missiles, and coastal patrol boats. The second phase was the introduction of ballistic missiles and Ilyushin 28 bombers, both capable of delivering nuclear weapons to the United States. These would be accompanied by four battle groups armed with tactical nuclear weapons.

There were to be four ballistic missile complexes, MRBMs (medium range ballistic missiles, with a range of about a thousand miles) and IRBMs (with a range of about two thousand miles).

By the time the missiles were removed there were forty-eight

---

as that in *Khrushchev Remembers,* that is, the missiles were placed in Cuba only to protect the island from invasion.

[23] Statement by Senator Everett McKinley Dirksen, Sep. 7, 1962. Quoted in David L. Larson, ed., *The "Cuban Crisis" of 1962—Selected Documents and Chronology,* Houghton Mifflin, Boston, 1963, p. 4.

[24] Hilsman, *To Move a Nation,* p. 159. The next two paragraphs rely heavily on the account in Hilsman's ch. 13.

MRBMs with twenty-four launchers, and sixteen working IRBM erectors.[25] Thus, when the sites were complete they would have been able to launch an initial salvo of about forty missiles (twenty-four MRBMs plus sixteen IRBMs),[26] each propelling a warhead of about three to four megatons. The MRBM launchers could be reloaded in a matter of hours to deliver another salvo of twenty-four missiles. Thus, there were potentially sixty-four missiles which could be fired at the United States; and it must be remembered that the Soviet plan was discovered before it was completed, so that in fact many more than sixty-four might have been the final number the Soviet government had in mind.

The Russians could not have been unaware of the risks of the adventure. President Kennedy had warned several times about the placement of "offensive" weapons in Cuba,[27] and the Soviet government must have realized the danger of provoking the United States into a first strike both against Cuba and possibly also the Soviet Union if the plan was discovered. Indeed, the danger of such a preemptive strike by the United States would have been even greater if the missiles had not been discovered until after they were operational, since the danger would have been immediate, and the United States government would have had far less time to deliberate.

Second, if the aim of the adventure was really to deter an attack on Cuba and nothing else, then this aim would have been better served, and would have been far less provocative, by making use of tactical short-range missiles. Such missiles could have had a range of a few hundred miles to destroy United States cities, airfields, and marshaling and embarkation points in the Florida area.[28] Such deterrence would have been deterrence *à la Suisse*.[29] It probably would not have prevented a determined attempt by the United States to invade Cuba, but it may have raised the cost of so doing to a prohibitive level.

[25] Briefing Feb. 6, 1963 by Mr. John Hughes, Special Assistant to General Carroll. Reprinted in Albert and Roberta Wohlstetter, "Controlling the Risks in Cuba," *Adelphi Papers 17*, London, Institute for Strategic Studies, 1965, p. 11.

[26] See also Elie Abel, *The Missile Crisis*, Bantam, New York, 1968, p. 47; and Hilsman, *To Move a Nation*, p. 200.

[27] See for example the statement made by President Kennedy on Cuba, Sep. 4, 1962. In Larson, *The "Cuban Crisis" of 1962*, p. 3.

[28] Arnold Horelick, "The Cuban Missile Crisis," *World Politics 16*, 1964.

[29] *Ibid.*, p. 2.

Lastly, why should the Soviet Union place ballistic missiles in Cuba when, as it had long claimed, it could launch a sufficiency of missiles from its own territory? *Tass* stated that

> there is no need for the Soviet Union to shift its weapons for the repulsion of aggression, for a retaliatory blow, to any other country, for instance Cuba. Our nuclear weapons are so powerful in their explosive force and the Soviet Union has such powerful rockets to carry these nuclear warheads, that there is no need to search for sites for them beyond the boundaries of the Soviet Union. . . . The Soviet Union has the possibility from its own territory to render assistance to any peace-loving states. . . ." [30]

This statement was made when Soviet missiles were already on board ships en route for Cuba. If the Soviet deterrent was indeed credible, then there should have been no need for placing missiles on Cuba itself. Just as the United States could achieve credibility with its threat of nuclear reprisals for any Soviet military incursion into western Europe, there is every reason to assume that the Soviet Union could achieve similar credibility in a defense of Cuba. If, however, the Soviet deterrent was not as powerful as had been claimed, and the United States government knew this; and further, in the tortured logic of deterrence games, the Soviet government knew that the United States government knew—then perhaps credibility could not be achieved with a threat of nuclear reprisals against the United States for interference in Cuba. This point will be elaborated on below.

THE POLITICAL EXPLANATION

The second main current of thought about Soviet motivations is that the missiles were placed in Cuba not so much because of the necessity to protect Cuba (although this may have been part of their purpose) but in order to stage a dramatic political "coup" against the United States, and reassert Soviet leadership in the Communist world. [31] This explanation denies that the missiles themselves had any really very great strategic significance in terms of the outcome of any nuclear exchange between the Soviet Union and the United States, or

[30] "Statement by the Soviet Union that a U. S. attack on Cuba would mean nuclear war," Sep. 11, 1962. In Larson, *The "Cuban Crisis" of 1962,* pp. 11–12.

[31] See especially Adam B. Ulam, *Expansion and Coexistence—the History of Soviet Foreign Policy 1917–1967,* Praeger, New York, 1969, pp. 660–77.

vis à vis the deterrence posture of either side. Any strategic implications were more psychological than actual—although of course psychology is an extremely important factor in deterrence. As President
Kennedy said, "It would have politically changed the balance of
power. It would have appeared to, and appearances contribute to
reality." [32]

The Soviet Union was caught in a cruel dilemma in its conduct of
foreign policy in the early 1960s. The main priorities in the minds of
the Kremlin leaders were to reassert their leadership in the Communist world—a leadership increasingly challenged by China and tiny
Albania—and to prevent China from acquiring nuclear weapons. [33]
Also they wished to prevent West Germany from obtaining such
weapons, and to reach a final settlement of the German question by
the signing of a German peace treaty. [34] This was a vicious circle. In
order to obtain some concessions from the West, the Soviet Union
had to preserve the appearance of bloc unity, and to do this required
the agreement of China. However, to obtain this agreement the Soviet Union also needed to put on a show of militancy. But this very
militancy jeopardized the peaceful solution of the very problems it
started with. [35]

Chairman Khrushchev, it was felt, had lost considerable "face"
with his repeated ultimatums over Berlin and the question of a German peace treaty, and his subsequent withdrawals. [36] True, the Wall
had gone up in Berlin, but this had by no means accomplished the
real Soviet goals.

Thus, the explanation of why the Soviet government put the missiles in Cuba is that it hoped at one fell swoop to resolve these di-
lemmas. Once in Cuba and ready to fire, the missiles would have become negotiable. There could be a German peace treaty containing
prohibition on nuclear weapons for West Germany, and possibly part
of the price the United States would have to pay for the removal of
the missiles would have been termination of its protection of Formosa. This would have then provided the Communist Chinese with a

[32] In an interview with the *Washington Post,* Dec. 18, 1962. Quoted in
Wohlstetter, "Cuba and Pearl Harbor," p. 13.

[33] Ghita Ionescu, *The Break-Up of the Soviet Empire in Eastern Europe,*
Penguin, Baltimore, 1965.

[34] Ulam, *Expansion and Coexistence,* p. 661.   [35] *Ibid.,* p. 661.

[36] Wilfrid Knapp, *A History of War and Peace 1939–1965,* Royal Institute
of International Affairs, Oxford University Press, London, 1967, pp. 483–88.

great incentive to cancel or at least postpone their own nuclear plans. Chairman Khrushchev would appear to the world to be a great peacemaker and the sagging status of the Soviet Union in the Communist bloc, as well as amongst the neutralists, would have been immeasurably enhanced.[37]

There is little doubt that if the Soviet plan had worked, that is, if the missiles had not been discovered before they were ready, then the Russians would have pressed for at least part, if not all, of the above. As Adam Ulam put it, "Granted the stakes involved, the risks were not too unreasonable." [38] But, we may raise the question, "weren't they?" In actual fact the risks were enormous.

First of all, there was the risk of discovery before the missiles became operational—which is what occurred. The United States had been making U-2 flights over Russia since 1956,[39] and it was not until the summer of 1961 (U-2 flights over Russia had been officially discontinued after Gary Powers had been shot down in May 1960) that conclusive evidence reached the Department of Defense concerning the actual Soviet ICBM strength.[40] The Soviet government may have concluded from this several year lag in intelligence that the U-2 was not such an efficient machine, and that they could hope to evade its cameras for the few weeks necessary to install the missiles in Cuba. It is clear, of course, that the Russians did hope to avoid detection, and went to some pains to convince the United States government that it had nothing to worry about concerning ballistic missiles in Cuba. For example, two days after the missiles were first spotted in Cuba, but before the Russians learned that the Americans knew—on October 16, 1962—Chairman Khrushchev told the American ambassador in Moscow, Foy Kohler, that the last thing that he (Khrushchev) wanted was to embarrass the President on the eve of the Congressional mid-terms, and that he need not worry about anything so untoward as Soviet ballistic missiles in Cuba.[41] However, the risk remained, even if the Russians thought they had dealt with it. As events proved, they clearly had not.

Second, there was the possibly greater risk of United States reaction to discovering the missiles after they had been made ready. Again it is clear that the Soviet leaders underestimated the pressure

[37] Ulam, *Expansion and Coexistence,* pp. 668–69.
[38] *Ibid.,* p. 669.   [39] *Ibid.,* p. 633.
[40] Hilsman, *To Move a Nation,* p. 163.   [41] Abel, *The Missile Crisis,* p. 37.

that would be put on the President to authorize a strike against either Cuba, or Russia, or both. The discussions which took place in EXCOM (the Executive Committee of the National Security Council —the ad hoc thirteen-man committee which was the main decision-making body during the missile crisis) after the discovery of the missiles reveal how much support there was for an American surprise attack on the missile sites. One of the key factors which had led to the decision to impose a "quarantine" rather than a military attack was the fact that the missiles were not yet operational. "Everyone in the room recognized that once they were operational the danger would take on a new dimension." [42] Among the powerful voices that spoke in favor of a strike were Dean Rusk, Secretary of State; General Maxwell W. Taylor, of the Joint Chiefs of Staff; John McCone of the C.I.A.; Dean Acheson, who joined EXCOM at the invitation of the President; Paul Nitze, one of McNamara's assistant secretaries; and Douglas Dillon, Secretary of the Treasury. [43]

Once more, one can ask if the Soviet leaders would have been prepared to take the great risk of provoking a pre-emptive United States strike against missiles that in themselves were of little strategic value, and perhaps even a strike against the Soviet Union itself. Would it have been worth placing the missiles in the center of the United States' historically private back garden—Latin America—on the raw nerve of Cuba, if the missiles themselves did little to alter the actual military balance?

And connected to these questions, another question arises. Would the missiles have served their ostensible political purposes if they had little real military value? The object of a deterrence threat is to achieve credibility. Even if missiles are never to be used, indeed *especially* if the missiles are never to be used, a threat must be credible. The other side must believe that missiles will be used if your demands are not met, and that the consequences of this will be worse than compliance. [44] If the missiles placed on Cuba really did little to

[42] *Ibid.*, p. 52.

[43] *Ibid.*, pp. 39–56. Although Abel mentions "the futility of trying to sort out the hawks from the doves" (p. 56) in EXCOM, because so many people changed their minds as to the best course of action, it is nevertheless clear that some members of EXCOM stuck more rigidly to their original hawkish stands than others. The people mentioned in the text took their "hawkish" positions early, and with the exception of Dean Rusk, tended to stick to them longest.

[44] Schelling, *The Strategy of Conflict*, chs. 2, 7, 8.

alter the military positions of the two sides, as a threat they were not credible. And if the strategic threat is not credible, political consequences are unlikely to be forthcoming. By allowing strategically worthless missiles to remain in Cuba, the Russians might have calculated that the Americans might lose some face in Latin America and elsewhere. But if there was no very real military threat, this would have been the worst consequence the United States could expect. The United States would have no reason to give in to Soviet demands in Berlin and concerning Formosa merely as the result of some marginal IRBMs and MRBMs in Cuba. The only way, therefore, for the threat to have worked, would have been for those missiles to have in some way greatly altered the strategic balance in favor of the Soviet Union.

THE STRATEGIC EXPLANATION

In order to begin understanding why the Soviet government was prepared to take the enormous risks involved in the Cuban venture, it is important to realize precisely to what extent the missiles placed in Cuba (and perhaps their intended successors) really did alter the strategic military balance.

The Appendix to this article is a table which compares Soviet and United States nuclear weapons delivery systems for October 1962. It can be seen from this table that the United States possessed at the time of the missile crisis two hundred and seventy-six ICBMs, one hundred and forty-four Polaris-type missiles (SLMs), six hundred and thirty long-range bombers, and nine hundred and forty medium-range bombers. All of these, except those medium-range bombers not stationed in Europe, were capable of delivering nuclear weapons into the Soviet Union. By contrast, the Soviet Union could strike at the United States with only seventy-five ICBMs and one hundred and ninety long range bombers. It had no SLMs, and its massive preponderance in MRBMs could be used only against targets in Europe. Similarly, the large number of medium bombers were effectve only in Europe. Because of United States strategic bases in and around Europe, almost all of its forces could have been, in case of need, directed at the Soviet Union. In terms of megatonage as well, the United States was at this stage also vastly superior. One authoritative source [45] has stated that the United States was in a position to dump

[45] American Security Council, *The Changing Strategic Military Balance USA vs USSR*—a study prepared for the House Armed Services Committee

between twenty-five thousand and thirty thousand megatons on the Soviet Union, while the Soviet reverse capability was between only five thousand and ten thousand megatons—most of which was targeted at Europe.

Without access to the relevant technical data concerning accuracy, hardening of sites, speed with which missiles can be launched, warning time, and the probability of intercepting incoming bombers with fighters and surface-to-air missiles, it is very difficult to say with any degree of certainty precisely what the outcome of any nuclear exchange would be. However, it is clear that in terms of strategic weaponry the United States was vastly superior to the Soviet Union. Whether this superiority was sufficient to give the United States the potential for a credible first strike against the Soviet Union is a moot point—and without the technical data referred to above, it would be impossible to guess realistically. The point is that if the United States should have wanted to launch such a pre-emptive strike (and given that it would have meant the almost certain obliteration of Europe) it might have succeeded in destroying a sufficiently large part of the Soviet ICBM force to seriously blunt a retaliatory strike. This task would have been made easier by the fact that it was widely believed that the Soviet ICBM sites were "soft" and that the liquid fueling system of the rockets would take sufficiently long to allow a very large number of Soviet missiles to be destroyed on the ground.[46] If enough of the Soviet long-range bombers could be destroyed either before take-off or while in the air on the long flight from the Soviet Union, then there was a possibility that the Soviet retaliatory blow would not inflict unacceptable damage on the United States.

An additional factor of great importance to this scenario is the fact, referred to above, that United States U-2 flights over the Soviet Union and other intelligence had by the summer of 1961 yielded conclusive evidence of Soviet ICBM strength, and the deployment of missiles.[47] Definitive knowledge by the United States of the positioning of these ICBMs made them even more vulnerable and "soft."

---

by the National Strategy Committee of the American Security Council, Washington D. C., 1967.

[46] *Ibid.,* p. 52; also Hilsman, *To Move a Nation,* p. 162; and the Stockholm International Peace Research Institute, *SIPRI Yearbook of World Armaments and Disarmament 1969/70,* Humanities Press, New York, 1970, p. 362.

[47] Hilsman, *To Move a Nation,* pp. 162–64; and Abel, *The Missile Crisis,* p. 27.

This stage in the argument, therefore, suggests not that the United States had any real intentions of launching a first strike, but that nevertheless it had the potential for so doing with at least some chance of success. Therefore, the Soviet Union during the period in question did not have a completely invulnerable second strike capability which would be certain to inflict unacceptable damage on the United States.

It will be recalled that the critical requirement for stability in nuclear deterrence is that both sides possess such retaliatory capability.

However, the mere discovery by the United States that the Soviet Union was considerably weaker in its missile strength and in the vulnerability of targets was not in itself destabilizing, if we make the assumption that it was not part of United States military doctrine to launch a pre-emptive first strike. So long as the Kennedy administration kept its knowledge of Soviet strategic weakness secret, deterrence might have been maintained. The raging debate in the United States in 1959 and 1960 about the "missile gap" must have proved to the Soviet government that even though it was strategically inferior, the opposite was thought to be the case by large sections of informed opinion in the United States. So long as the extent of Soviet weakness was not known to the American administration, deterrence was secure.

But in fact the logic of the situation requires an extra element. Deterrence was secure so long as the Soviet government thought that the United States government was ignorant of the true state of affairs, both sides feeling assured not only of their own second strike capability but of the opponent's also. However, as soon as the United States made it clear to the Soviet Union that it was aware of the real nature of Soviet strategic weakness, then the situation would become unstable. So long as the Soviet Union thought that its weakness was concealed, it would think itself safe from a United States first strike, because the United States would fear retaliation. As soon as the Soviet government became aware that the United States government knew the truth, then it could reasonably fear becoming the victim of a first strike. For then the United States might have been able to strike with relative impunity.

The destabilizing factor, therefore, was the public announcement in November 1961 by Deputy Secretary of Defense Roswell Gilpatric that the United States government was finally aware of the truth. The Gilpatric speech was followed by briefings to United States allies —deliberately including some that were known to have been penetrated by Soviet intelligence—so as to make certain that the message reached the Russian government.[48]

There were, however, several other factors which contributed to the instability of the situation.

Soviet military doctrine concerning the use of nuclear weapons was in a strange kind of flux. As has been mentioned, United States nuclear doctrine was moving from massive retaliation to graduated response—which in itself had budgetary consequences alarming to the Soviet Union. (This argument is elaborated below.) Meanwhile, Soviet doctrine had shifted from the Stalinist idea that nuclear weapons would be indecisive and that mass land armies would decide the outcome of future wars to the theory that nuclear weapons could prove decisive.[49] The earlier anti-nuclear doctrine, of course, had not prevented the Soviet Union from making strenuous efforts to develop first atomic, then hydrogen bombs. At the same time the space program had provided large rockets with thrusts of about 800,000 pounds that could escape the earth's atmosphere to launch Sputniks as well as carry the twenty-five to fifty-megaton warheads the Soviets had succeeded in developing.

In the late 1950s Soviet military thinkers began to develop the doctrine of the pre-emptive strike. Realizing the potency of nuclear weapons, they argued that by striking first, just before the enemy was about to strike you, and "knocking the weapon from his hands," [50] the war would be won. But, just as in Stalin's time, doctrine was at variance with policy; and in the latter period the weaponry actually developed by the Soviet Union was far more suited to retaliation than to pre-emption. The reasons for this were at least in part bud-

---

[48] *Ibid*. Hilsman explains the decision to tell the Soviet Union what had been discovered in the following way: "The American decision to let the Soviets know what we knew was deliberate. But it was made only after much agonizing, since everyone involved recognized that telling the Soviets what we knew entailed considerable risk. Forewarned, the Soviets would undoubtedly speed up their ICBM program. They would do so anyway, of course, but this action to let them know what we knew meant the speed-up would be sooner rather than later. On the other hand, Khrushchev's several ultimatums on Berlin indicated that, if he were allowed to continue to assume that we still believed in the missile gap, he would probably bring the world dangerously close to war. Thus the decision was reached to go ahead with telling the Soviets that we now knew." (p. 163)

[49] John Strachey, *On the Prevention of War,* St. Martin's Press, New York, 1963, pp. 36–37.

[50] *Ibid.,* quotation from the Soviet publication *Military Thought.*

getary. A pre-emptive strike, to be successful, must destroy the majority of the opponent's retaliatory force, and bring him below the level of what would be unacceptable damage to the pre-emptor. This requires a much larger number of rockets than the opponent, since to ensure destruction of his missiles one's own missiles must be extremely accurate. The number of weapons required to destroy a missile and its warhead sheltered to a sufficient degree will, within relevant limits, vary as the square of the average aiming accuracy. That is, double the inaccuracy and four times the number of attacking vehicles are required; treble the inaccuracy and nearly ten times the number of attackers are needed.[51] The Soviet Union instead developed a small number of ICBMs with very large warheads, which, assuming they could survive a first strike against themselves, would be adequate vehicles for a retaliatory countercity blow. As long as the United States remained in ignorance of the sites and numbers of these missiles, all would be well. But by the time of Gilpatric's speech, it was clear that the United States had so great a preponderance of delivery vehicles, and such detailed knowledge of the Soviet installations, that instead a United States first strike appeared to be a credible threat.

In effect, the Soviet government had been trying to bluff its way to nuclear security by exaggerating the number of its missiles and the strength of its strategic deterrent. The doctrine of the pre-emptive strike was one of the ways this was done. Officially of course, the Soviet government espoused the doctrine of retaliation—but the use of such unofficial military sources as the magazine *Military Thought* was a convenient way of adding to the impression of Soviet military might.[52]

Not only Soviet foreign policy but also Soviet domestic policy was in a dilemma in the early 1960s. By 1959–1960 Chairman Khrushchev found it expedient to push for an increase in the availability of consumer goods in the Soviet Union.[53] This would mean that heavy industry and military expenditures would have to have a reduced share in the economy. Throughout the Khrushchev period of government, the dilemma of allocating between heavy and light industry had been part of the political struggle, a factor in Khru-

---

[51] Albert and Roberta Wohlstetter, "Controlling the Risks in Cuba," p. 11.

[52] Strachey, *On the Prevention of War,* pp. 39–41.

[53] Zbigniew Brzezinski and Samuel P. Huntington, *Political Power USA / USSR,* Viking Press, New York, 1964, pp. 272–83.

shchev's own rise to power, and a genuine dilemma for the Soviet leaders. They were caught on the one hand between the dictates of doctrine—the demands of heavy industry and the military, and the desire to "catch up" with the West—and on the other by pressures from the population and certain factions in the bureaucracies to ease restrictions and increase the standard of living.[54]

Early in 1959, in outlining the Seven-Year Plan for 1959–1965 Khrushchev said that one of the main Soviet tasks was "to attain the world's highest standard of living. In this stage of the competition, the Soviet Union intends to surpass the United States economically."[55] It is clear that attaining this objective was greatly hampered by the requirements of military defense. The change in emphasis from the needs of conventional armaments to reliance on nuclear weapons was an attempt to keep down the costs of defense. Also the dual utility of rockets, which were being developed for the space program and could also serve as delivery vehicles for nuclear weapons, promised an alluring "two for the price of one." However, it is also true that the decision not to develop smaller, less cumbersome missiles, but to use the existing rocketry, made these missiles far more vulnerable when their real strength and numbers were discovered.[56] Thus, economic imperatives were a large factor in the decision to rely far more on the hopefully less costly nuclear deterrent. This was shown very clearly in January 1960 when Khrushchev announced to the Supreme Soviet that the combined strength of the Russian armed forces would be reduced by 1,200,000 to a total of 2,425,000 men. Later in the same speech, the Chairman also said,

Even if we accept for a minute that it (some State) would succeed in delivering a surprise blow—would the attacking side be able to put out of action at once all the stocks of nuclear weapons, all the rocket installations on the territory of the power attacked? Of course not! A State subjected to a surprise attack—provided of course it is a big State—will always be able to give the aggressor a worthy rebuff.

We are aware that our country is ringed with foreign military bases. That is why we locate our rockets in such a way as to ensure a double and even treble margin of safety. We have a vast territory and we are

[54] *Ibid.* See also Alec Nove, *The Soviet Economy,* Praeger, New York, 1966; Mark Frankland, *Khrushchev,* Penguin, Harmondsworth, 1966; and the other basic texts on Soviet government such as Merle Fainsod, *How Russia is Ruled,* Harvard University Press, Cambridge, 1965 and Lloyd G. Churchward, *Contemporary Soviet Government,* Routeledge & K. Paul, London, 1968.

[55] Brzezinski and Huntington, *Political Power USA / USSR,* p. 273.

[56] Hilsman, *To Move a Nation,* p. 162.

able to disperse our rockets and camouflage them well. We are developing such a system that if some means of retaliation were knocked out, we could always fall back on others and strike the enemy from reserve installations.[57]

Just how large the burden of defense was on the Soviet economy is a matter of some controversy. In the United States in 1959 and 1960 the Gross National Product was running at 482 billion dollars and 503 billion dollars respectively. National Defense Spending in those years was 46 billion dollars and 45 billion dollars. As a proportion of the GNP this was 9.5 per cent and 9.0 per cent respectively.[58] However, making direct comparisons with the Soviet Union is very difficult, since accounting techniques for the GNP are different, and since converting the rouble into dollars at the official exchange rate undervalues the real purchasing power of the rouble. Another problem is that there is no obvious price index to use in order to arrive at the "real" comparable costs of the same type of equipment in both countries. Finally, it is generally believed that the announced Soviet Defense Budget understates the true size of the allocation since it excludes items which are included in the United States Budget, such as certain Research and Development costs.[59] However, the Stockholm International Peace Research Institute (SIPRI) makes an estimate of the Soviet Defense Budget allowing as much as possible for the above variables in the years 1959, 1960, 1961, and 1962 as being, respectively, 22 billion dollars, 22 billion dollars, 27 billion dollars, and 30 billion dollars.[60] The authoritative Institute for Strategic Studies, placing its estimate of the 1962 Soviet Defense Budget slightly higher than the SIPRI—at 33 billion dollars—concludes that this accounted for nearly 19 per cent of the Soviet GNP.[61] For the United States in 1962, Defense spending was 52 billion dollars [62]— about 11 per cent of the GNP.[63]

[57] Quoted in Strachey, *On the Prevention of War*, p. 45.

[58] Samuel P. Huntington, *The Common Defense*, Columbia University Press, New York, 1961, p. 282.

[59] For a detailed discussion of these problems see SIPRI *Yearbook 1969/70*, pp. 259–65; and United States Arms Control and Disarmament Agency, *World-Wide Defense Expenditures and Selected Economic Data, 1964*, Washington, D.C., 1966.

[60] SIPRI *Yearbook 1969/70*, pp. 268–69.

[61] Institute for Strategic Studies, *The Military Balance 1962–63*, London, p. 25.

[62] SIPRI *Yearbook 1969/70*, pp. 268–69.

[63] ISS, *The Military Balance 1962–63*, p. 25.

Even allowing for the tenuous nature of these estimates, it is clear that in the late 1950s and early 1960s the Soviet Union was spending in absolute terms between one half and two-thirds of what the United States was spending on defense—and that this smaller sum involved a far greater proportion of real national resources. In the year of the missile crisis the Soviet effort was proportionally almost twice as much as the United States—19 per cent of the GNP as against 11 per cent—an enormous economic burden and a serious obstacle to expanding the consumer goods program.

In addition, the international situation appeared to the Soviet government to be deteriorating seriously by 1960,[64] and there is little doubt that strong reservations were voiced in the Kremlin about the advisability of reducing the armed forces and proceeding to a further reallocation of resources away from Defense. Indeed, between 1960 and 1961 the Soviet government increased its Defense spending from the level of nine billion roubles (where it had remained fairly constant since 1956) to eleven and a half billion roubles.[65]

In the autumn of 1961 planned cuts in the size of the army were canceled, and in September nuclear testing was resumed. The explosion of fifty-megaton bombs by the Soviet Union at this time—that is, at about the same time as the United States government discovered the true state of Soviet strategic weakness—may even have been an attempt to cover up this weakness and make the world believe that the Russian deterrent was a great deal stronger than it actually was.[66]

The new Kennedy administration came into office with its strategic doctrine of graduated response, which meant in effect that an increase in both conventional capabilities and increased flexibility in nuclear capabilities was required. Secretary of Defense Robert McNamara conducted a review of defense on taking over, and by March 1960 the review had advanced sufficiently for President Kennedy to request from Congress an additional 650 million dollars for the Defense Budget.[67] The entire Defense Budget jumped from 45 billion dollars in 1960 to 47 billion dollars in 1961, to 52 billion dollars in 1962.[68]

[64] *Ibid.*
[65] SIPRI *Yearbook 1969/70*, p. 271.
[66] This theory is elaborated in Strachey, *On the Prevention of War*, p. 48.
[67] Schlesinger, *A Thousand Days*, p. 297.
[68] SIPRI *Yearbook 1969/70*, pp. 268–69.

To sum up the argument so far, it may be surmised that Defense expenditures imposed a crushing burden on the Soviet economy, and that this burden greatly retarded the consumer goods program which Khrushchev clearly felt was important both in itself and as a factor in his own power relationships inside the Kremlin. This economic burden had led to an attempt to keep down Defense costs by relying on rocketry developed essentially for another purpose, and by developing warheads of large megatonage suitable only for what Western strategists would call countercity retaliation. A further factor here was the attempt to pretend to the world that this deterrent was much stronger than it actually was. For a long time this policy achieved great success—as the "missile gap" debate in the United States showed. Soviet strategic weakness became more worrying to the Soviet leaders as the international situation deteriorated, and as the Soviet Union failed to reach its objectives over the Berlin question and Germany. In addition, the Soviet government was faced with increasing intrabloc problems concerning Albania and China. All of these factors further undermined Khrushchev's domestic political position, and forced him to a display of militancy vis à vis the West. This was shown by his confrontation with President Kennedy in Vienna, his intractability over Berlin, the cancellation of planned army cuts, the increase in the size of the military budget, and the testing of fifty-megaton nuclear warheads. The Kennedy administration, partly as a result of its own adopted policy of graduated response, and partly as a reaction to this display of Soviet militancy, sharply increased United States military expenditures. In order to compete, therefore, in an apparent new lap of the arms race, the Soviet government would have had to devote even more of its efforts to defense and away from consumer goods. This would create still further problems for Khrushchev.

Finally, the ultimate destabilizing factor was the discovery by the United States of the true nature of Soviet strategic weakness, and the realization by the Soviet government that either the United States already possessed a first strike capability, or would very shortly possess one, unless the Soviet Union embarked on a new and very costly crash missile building program. And to do this would have been extremely costly politically to Chairman Khrushchev.

Thus, the decision to place missiles in Cuba was taken very much out of a sense of desperation and, considering the immense risks involved, as a last resort.

The question then arises—precisely what were these missiles designed to achieve? Missiles with nuclear warheads were placed in Cuba in response to an increasing and seemingly irreversible deterioration in Soviet foreign policy and domestic economic plans, as well as in response to the corresponding deterioration in Khrushchev's own political power. How then was it hoped that these missiles would correct the situation?

As has been mentioned above, the number of missiles placed in Cuba could deliver an initial salvo of forty missiles propelling three- to four-megaton warheads, and then deliver a second salvo of twenty-four. Thus, when the missiles were prematurely discovered by the United States government on October 15, 1962, there were already sixty-four missiles; and as there were ships en route for Cuba containing more missiles when the blockade was imposed on October 22, we can assume that the final number of missiles was certainly in excess of this number. The Appendix shows that in October, 1962, the Soviet Union possessed only seventy-five ICBMs capable of hitting the United States. Thus, it seems fair to conclude that if the Cuban missiles had become operational they possibly would have more than doubled the number of Soviet missiles capable of reaching the United States.

Many critics of President Kennedy's actions regarding the missile crisis have placed a great deal of blame on Secretary of Defense Robert McNamara's initial reaction to the news of the Soviet missiles in Cuba, which was that "a missile is a missile. It makes no great difference whether you are killed by a missile fired from the Soviet Union or from Cuba." [69] The Secretary of Defense, although he later changed his opinion, clearly felt that the missiles in Cuba made very little real difference to the deterrence relationship of the United States to the Soviet Union, and that Soviet missile strength was already sufficient deterrent to the United States without missiles in Cuba. Most of the evidence we have, however, indicates simply that the Secretary made a mistake, and that he later acknowledged this. Also, most of the members of EXCOM disagreed then, as now, with McNamara's initial judgment. [70] Apart from the fact that the number of Soviet missiles capable of reaching the United States would have

[69] Quoted in Abel, *The Missile Crisis,* p. 38.

[70] *Ibid.,* pp. 31–53; also compare the accounts in Hilsman, *To Move a Nation,* ch. 13; Schlesinger, *A Thousand Days,* ch. 30; and Robert F. Kennedy, *13 Days: A Memoir of the Cuban Missile Crisis,* Norton, New York, 1969.

been doubled, there would have been other military effects. Paul Nitze, then Assistant Secretary of Defense, argued that missiles in Cuba would expose a large part of the American strategic bomber force, based in the southeastern states, to surprise attack, and that these missiles being behind the Ballistic Missile Early Warning System, would cut warning time from fifteen to three minutes.[71]

One of the main problems confronting those who have attempted to analyze the Cuban Missile Crisis has been this problem of what precise function the missiles were supposed to have performed. Those who are sceptical of whether, even if the missiles could have been fired, they would have amde any real difference to the result of a nuclear exchange,[72] take refuge in McNamara's early judgment. Further evidence for this viewpoint was a later statement by President Kennedy to the effect that "these Cuban missiles did not substantially alter the strategic balance in fact. . . ."[73] In other words the crisis was seen as a confrontation involving merely "face" and "prestige." Implicit in this judgment is the theory, discussed earlier, that the missiles had the function merely of protecting Cuba and possibly embarrassing the United States government in Latin America and elsewhere.

In contrast, those who maintain that the missiles had a larger political purpose—the solution of the Berlin and China problems [74]—are unable to cope with the objection that if the missiles did not in fact serve some real strategic purpose, then this would provide no reason for the United States to give in to Soviet demands concerning what were regarded as vital United States national interests.[75]

However, even those who concede that the missiles really must have altered the military balance in some way in order to achieve their goals, are puzzled by precisely what military function they were designed to serve.

Arnold Horelick,[76] who concedes that the Cuban affair was in many ways intended by the Soviet government as a method of achieving a substantial and inexpensive improvement in the strategic balance, concludes that in effect he does not quite see how it would

---

[71] Abel, *The Missile Crisis,* p. 40.

[72] For example, I. F. Stone, "What if Khrushchev Hadn't Backed Down?", *In A Time of Torment,* Random House, New York, 1969, pp. 18–19.

[73] *Ibid.*

[74] See above, and Ulam, *Expansion and Coexistence,* pp. 660–67.

[75] See above.   [76] Horelick, "The Cuban Missile Crisis."

have achieved this. The missile sites themselves were very close to the United States, very "soft," and consequently very vulnerable to a United States first strike even with conventional bombs. Furthermore, says Horelick, the missiles were not sufficient in number (even allowing for the fact that the final number of missiles envisaged in the plan is not known) to have been an effective counterforce first strike against the United States. In other words, they were too vulnerable for retaliation and too few for pre-emption. Horelick is forced to conlude, therefore, that all the missiles would really have done would have been to complicate a United States first strike, or maybe blunt a United States counterattack if the Soviet Union struck first. A similar conclusion is reached by Albert and Roberta Wohlstetter, who write that the Cuban missiles were "weapons that in case of need during a grave crisis of escalation, would help to blunt an American retaliation." [77]

However, it is clear that if the previous analysis of Soviet motivations is correct, then these explanations are insufficient.

First, would the Soviet Union have undertaken the immense risks involved merely in order to "blunt an American retaliation"? With the United States at this time possessing an overkill factor of about ten against the Soviet Union,[78] does it seem reasonable that such enormous risks (that is, the risk that the missiles in Cuba would provoke the United States to the very act they were supposed to deter —a United States first strike against the Soviet Union) would be taken merely to blunt an attack which could in any case devastate the Soviet Union ten times over?

Second, even if the missile adventure was merely a temporary method of rectifying the strategic imbalance, it would not have helped solve the fundamental economic dilemma of the Soviet government—the dilemma of how to compete with the United States in defense expenditures, and at the same time devote more resources to consumer goods and away from heavy industry. The Soviet Union would still have to think about its long-term stand, and devote resources to a new missile program, just as Khrushchev's successors have felt compelled to do.

[77] Albert and Roberta Wohlstetter, "Controlling the Risks in Cuba," p. 10.

[78] I. F. Stone, "Theatre of Delusion", *New York Review of Books,* April 23, 1970. Overkill is defined as the number of times that the USA could devastate the USSR if all its megatonage were to be distributed evenly across the country. Stone gives estimates which indicate that the US stockpile in 1962 of 30,000 megatons could destroy the USSR ten times over.

Third, and most important, the dilemma that analysts have faced in deciding the "real purpose" of the Soviet missiles stems from the preoccupation with what occurred after the missiles were discovered. It is very easy to forget that the missiles in Cuba were discovered before they became operational. Clearly, the Soviet plan misfired, and the missiles were not supposed to have been discovered, or revealed before they were ready to launch. Thus, in order to reach an understanding of what function the missiles were supposed to have performed, it is necessary to look from the Russian point of view had the plan succeeded. In other words, what could the Russians have hoped to gain by having sixty or seventy (or more) missiles with nuclear warheads pointing at the United States; missiles, moreover, that were incapable of a credible counterforce first strike, and too vulnerable to be a credible retaliatory force?

If the hypothesis is correct that the Soviet move was motivated by the deterioration in international, domestic, and economic conditions, and as a result of the precariousness of the Soviet leader's power base, then we must ask how it was that the placement of missiles in Cuba could have rectified the situation? The answer is to be found in the theory of threats.

Thomas Schelling has written, "The creation of a risk—usually a shared risk—is a technique of compellence that probably best deserves the name of 'brinkmanship'. It is a competition in risk-taking. It involves setting afoot an activity that may get out of hand, initiating a process that carries some risk of unintended disaster. The risk is intended but not the disaster." [79] Elsewhere he has written, "Brinkmanship is thus the deliberate creation of a recognizable risk of war, a risk that one does not completely control. It is the tactic of deliberately letting the situation get completely out of hand just because its being out of hand may be intolerable to the other party and force his accommodation." [80]

It is a commonplace that the Cuban missile venture was an exercise in the art of "brinkmanship". What has been less obvious is precisely how the brinkmanship threat was supposed to work, and precisely why the missile force the Soviet government chose for this operation was constructed in quite the way it was.

Clearly, the missiles had minor functions, such as those pointed out by the Wohlstetters and others, of complicating a United States first strike and possibly blunting a United States retaliation. But these

[79] Schelling, *Arms and Influence*, p. 91.
[80] Schelling, *The Strategy of Conflict*, p. 200.

were only fringe benefits. The whole point of placing a large, strategically highly significant, and very vulnerable missile force on Cuba
was the very fact of their vulnerability. The Soviet government must
have known that the missiles were "soft" and that therefore they
could easily be destroyed either in a United States first strike or
merely by conventional bombs. But, remembering that from the
Russian point of view the missiles were supposed to have been operational (that is, could have been launched at a few minutes notice)
before they were discovered, the Soviets must have calculated that
the United States too would realize that the missiles were of use only
in a Soviet first strike. In other words, it was the very vulnerability of
the missiles which constituted the threat. If the United States made
any move either to destroy or threaten those missiles, the United
States would have known that for them to be of any use at all to the
Soviet Union they would have to be fired immediately. Thus, after
the missiles had become operational the United States would have
been forced into the position that even the slightest movement
against those missiles could result in their being launched. They were
so vulnerable that should the Soviet Union hesitate even for a few
minutes, the missiles could have been wiped out. In other words, the
missiles constituted a shared risk, over which the Soviet Union had
less than complete control itself.

Of course this is speculation, since the missiles were in fact discovered before their construction was completed. However, as has
been said, in order to understand their true function we must imagine
some kind of scenario in which the missiles were in fact completed in
the numbers the Russians had in mind, and then somehow revealed
to an astonished world. Under these circumstances the Soviet Union
would have possessed a missile force at least twice its previous size
targeted behind the United States Ballistic Missile Early Warning
System, and aimed at major cities and military installations. The
United States would be aware that for these missiles to have been
useful to the Soviet Union they would have to be fired first, since
they were so "soft" and vulnerable. The United States would perhaps
have been warned that the first sign of any military action to remove
the missiles would result in their being fired, since they were so exposed that the Soviet Union could not afford to wait. Thus, the threat
would be that the situation was so precarious that any move at all by
the United States—troop deployment, dispersal of planes, putting the
armed forces on alert, preparations to bomb or invade Cuba, and so

on might have resulted in the Soviet Union being forced to launch the missiles, since to wait might be to court disaster. The situation would have resembled the classic "Schellingian" situation of "the threat that leaves something to chance".[81] Indeed, Khrushchev later used language that evoked that kind of threat when he said that during a crisis "other forces and other laws would begin to operate—the laws of war" [82]—implying that events would have a momentum of their own which could not necessarily be halted. In the event this threat had far less credibility since when the words were spoken the missiles were still in a state of unreadiness.

Under conditions of such instability, the missiles in Cuba would have provoked a crisis in which almost any military move by the United States, not necessarily to attack, but even to look as though it might attack, would probably have led to a major war. This kind of threat, in which the Soviet Union put itself deliberately into a situation that in order to have any chance of survival it would have to strike first, would have been so precarious and entailed so great a risk of mutual destruction that it might well have forced the United States to capitulate on certain of the political moves the Soviet government had in mind, for example, Berlin. Also it may well have led to a realistic arms control agréement, which would have helped solve Khrushchev's domestic problems. That is, the missiles would have become a bargaining counter, and the incentive for the United States to agree would have been the very precariousness of the threat. The longer the missiles remained in Cuba, the greater the danger that the Soviet Union might panic and fire first.[83] And of course there had to

---

[81] *Ibid.*, ch. 8.

[82] Letter from Chairman Khrushchev to President Kennedy, Oct. 27, 1962. In Larson, *The "Cuban Crisis" of 1962*, p. 155.

[83] There is no parallel, in terms of the threat involved, between United States Jupiter missiles in Turkey, and Soviet missiles in Cuba. The crucial difference is that the United States in no way relied on the Jupiter missiles, in 1962, for adequate deterrence against the USSR. Even if the Jupiters were wiped out at a blow, the US had enough missiles and bombers remaining to obliterate the USSR. Thus, although the Jupiter missiles were extremely vulnerable, and were therefore by implication a first strike weapon, they were in fact really quite unimportant to the US deterrent. This was demonstrated when President Kennedy ordered their removal from Turkey in August 1962—an order that was apparently never carried out. (See Abel, *The Missile Crisis*, pp. 170–71.) What made a Soviet missile threat from Cuba more credible, and less stable, was the fact that the missiles were so strategically important to the USSR.

be a very significant number of missiles for several reasons. First, the United States might, despite risks, have tried to knock them out by an air strike or invasion. The larger the number, there would be less chance of this being successful.[84] Second, the larger the number of missiles, the greater the threat. Used as a first strike, they could possibly have destroyed a considerable portion of the Strategic Air Command in the southern United States, and also threatened the lives of enough Americans to help pressure the United States government into compliance.

The View From the United States— Why Get the Missiles Out?

It is now necessary to shift the viewpoint somewhat, and look at the situation from an entirely different perspective. As is well known, the Soviet threat did not materialize in the way the Soviet government had clearly hoped, since United States U-2 flights over Cuba in the autumn of 1962 eventually found decisive evidence that Soviet troops and technicians were deploying medium- and interme- diate-range ballistic missiles with nuclear warheads on the island of Cuba.

A great deal has been written on how the Kennedy administration, and in particular EXCOM, handled the crisis, and therefore there is little value in going over the same ground. From the point of view of this paper, two significant facts emerge. The first was that the mis- siles had been discovered before they were operational, and in the EXCOM meeting on October 17 it was assumed that it would take at least one more week before they became so.[85] In fact, over a week later, on October 25, despite the continuation by the Russians of the development of the sites, the missiles were not yet ready to fire.[86] The first important item, therefore, was that the United States had quite a long time to consider what to do before it became subject to any real danger. The second important factor was that to a very great extent the interests of the United States and the Soviet Union coin- cided. This was not a game of "pure" conflict, since both sides had an interest in avoiding a nuclear war. Thus, the "game" became what game theorists call a mixed-motive variable-sum game, combining el- ements of cooperation as well as conflict.[87]

---

[84] See above.   [85] Abel, *The Missile Crisis,* p. 50.   [86] *Ibid.,* p. 200.
[87] Albert and Roberta Wohlstetter, "Controlling the Risks in Cuba," pp. 13–14.

These two factors account in large part for the United States response to the potential missile threat. The fact that the missiles were not yet operational gave President Kennedy and his advisors time to consider all the alternatives and to initiate a policy of a slowly escalating series of threats to impress Khrushchev with their determination, while the common interest in avoiding a nuclear clash led to caution on both sides, and a desire within limits to accommodate the adversary.[88]

It is difficult to generalize about precisely how the missle threat was perceived by the members of EXCOM. The decision made by the President as a result of the EXCOM deliberations has been characterized as an example of "bureaucratic politics," of "the pulling and hauling of various players, with different perceptions and priorities, focusing on separate problems, and yielding outcomes that constitute the action in question." [89]

However, it is fairly clear that most members of EXCOM did not in fact perceive the missile threat in quite the way that it was intended. This stems partly from the fact that the missiles were not yet ready to fire, and partly from the fact that the precise military implications were not clear. In EXCOM, judgments varied from McNamara's "a missile is a missile" argument to Paul Nitze's less sanguine observations concerning the vulnerability of United States bomber bases in the South. If generalizations are at all possible, it can be said that there was almost unanimous agreement in EXCOM that the missiles would have to be removed and that, military considerations aside, the political threat was manifest.

After the Bay of Pigs fiasco in April 1961, the administration had decided on the approach of trying to isolate Castro diplomatically and applying economic pressures. During the Soviet military build-up in Cuba in the summer of 1962, the Republicans had made it clear that Cuba was going to be one of the major issues in the forthcoming Congressional mid-terms, and that they could charge the administration with weakness and vacillation. President Kennedy, to calm matters, had made speeches explaining that the military build-up in Cuba did not constitute any real threat to the United States. He did this partly in response to charges by Senator Keating and others, and partly to make his position perfectly clear to the Russians—and he warned against the introduction of "offensive" weapons into Cuba.

[88] *Ibid.*, pp. 14–18; and Schlesinger, *A Thousand Days*, p. 735.
[89] Graham T. Allison, "Conceptual Models and the Cuban Missile Crisis," *American Political Science Review*, Sep. 1969.

The President had therefore publicly pledged himself to act if long-range missiles were introduced into Cuba. When the missiles were finally discovered in October, a month before the Congressional elections, it was obvious to all the members of EXCOM that "the United States might not be in mortal danger but the Administration certainly was." [90]

Thus, one of the salient issues in the United States response was certainly the domestic political scene, and the administration's vulnerability over Cuba.

Initial discussion in EXCOM centered around precisely what the Soviet government hoped to gain from the missiles. [91] Many possibilities presented themselves, and much weight was given to the idea that the Berlin problem remained at the heart of the matter. The discussion has been summarized as follows:

the alternatives for the United States were ugly. If the President did nothing the Soviets would certainly succeed in exposing the hollowness of the Monroe Doctrine and the Rio Treaty, indeed of all United States treaty commitments to use its great power in defense of smaller nations anywhere. "To the Latins, Khrushchev would have looked like a winner," one State Department official said. Douglas Dillon recalls: "The first reaction of the President and the others, in full agreement, was that we simply could not accept the fact of Soviet missiles in Cuba trained on the United States." [92]

Not very much attention was paid to the exact manner in which the threat was to be carried out, or to the implications for strategic theory. In a sense, of course, all that was irrelevant at the time, since the threat had not yet materialized and what was important was to stop it from materializing. No one in EXCOM really felt that the Cuban missiles would have seriously undermined the credibility of the United States retaliatory strength since there were, after all, still one hundred and forty-four Polaris missiles at sea which by themselves were a fairly adequate deterrent. It was around the concepts of "appearances" and "political considerations" that the Soviet threat was evaluated. It was generally felt that this was a piece of Soviet "adventurism"—a judgment the Communist Chinese later echoed—not an example of a very desperate Soviet gamble.

As is well known, the response chosen by President Kennedy in

[90] Hilsman, *To Move a Nation,* p. 197.
[91] Abel, *The Missile Crisis,* p. 35.   [92] *Ibid.,* pp. 35–36.

consultation with EXCOM was to impose a blockade or "quarantine" around Cuba using the United States Navy to prevent the Soviet Union from bringing more missiles and strategic equipment into the island. In itself, a blockade would not remove the missiles, nor would it prevent the Soviet Union hurrying to complete the construction of those already inside Cuba. But after intensive discussions lasting from October 16 until October 21, when the President confirmed the blockade decision, it was felt that the blockade option had the best chance of success.

First, although not actually directly affecting the missiles, it was technically an act of war and would thus impress Khrushchev with the seriousness of United States intentions.

Second, as McNamara had pointed out in his now famous argument, it would "maintain the options." [93] The blockade decision left open to the President the use of an escalating series of pressures, not excluding, should it prove necessary, an air strike or invasion of Cuba. The blockade would be a minimal use of force that would permit escalation later if that was deemed to be desirable. Nothing would be lost by starting at the bottom of the scale.

Third, the blockade with its underlying message of possible escalation if the missiles were not removed, was able to rely on the overwhelming United States military superiority in the Carribean. Even before the blockade decision was taken, a Navy-Marine amphibious exercise in the area, previously scheduled for that week, provided a convenient cover-up for a task force of 40,000 Marines—as well as the 5,000 in Guantanamo. The Army's 82nd and 101st Airborne Divisions were made ready, while 100,000 troops were deployed ready for embarkation in Florida. SAC bombers left Florida airfields to make room for tactical fighter aircraft, and, just in case, to make them less vulnerable to a surprise nuclear attack.[94]

Fourth, the blockade would put the ball very much in Khrushchev's court. It would catch him off guard and force him either to directly challenge the blockade, and thus be the first to initiate violence, or to acquiesce by ordering his ships not to try and cross the American line.

The only real disadvantage, given the fact that the United States had time before the missiles were made ready, was simply that the Russians need not have bothered to challenge the blockade, but could

---

[93] *Ibid.*, p. 67.   [94] Schlesinger, *A Thousand Days*, p. 735.

have merely continued to make their missiles ready for use. The blockade did not prevent this, but as McNamara had pointed out, if that occurred then the other military operations could be initiated. In order to exclude this latter possibility—that is, the possibility that the Russians could just sit tight and wait on events—the United States decision was not only the initiation of a blockade but also the initiation of an escalating series of threats culminating eventually in an ultimatum.[95]

Several threats were contained in President Kennedy's address to the nation on October 22, which publicly announced the missile threat and the United States response. The first threat was the announcement of the "quarantine." The second was the oblique reference to the possibility of further direct military action against Cuba when the President said, "I have directed the Armed Forces to prepare for any eventualities; and I trust that in the interests of both the Cuban people and the Soviet technicians at the sites, the hazards to all concerned of continuing this threat will be recognized." The third was the statement that "it shall be the policy of this nation to regard any nuclear missile launched from Cuba against any nation in the Western Hemisphere as an attack by the Soviet Union on the United States requiring a full retaliatory response upon the Soviet Union." [96] Several commentators [97] have remarked that this latter statement does not sound like the doctrine of "graduated" or "controlled" response that was the administration's official nuclear-use doctrine. Indeed, it sounds much more like the "massive retaliation" of the earlier era. Thus, what the President was threatening was indeed an escalation of military pressure on the missile sites, and that should this provoke the Soviet Union to completing the sites and using, even by accident or miscalculation, just one of those rockets, it could expect a "full retaliatory response" from the United States.

The actions of the President did not, however, stop at this. On October 23, Kennedy learned that Russian submarines were beginning to operate in the Carribbean. "The President ordered the Navy to give the highest priority to tracking the submarines and to put into

[95] Alexander L. George, David K. Hall, and William E. Simons, *The Limits of Coercive Diplomacy—Laos, Cuba, Vietnam,* Little-Brown, Boston, 1971.

[96] These quotations are all from President Kennedy's address to the nation on October 22, 1962. In Larson, *The "Cuban Crisis" of 1962,* pp. 41–46.

[97] See Horelick, "The Cuban Missile Crisis"; and Albert and Roberta Wohlstetter, "Cuba and Pearl Harbor."

effect the greatest possible safety measures to protect our own aircraft carriers and other vessels." [98] From then on, the United States Navy continued to harrass Soviet submarines, at least six of which were forced to surface in the presence of United States military ships, while the build-up of other United States military forces continued. Thus, although the President on the evening of October 23 ordered that the blockade line, originally drawn 800 miles from Cuba, be pulled back to 500 miles, in order to give the Soviet leader more time to think, this was accompanied by so many other menacing moves as to signal United States determination. As almost all the commentators have pointed out, the President was determined to slow down as much as possible the pace of events and to keep matters as much under his direct control as possible. Once an actual military clash took place it was realized that events could easily get out of hand. The object was to signal determination while at the same time avoid war—hence the combination of toughness and conciliation.

The problem was to find some action or combination of actions that would communicate the threat to the Soviet Union; an action moreover that would promise damage if the Russians did not comply, but minimum damage if they did. Further, it had to be an action that would leave the next move up to the Russians, if war was to be averted. The blockade would not by itself make the missiles go away or prevent them being completed, but it did however "threaten a minor military confrontation with major diplomatic stakes." [99] It meant that the Soviet Union had the opportunity to turn aside, but the public nature and obvious resolve of the United States' action meant that the United States could not itself avoid the encounter once the blockade was in place.

The View From the Soviet Union— Why Acquiesce?

The Soviet Union had hoped to present the United States government with a *fait accompli*. Instead, it found itself presented with one —the blockade of Cuba. The blockade shifted the Soviet position regarding the precipitation of violence; that was now up to the Soviet

[98] Robert Kennedy, *13 Days*, p. 68.
[99] Schelling, *Arms and Influence*, p. 81.

Union, not as had been hoped, up to the United States, in circumstances of Russia's own choosing. In effect this gave the Soviet government three choices. They could submit to the humiliation of being searched and of having ships turned back if they contained forbidden cargo; they could refrain from entering the quarantine area; or they could violate the quarantine and thereby initiate violence which might be very difficult to control, and in which in any case they stood little chance of success because of the overwhelming United States conventional superiority in the Carribbean.[100]

Out of these choices sprang other choices. If the Soviet government opted for not challenging the quarantine, they still had other courses of action open to them. On October 24 came reports that some Soviet ships bound for Cuba had stopped dead in the water. A decision had been made, at least for the moment, not to challenge the blockade—as Dean Rusk put it, "The other fellow just blinked." [101] But in fact this course of action resolved very little and still left the situation ambiguous. Work continued apace at the missile sites: in other words the Soviet Union had exercised an option to continue work on the missiles. In many respects the crisis could have been attenuated to a great degree at that point by the simple expedient of stopping work on the sites—while leaving the missiles themselves in Cuba.[102] This might well have taken the wind out of the Kennedy administration's sails, and left time for bargaining in which the Soviet Union might have been able to extract more than it later did from the affair. However, this option was not exercised, and for reasons that must remain guesswork. Presumably this was thought of by the Russian leaders and rejected, although it is of course possible that it simply did not occur to them.

Another option, the one which the United States leaders feared the most, was that the Soviet Union would exert pressure elsewhere in the world to correspond to the United States pressure in Cuba. What most people had in mind was a blockade of Berlin. Again, however, this option was not exercised by the Soviet government. Later, Foreign Minister Gromyko told the Supreme Soviet that, "This (Cuban) crisis . . . made many people think how the whole matter might have developed if yet another crisis in Central Europe had been

[100] Horelick, "The Cuban Missile Crisis," part III—"Soviet Crisis Calculations."

[101] Quoted in Hilsman, *To Move a Nation*, p. 215.

[102] See George *et al.*, *The Limits of Coercive Diplomacy*, p. 119.

added to the critical events around Cuba." [103] Although this is not much to go on, it suggests that the Soviet government analyzed, and rejected, the possibility of a reply in Berlin for fear of the situation really getting out of control and leading to a nuclear confrontation.

This was true, despite the fact that it was generally considered that in Berlin the Soviet Union could match the enormous military superiority which the United States possessed in the Carribbean. Horelick writes, "Soviet quiescence in Berlin during and immediately after the Cuban missile crisis demonstrates the severe limitations of even overwhelming military superiority in the hands of a strategically inferior power. . . ." [104] Thus, Horelick sees the Soviet attitude to Berlin at this time as being determined by their nuclear inferiority. This was paradoxically, therefore, the same inferiority which prompted the Cuban adventure in the first place. In fact, however, while this may have been a consideration, there were two other reasons why the Soviet Union was unable to force a Cuba/Berlin equation.

One is simply that the stakes were different. The United States had limited aims in Cuba—the removal of offensive missiles. To get them removed it had demonstrated its intentions by a blockade and a military build-up designed as the preparation for a strike against the sites if necessary. There was no corresponding way for the Soviet Union to use Berlin. A blockade there would not really affect the Cuban situation, nor alter United States resolve. A tit-for-tat arrangement would not lead anywhere, except, as the Soviet government appeared to see, to greater tension.

Second, as Thomas Schelling has written,

Equally significant was the universal tendency—a psychological phenomenon, a tradition or convention shared by Russians and Americans—to *define* the conflict in Carribbean terms, not as a contest, say, in the blockade of each other's island allies, not as a counterpart of their position in Berlin, not as a war of harrassment against strategic weapons outside national borders. [105]

As the pressure on the Soviet Union increased, it became clear to the Soviet leaders that a military strike against Cuba was imminent. In the messages sent to the Russians it was relayed that the United

[103] *Pravda,* Dec. 14, 1962.
[104] Horelick, "The Cuban Missile Crisis," p. 388.
[105] Schelling, *Arms and Influence,* p. 87 n.

States government was on the verge of military action. This was done formally by the Attorney-General Robert Kennedy conferring with Ambassador Dobrynin on October 26, when the President's brother indicated that action could not be deferred for more than two days, and informally in the exchanges between newspaperman John Scali and Soviet Official Aleksander Fomin.[106] Later, on December 12, 1962, Khrushchev made a speech to the Supreme Soviet in which he said,

In the morning of October 27, we received information from our Cuban comrades and from other sources which directly stated that this attack would be carried out within the next two or three days. We regarded the telegrams received as a signal of utmost alarm, and this alarm was justified. Immediate actions were required in order to prevent an attack against Cuba and preserve the peace.[107]

Thus, in a situation in which the United States had both strategic and conventional superiority, the Soviet government backed down. They received no direct *quid pro quo* concerning the removal of United States Jupiter missiles in Turkey, but they did receive assurances about United States noninvasion of Cuba, permitting some degree of face-saving. It is clear that the Soviet Union stepped down in order to avoid a clash of conventional forces, which in the Carribbean the Soviet Union would have lost. To avoid this, it would have been necessary either to shift the locus of events, for example to Berlin, which the Soviet government was unwilling to do, or it would have been necessary to escalate the conflict to higher, probably nuclear levels, in which the Soviet Union was extremely weak in any case. Indeed, the Berlin ploy would only have made the use of nuclear weapons more likely.

Conclusion

An analysis of the crisis on which this paper has relied heavily reaches the conclusion that "as long as the West maintains a favora-

[106] Hilsman, *To Move a Nation*, pp. 217–23. John Scali was a State Department correspondent for ABC who was approached by a senior Soviet official in the Soviet Embassy, Aleksander Fomin, and was used during the crisis as a go-between for the US Government and the Kremlin.

[107] Quoted from *Pravda*, Dec. 13, 1962, in George *et al.*, *The Limits of Coercive Diplomacy*, p. 126.

ble strategic balance, the Soviet Union cannot use West Berlin as a hostage to cover Soviet offensive moves and probes in other parts of the world. . . ." [108] This statement has an important implication. It suggests that the attempt to put missiles in Cuba was a "probe" by the Soviet government, which was forestalled at least in part—the part that could have led to pressure being applied in Berlin—by Western strategic superiority.

But, it emerges from the analysis in this paper that the Soviet move in Cuba was largely a result of its strategic inferiority. In other words, Horelick's conclusion puts the cart before the horse. Strategic inferiority may have been one of the factors which denied the Soviet Union success; but more important, it was the factor which prompted the move in the first place. Thus, the conclusion of this paper is very much the opposite of Horelick's. In order to maintain stability in a deterrence relationship, as much as in an arms race, it is important that neither side get too far ahead of the other. This is what had occurred by 1962, and this is what prompted the Soviet Union to find a quick way to get even. The turning point was the discovery by the United States that the Soviet Union was as weak as it was, and the transmittal of this information back to the Soviet government. But what was unstable in the deterrence relationship was the fact that the United States had gotten so far ahead of the Soviet Union that the key element in the equation of stability was lacking. It was not certain that both sides could inflict unacceptable damage on the other in a retaliatory strike.

A second conclusion is the influence on the moves of both sides, both before and during the crisis, of domestic political considerations that had little directly to do with the foreign policy problem. Thus, Khrushchev was forced into the missile venture in the first place at least in part because of his precarious domestic political position, while President Kennedy's response was similarly influenced. In this way the deterrence relationship can become distorted and perhaps destabilized by the influence of domestic political considerations that have little directly to do with "the military balance" as such.

Third, it is clear that although both sides adhered to a particular strategic doctrine, neither side stuck very rigidly to its avowed policies. The Soviet Union would have been forced to threaten a first

---

[108] Horelick, "The Cuban Missile Crisis," p. 389.

strike in order to obtain its objectives had the original plan worked out, while official government policy advocated retaliation only. The United States, having recently espoused the doctrine of controlled response, threatened the Soviet Union in effect with a more massive kind of retaliation if any missile from Cuba should be fired. Thus, strategic doctrine does not necessarily shape policy, but is often itself molded by the day-to-day needs of governments.

This is particularly true when governments make threats. It is not certain that the United States would in fact have retaliated in a massive way if any missiles were launched from Cuba, but the threat was used to deter the Soviet Union from completing construction of the sites. Similarly both sides were well aware of the danger of war-by-miscalculation, and also of the good use that could be made of a threat based on the assumption that events might get out of hand. After the start of the crisis itself, control was evident in almost everything that both sides did, but far less noticeable in what they said.

Deterrence theory as usually expounded frequently fails to take these kinds of variables into account. Governments respond to threats and crisis situations in ways which are not immediately predictable from the "pure" deterrence relationship. All sorts of external factors can enter the picture to distort events, and in particular the arms race implied by a deterrence relationship can prove to be highly unstable. Both sides must be aware that the race is not one in which the object is to win, but one in which the object is to a large extent to accommodate the adversary. If this is not done he may feel so insecure that he will resort to desperate and dangerous methods to close the gap.

Appendix: The Military Balance USA / USSR October 1962

	USA			USSR		
missiles		90 Atlas	*missiles*			
		36 Titan				
		150 Minuteman				
ICBM	—	276	ICBM	—	75	
MRBM	—	45 Jupiter *	MRBM	—	700	
SLM	—	144 Polaris	SLM	—	0	
bombers			*bombers*			
LONG RANGE	—		LONG RANGE	—	70	Bears
					120	Bisons
		630 B52's			190	
MEDIUM RANGE	—		MEDIUM RANGE	—		
		850 B47's				
		90 B58's				
		940			1000	Badgers

Source: Institute for Strategic Studies., *The Military Balance,* 1962–63.
* For some reason the ISS estimate of MRBM's belonging to the USA does not include 60 Thor missiles stationed in Europe.

Megatonage (1962)

USA	USSR
25–30 thousand megatons	5–10 thousand megatons

Source: American Security Council, *The Changing Military Balance USA/USSR*

BIBLIOGRAPHY

Readers interested in a further investigation of the subject of this article may wish to consult:

Abel, Elie. *The Missile Crisis,* Bantam, New York, 1968.
Allison, Graham T. "Conceptual Models and the Cuban Missile Crisis," *American Political Science Review,* Sept. 1969.
American Security Council. *The Changing Military Balance USA vs USSR,* a Study prepared for the House Armed Services Committee by the National Strategy Committee of the American Security Council, Washington, D. C. 1967.
Aron, Raymond. *The Great Debate*—Theories of Nuclear Strategy, Doubleday Anchor, New York, 1965.

Boulding, Kenneth E. *Conflict and Defense—A General Theory,* Harper Torchbooks, New York, 1963.

Brzezinski, Zbigniew, and Samuel P. Huntington. *Political Power USA / USSR,* Viking Press, New York, 1964.

Churchward, Lloyd G. *Contemporary Soviet Government,* Routeledge & K. Paul, London, 1968.

Deutsch, Karl. *The Analysis of International Relations,* Prentice-Hall, Englewood Cliffs, N.J., 1968.

Fainsod, Merle. *How Russia is Ruled,* Harvard University Press, Cambridge, 1965.

Frankland, Mark. *Khrushchev,* Penguin, Harmondsworth, 1966.

George, Alexander L., David K. Hall, and William E. Simons. *The Limits of Coercive Diplomacy—Laos, Cuba, Vietnam,* Little-Brown, Boston, 1971.

Green, Philip. *Deadly Logic—the Theory of Nuclear Deterrence,* Ohio State University Press, 1966.

Henkin, Louis. *How Nations Behave,* Praeger, New York, 1970.

Hilsman, Roger. *To Move a Nation—the Politics of Foreign Policy in the Administration of John F. Kennedy,* Delta, 1967.

Horelick, Arnold. "The Cuban Missile Crisis," *World Politics 16,* 1964.

Huntington, Samuel P. *The Common Defense,* Columbia University Press, New York, 1961.

Ikle, Fred Charles. *How Nations Negotiate,* Praeger, New York, 1968.

Ionescu, Ghita. *The Break-Up of the Soviet Empire in Eastern Europe,* Penguin, Baltimore, 1965.

Institute for Strategic Studies. *The Military Balance 1962–63,* London.

Kennedy, Robert F. *13 Days: A Memoir of the Cuban Missile Crisis,* Norton, New York, 1969.

Khrushchev, Nikita S. *Khrushchev Remembers,* from *Life,* Dec. 18, 1970.

Kintner, William R., and Harriet Fast Scott. *The Nuclear Revolution in Soviet Military Affairs,* University of Oklahoma Press, 1968.

Kissinger, Henry A. *Nuclear Weapons and Foreign Policy,* Norton, New York, 1969.

Knapp, Wilfrid. *A History of War and Peace 1939–1965,* Royal Institute of International Affairs, Oxford University Press, London, 1967.

Larson, David L. ed. *The "Cuban Crisis" of 1962—Selected Documents and Chronology,* Houghton Mifflin, Boston, 1963.

Mongar, Thomas M. "Personality and Decision Making," *Canadian Journal of Political Science,* 1969.

Nove, Alec. *The Soviet Economy,* Praeger, New York, 1966.

Schelling, Thomas C. *Arms and Influence,* Yale University Press, New Haven, 1967.

——*The Strategy of Conflict,* Oxford University Press, New York, 1969.

Schlesinger, Arthur M. *A Thousand Days—John F. Kennedy in the White House,* Fawcett, New York, 1967.

Stockholm International Peace Research Institute. *SIPRI Yearbook of World Armaments and Disarmament 1969/70,* Humanities Press, New York, 1970.

Stone, I. F. *In A Time of Torment,* Random House, New York, 1967.

——"Theatre of Delusion," *New York Review of Books,* April 1970.

Strachey, John. *On The Prevention of War,* St. Martin's Press, New York, 1963.

Ulam, Adam B. *Expansion and Coexistence—the History of Soviet Foreign Policy 1917–67,* Praeger, New York, 1969.

United States Arms Control and Disarmament Agency. *World-Wide Defense Expenditures and Selected Economic Data, 1964,* Washington D. C. 1966.

Wohlstetter, Albert and Roberta. "Controlling the Risks in Cuba," *Adelphi Papers 17,* Institute for Strategic Studies, London, 1965.

Wohlstetter, Roberta. "Cuba and Pearl Harbor," *Foreign Affairs 43,* 1965.

Disintegration and Integration
in Southeast Asia

MARGARET ROFF

The impressive body of theoretical literature that has been built up concerning the European integrative effort of the past two decades makes somewhat depressing reading when one comes to consider its relevance to regional integrative efforts in the underdeveloped world. So many of the background features or preconditions for successful integration discovered by scholars—for example, "interdependence," "mutual responsiveness," and "mutual attentiveness"—are apparently absent or lacking in the Third World, that one is tempted to prejudge all efforts at regional cooperation as doomed to failure before they start.

In the Southeast Asian context this is a *fortiori* true. Postindependence intraregional disagreements have exacerbated long-standing hostilities and distrust indulged in by the precolonial polities. All countries of the region were absorbed into one or more of the Portuguese, Spanish, Dutch, British, French or American empires (with the notable exception of Thailand), and all gained independence in the decade 1947–57. This disparate colonial experience heightened intraregional differences by imposing a multiplicity of trading and cultural foci,[1] and also, as the imperial powers were not much con-

[1] Even today 80 per cent of the trade of the countries of southeast Asia is without the region, and although the situation is changing for the better, many cultural, educational, and communication lines still go back to the erstwhile metropolitan powers rather than to other capitals in the area. I recall, for example, that on one occasion both the Malay and the English language press of Kuala Lumpur devoted far more space to a British by-election than to an all-important national election in neighboring Thailand. Over-dependence upon international wire-services is, however, slowly ceasing to be a feature of the press of the region.

cerned with the human realities and complexities of ethnicity, language, and religion, they bequeathed many problems in terms of minorities at odds with the prevailing norms of the nation-states within whose borders they found themselves.

The intention of this paper is first of all to outline briefly those factors working against any attempts toward regional cooperation and integration in Southeast Asia, together with some allusion to the more dramatic disintegrative episodes of the past decade. Thereafter it is proposed to investigate integrative efforts and experiments that have been launched notwithstanding, and to make some sort of assessment of the reality and persistence of forces working toward a transcendence of national barriers and an efflorescence of cooperative schemes.

While it is possible to argue a certain cultural homogeneity among the peoples and countries of Southeast Asia,[2] what immediately strikes the casual observer of the ten independent nation-states (Burma, Thailand, Cambodia, Laos, North and South Vietnam, Malaysia, Singapore, Indonesia, and the Philippines) is their enormous diversity. The languages of the region are much more numerous than the nation-states, but each of the latter has adopted a "national language," all of which are mutually unintelligible except for the shared tongue of the two Vietnams, and the similarity of Malay and Indonesian. Frequently it is the languages of the former imperialists which must be used for communication internationally within the region, especially between members of the respective educated elites. Most major religions of the world with their radically different world views—Islam, Buddhism, Taoism, and Christianity—have numerous adherents among the 250 million people of the region, and although there have been no modern-day religious wars between countries in the area, there are still innumerable pressure points within and between nations, of which religion becomes the focus.[3]

And religion and language are just two of the most obvious facets

[2] See, for example, David Joel Steinberg *et al., In Search of Southeast Asia,* (New York, Praeger, 1970), especially Part I.

[3] Buddhist/Catholic strains within South Vietnam have been well publicized, as have Cambodian/Thai quarrels over possession of border temples. Less widely known are Malaysian/Thai strains over the conversion to Buddhism of many hitherto Muslim Malays of southern Thailand; allegations of forced Islamization of Roman Catholic and other tribesmen in Sabah; and Catholic/Muslim violence in the southern Philippine islands.

of the more complex diversity subsumed under the rubric "ethnicity."
Speaking in the most general possible terms, the majority of the
many diverse peoples of Southeast Asia can be divided into the insu-
lar, maritime, Malayo-Polynesian people of Malaya, Indonesia, and
the Philippines, and the more sinicised peoples of the former territories of French Indo-China and of Thailand. Complicating this picture
is the presence of large numbers of immigrant Chinese (Singapore is
in effect a Chinese city-state, the Chinese in Malaysia form approximately 40 per cent of the population, and the other countries of
Southeast Asia also have considerable minorities, significant particularly by virtue of their economic power) and Indians (particularly in
Malaysia and Burma), and the survival of unassimilated hill-tribe
peoples in most of the region.[4] Historically the mainland/maritime
division has been an important one, and it is not without significance
that most of the more successful efforts at transnational cooperation
have been within one or the other division (with Thailand a central
"neutral" participant, able to move with either group). Finally, in ad-
umbrating possible or potential centrifugal tendencies in the region
and sources of discord, it is important to remember that prior to European colonization much of the area consisted of a plethora of tiny
independent kingdoms and sultanates, some of which from time to
time were able greatly to extend the area of their power and influence, but all of which were prone to warring with neighbors or in-
truders. In particular the Mon, Khmer, Shan, Karen, Lao, and Thai
people of present-day eastern Burma, northern Thailand, Cambodia,
and Laos have long memories of competing for land and power, and
from time to time it has suited the purposes of modern politicians to
revive these ancient rivalries.

The Vietnam war has unquestionably been the most damaging and
disruptive phenomenon of postindependence Southeast Asia (although it depends upon one's point of view whether it be termed an
international dispute or a civil war).[5] The French had welded the five

[4] The most exhaustive survey of the Nanyang Chinese is Victor Purcell, *The
Chinese in Southeast Asia,* (London, Oxford University Press, 1965). For discussion of the immigrant Indians, see Usha Mahajani, *The Role of the Indian
Minorities in Burma and Malaya,* (Bombay, Vora and Co., 1960). The tribal
groups are most extensively discussed in Peter Kunstadter (ed.), *Southeast
Asian Tribes, Minorities and Nations,* 2 vols., (Princeton, N. J., Princeton University Press, 1967).

[5] This is not the place for a discussion of the nightmare. Among the more
insightful books on the subject are John T. McAlister Jr., *Vietnam: The Ori-*

parts of their Asian empire—Annam, Tonkin, Cochinchina, Laos, and Cambodia—into a customs union, and had imposed a number of unifying administrative, educational, and cultural institutions. Two decades of warring and incursions between the four successor states have shattered what integrative apparatus there was, but to a surprising extent remnants of French culture have survived, and this, together with majority adherence to Buddhism, constitutes some possible basis for future cooperation and coincidence of interest if peace can be restored.

The only other intraregional war of the post World War Two period has also been between what might be thought of as "fraternal" states—Indonesia and Malaysia.[6] Sukarno's "Konfrontasi" of the extension of the Federation of Malaya to include Singapore and the Borneo territories of Sabah and Sarawak was multimotivated, and both the Army and the Indonesian Communist Party, for completely different reasons, went along with him. Although it was diplomatically and otherwise trying for Malaysia, the violence and damage wrought was minimal (except perhaps along the Sarawak border), and it might be argued that the "ordeal by fire" served the purpose of welding together an otherwise reluctant polity. Certainly Singapore's ejection from Malaysia came not because of external pressure but because of internal, Malay/Chinese strains.

Before moving on to consideration of more hopeful trends and developments in Southeast Asia two other "disruptions" of the harmony of the region ought perhaps to be mentioned. These both involved territoriality, and although neither is at present being focused upon by the governments involved, neither has been finally or satisfactorily resolved. These two cases are the Philippines' claim to part of Sabah (which since 1963 has been incorporated in Malaysia), and Cambodia's several border disputes with Thailand. Tiny modern Cambodia is the successor state to the once extensive Khmer Empire which controlled virtually all of Indo-China and large areas of present-day Thailand. In these circumstances it is not surprising that Si-

---

gins of Revolution, (New York, Alfred Knopf, 1969) and Paul Mus, *Vietnam: Sociologie d'une guerre,* (Paris, Editions du Seuil, 1952).

[6] This has received various treatments, for example, Bernard K. Gordon, *Dimensions of Conflict in Southeast Asia,* (Englewood Cliffs, N. J., Prentice Hall, 1966), Chapter 3; but the definitive work on confrontation (by J. A. C. Mackie) is to be published by Oxford University Press, Kuala Lumpur, later this year.

hanouk, in particular, was acutely sensitive about every last inch of remaining Cambodian territory. The greater conflicts in the area have for the moment pressed boundary disputes into the background, but further trouble concerning them is always possible.

The Philippines/Malaysian dispute had no such historical antecedents; indeed Manila/Kuala Lumpur relations since independence had been particularly cordial, and it came as a considerable shock to the Malaysian government when the Philippines joined Indonesia in harassment of the new federation. Based on an 1878 treaty between the Sultan of Sulu and the British North Borneo Company, Macapagal's claim probably had more to do with internal Philippine politics than with international realities,[7] but it was pursued with sufficient fervor to seriously disrupt what had been one of the more promising attempts at regional cooperation. One other potential border dispute (between Malaysia and Thailand; in the nineteenth century Thailand had suzerainty over some of the northern Malay states, and present-day southern Thailand includes several ethnically "Malay" states) has been carefully not pursued by either party, each recognizing that the price of discord is more than they wish to pay.

At this point the integration theorist—especially if his area of expertise is Europe—might well exclaim in horror that the situation is utterly inimical to integration; that even though the misguided participants might choose to call the game "integration" they delude themselves; and that the ground rules are obviously unrecognizable. While tending to agree up to a point—the efforts at regional cooperation I am about to discuss have been limited in both extent and duration— it seems to me that the very persistence of the idea of the desirability of regional integration (despite the previously mentioned regional disruptions) must be accorded serious attention. A remarkable cross-section of the elites, and almost all serious politicians of the area, are convinced of the desirability of integration. (In this respect, at least, Southeast Asia is not too dissimilar from Europe.) "Cooperation," the theoretician might argue, "is not integration, even if cooperation is extensive and successful," and the politicians of South-

[7] See K. G. Tregonning, "The Claim for North Borneo by the Philippines," *Australian Outlook*, XVI, 3, 1962; Michael Leifer, *The Philippine Claim to Sabah*, (Zug, Switzerland, IDC Co., 1968: Hull Monographs on Southeast Asia, No. 1); and M. O. Ariff, *The Philippines' Claim to Sabah: Its Historical Legal and Political Implications*, (Kuala Lumpur, Oxford University Press, 1970).

east Asia who have successively put together ASA (Association of Southeast Asia), MAPHILINDO (Malaysia, the Philippines and Indonesia), and ASEAN (Association of Southeast Asian Nations) are aware that they are taking only the first steps in a long and perilous journey. But they would argue, and I would agree, that cooperation is cumulatively integrative, and hopefully will develop an inner dynamic of its own.[8] One important feature of ASA and ASEAN in particular is that they stemmed from initiatives *within* the region, unlike, for example, ECAFE, the Asian Development Bank, or the Columbo Plan (which do not in any case confine their activities to Southeast Asia). "Asian solutions for Asian problems" has become something of a battle cry in the region, and it is interesting to speculate that a sort of Southeast Asian-centricity might make a useful and acceptable emotional substitute for rampant nationalism and, hopefully, a spur to self-propelling development.

ASA, as the first formalized regional grouping to pursue economic and other cooperative ends, warrants examination as to the manner of its formation, its goals and achievements. Originating in Kuala Lumpur, the idea behind the proposed "Southeast Asia Friendship and Economic Treaty" was the inclusion not just of the Western-supporting states (Malaysia, Thailand, and the Philippines) but also of neutrals such as Burma, Indonesia, and Cambodia. Despite this, both Thailand and the Philippines welcomed the idea as a "bulwark against Communism," thus ensuring that the neutralist nations would view it with suspicion and refuse to join.[9] ASA started life therefore (in Bangkok on July 31, 1961) with only three members—Malaya, Thailand and the Philippines. All three were allied with the West (Thailand and the Philippines through SEATO and Malaya by virtue of its defense treaty with Great Britain), and in the decade 1950–60, operating free-enterprise economies, the three had had the highest growth rates in the region (together they produced half the world's tin, natural rubber, and palm oil).

[8] See, for example, Augustine H. H. Tan (Member of Parliament, Singapore), "Singapore and Regional Cooperation", *Singapore Newsletter,* III, 3, March 1971; and S. Rajaratnam (Singapore's Minister for Foreign Affairs), "ASEAN after Four Years", *Singapore Newsletter,* III, 5, April 1971.

[9] For discussions of this see, for example, Vincent K. Pollard, "ASA and ASEAN 1961–67: Southeast Asian Regionalism", *Asian Survey,* X, 3, 1970; and Bernard K. Gordon, "Regionalism and Instability in Southeast Asia" in Joseph Nye (ed.), *International Regionalism,* (Boston, Little Brown, 1968).

The "Bangkok Declaration," with which ASA was launched, after calling for "common action to further economic and social progress in Southeast Asia" went on to enumerate seven specific fields of proposed action and cooperation. These were: preferential trade agreements among members; free trade in certain commodities; lowering of tariffs; easing of customs rules and procedures; standardization and control of exports; joint business ventures; and cooperation in commercial aviation and shipping.[10]

Conceived primarily as being concerned with economic cooperation and development, ASA became principally the responsibility of Malayan, Thai, and Filipino civil servants who were already involved in their own state's developmental efforts. A decision was made not to establish a central administrative organization, but to proceed by means of national working parties for specific problems, submitting reports and recommendations to periodically assembled joint working parties. Heads of Government and Foreign Ministerial conferences were to be held at least annually, and meetings of Education Ministers, Agriculture Ministers, and other officials as the need arose. Through 1962 and 1963 evidence of greater communication between bureaucratic elites of the three capitals was readily apparent.

With intra-ASA trade then running at no more than 7 or 8 per cent per annum [11] it was clear that more than merely lowering trade and customs barriers was necessary if regional prosperity were to be increased. It was necessary also to "encourage a vigorous policy of regional cooperation in spreading industrial know-how and promoting investment in a wide range of diversified production." [12] Regional industrial specialization was seen to be necessary if individual nation-states were not to find themselves competing for scarce investment resources. After the initial high-flown statements about long-range goals and aspirations, the various committees of ASA grappled with the concrete problems of simplifying customs procedures, adopt-

---

[10] This list is to be found in various places, but see, for example, Hugo Durant, "ASA—Prospects and Results," *Eastern World,* XVIII, August 1963. One month later the foreign ministers of the ASA countries met and issued a more detailed document outlining the specific goals and plans of the organization, but this did not differ in essentials from the Bangkok Declaration.

[11] For details see Theodore Morgan and Nyle Spoelstra, *Economic Interdependence in Southeast Asia,* (Madison, Wisc., University of Wisconsin Press, 1969), especially chapters 1, 5, 7, 8, and 12.

[12] Lim Tay Boh, "Regional Trade Cooperation among Asian Countries," *Pakistan Development Review,* Spring 1962, p. 550.

ing compatible tax regulations, facilitating increased educational, technical, and business exchanges, and developing an essential communications network between proximate territories whose histories had been sundered by three hundred years of colonial intrusion. Advances were small but measurable, and were considered significant by the respective national bureaucracies. Development planning was co-ordinated to some degree, and exchange of technical competence facilitated.

Although the bureaucrats were highly pleased with the progress they were making, "politics" reared its ugly head. Macapagal's decision to lay claim to Sabah escalated to the point where Manila broke off diplomatic relations with Kuala Lumpur. For regional cooperation and for ASA this was obviously disastrous, and yet strangely it was not the death blow one might have supposed. ASA projects were not dismantled, nor was the Bangkok Declaration repealed. The whole thing was merely put on ice. Ministerial meetings were "postponed," not canceled, and until Marcos's presidential victory and the decision to resume diplomatic ties the two sides were indirectly kept "talking to each other" through the good offices of Thailand's foreign minister. There was very evident reluctance to bury the region's first indigenously inspired attempt at inter-national cooperation. Following the downfall of both President Sukarno and the Indonesian Communist Party, and Indonesia's adoption of a less militant foreign policy and a more rational domestic policy, ASA was in fact briefly revived before bowing out graciously and subsuming itself within the enlarged cooperative endeavour, ASEAN.

Before coming to examine ASEAN, MAPHILINDO, a brainchild of President Sukarno for regional cooperation, should be mentioned briefly. Looking for a face-saving way of calling off his confrontation with Malaysia, President Sukarno at a conciliatory conference in Manila in early 1964 proposed a union of the "Malay" people of Malaysia, the Philippines, and Indonesia. The idea understandably alarmed the non-Malay peoples of the countries concerned (in particular the 40 per cent Chinese minority in Malaysia), and by definition excluded Thailand, which had hitherto been most assiduous in pursuit of regional accord and cooperation. So anxious were Malaysia and the Philippines to see an end to disruption and to confrontation that at first they expressed real interest in Sukarno's scheme, but when it came to the business of implementing it they drew back. The proposal did, however, highlight the absurdity of Indonesia's non-

membership in ASA, and may have made it easier for her subsequent leaders to participate in ASEAN.[13]

On August 8, 1967, ASEAN (Association for Southeast Nations)
was set up, the signatories to the agreement being the three former
ASA states, plus Singapore and Indonesia. (For at least part of the
life of ASA Singapore had been within Malaysia.) The ASEAN
Declaration stated that the purpose of the organizeation was "to col-
laborate more effectively for the greater utilization of agriculture and
industry, the expansion of trade including a study of the problems of
international commodity trade, the improvement of transportation
and communication facilities, and the raising of the living standards
of the people." [14] ASA did not immediately go out of existence, but
waited to see if ASEAN's viability were firmly established. In a year
they were so convinced, and ASA projects and funds were transferred to ASEAN and ASA formally dissolved. While ASA had
been in effect "anti-communist," ASEAN was avowedly neutral internationally and ideologically. But all the participating governments
(including the post-Sukarno Indonesian leaders, and the ethnically
Chinese "socialist" leaders of Singapore) remained perilously aware
of the proximity of China, and unalterably hostile to communist activities within their borders.

As with ASA, it was decided that ASEAN should have no permanent supranational authority, but should operate through national
secretariats and regular meetings at ministerial and subministerial
levels. Economic growth and diversification were immediately focused upon as a prime goal (particularly in the light of population
projections for the coming decades), and plans were drawn up to examine ways to facilitate this through cooperative endeavor.[15] It was
agreed that national and regional interests were in no way conflicting
and that a necessary precondition for "effective and meaningful re-

[13] See, for example, Jose Ma Sison, "Prospects for MAPHILINDO," *Eastern
World,* XVIII, July 1964.

[14] See, for example, Augustine Tan, "Singapore and Regional Cooperation,"
(unpublished paper delivered at the Regional Development Seminar, organized
by the Southeast Asia Development Advisory Group, East-West Center, Honolulu, July 6, 1970).

[15] For discussions of the functioning and achievements of ASEAN see, for
example, V. Kanapathy, "Towards a Strategy of Regional Economic Development," *Economic Review,* V, 2, 1969; and Barbara French Pace (and others),
*Regional Cooperation in Southeast Asia: The First Two Years of ASEAN,
1967–69,* (McLean, Va., Research Analysis Corporation, 1970).

gional growth is the emergence of dynamic national economies." [16]

Following discussion of this regional prosperity, let us now look at some of the concrete agreements and achievements of ASEAN. Indonesia, Thailand, and Malaysia, the tin-producing countries of the region, were able within the framework of ASEAN to come to an agreement on production and buffer stock arrangements in an effective effort to regulate fluctuations in the world price of the commodity. When prices fell all agreed to withhold stocks until recovery to a certain point was reached. As Malaysia, in particular, is critically dependent upon tin exports for foreign revenue, this agreement and its successful operation has been of enormous consequence. Educational, technological, and research cooperation has proceeded apace. In order to ensure concentrations of skills, and to avoid duplication, ASEAN has established centers for tropical biology in Indonesia, for mathematics and science in Malaysia, for agriculture in the Philippines, for tropical medicine in Thailand, and for English language study in Singapore. Determined to lessen the region's dependence upon the higher educational facilities and research skills of the erstwhile metropolitan powers, the ASEAN Ministers of Education conference has pushed ahead with schemes for mutual recognition of degrees, encouraging excellence in institutions where it already exists by judicious investment, and formulating and encouraging research programs of direct economic consequence to the region. Avoiding duplication of efforts has been considered of primary importance, and a Southeast Asia Iron and Steel Institute is to be established in Singapore. Tourism has been recognized as an area for potentially fruitful cooperation, and resources have been pooled and planning coordinated in an effort to attract more international tourists to the area, and once there to persuade them to explore beyond the chief tourist attractions of Bangkok, Singapore, and Bali. Aviation cooperation has resulted in a policy of equal traffic rights, and plans are under way to set up a joint ASEAN aviation "university" to lessen the dependence of the region's airlines on "expatriate" pilots. Shipping

[16] Mr. S. Rajaratnam, Singapore's Minister for Foreign Affairs, in his speech to the ASEAN meeting of foreign ministers held at Manila on March 12, 1971. (Published in full in *Singapore Newsletter,* III, 5, April 1971). Singapore, be it noted, has the most "dynamic" national economy in the area, yet the government realizes that this is threatened if the region as a whole does not prosper. The Singapore government itself invests in development projects in the region, and by tax concessions also encourages private capital to remain within Southeast Asia.

too is seen as an area of mutual concern and possible cooperation, although the capital investment necessary to establish a regional shipping line has yet to be found. Double-tax agreements have been reached between various ASEAN partners, and more are being negotiated. Although ASEAN is far from being a common market, considerable progress has in fact been made with trade liberalization, and the encouragement of intraregional trade. (It is estimated that in the past five years it has risen from 7–8 per cent to something in the order of 20 per cent.) Preferential tariffs have been designed to encourage manufacture of certain goods within the region (such as textiles, footwear, household appliances, light machinery, and plastic products) rather than importing them from outside. It is hoped to avoid competitive industrialization, so that cooperation in planning industrial development is going on at all levels. All the countries of the region are determined upon policies of self-sufficiency in food crops, but it is recognized that a common agricultural marketing policy in rubber, palm oil, and copra would be to the economic betterment of the area in the way that the tin agreement has been. Such a common agricultural marketing policy has yet to be agreed upon, but all concur as to its desirability, and work is proceeding toward it. Trade credit provisions have been liberalized and steps taken to encourage commercial banks to invest in development schemes. New links between the stock exchanges of the region have been established, and a progressive liberalization of trade shares is hoped for. Common efforts to attract investment to the region have been embarked upon with some success. Visa regulations have been modified, and it is hoped to phase them out altogether. Regional associations of such organizations as Chambers of Commerce, Manufacturers' Associations, and professional bodies and students' associations have burgeoned. Businessmen, in particular, have shown a rapid appreciation of the possibilities of intraregional cooperation, and the number of cross-national business ventures has been increased greatly. With each small success confidence is gained to venture more, and there is considerable talk now of the possible need for the establishment of a centralized bureaucracy and planning body to carry out the growing number of ASEAN projects and plans. Although there is still occasionally visionary talk of full regional integration, it should be stressed that on the whole the emphasis is pragmatic, and practical projects with the greatest chance of fairly immediate success appeal most.

Compared with European integrative achievements, all this may appear puny. But, given economic and political realities, it seems that successful completion of small tasks is likely to encourage further economic cooperation, whereas failure of grandiose schemes would have a deleterious effect on any movement toward ultimate regional integration. Even the theoreticians seem to concede that "developmental regionalism" or "developmental integration" might well be best suited to the nonindustrialized nations of the world in their efforts for economic growth,[17] and that the economic differences in these regions are so startlingly in contrast to those in Europe that the European model for integration may have little relevance to them. It is conceded that a more practical policy of regional integration for the less-developed countries "will have to devise more limited forms of integration," and that "the important thing is not so much free trade for the handful of existing industries, as it is the assurance of region-wide markets for new industries." [18]

Regionalism has attracted the political leaders of independent Southeast Asia as a possible way of improving the economies of their nations. It is sometimes suggested that fears of big-power domination have also been a goad, but analyzing the pronouncements of those politicians pressing for regional cooperation, one finds far greater stress upon economic considerations. So long as ASEAN is seen to be beneficial in this way so long will it be supported, and there is little doubt that its initial modesty has paid dividends in terms of feelings of achievement, and given it some built-in dynamism of its own. Since Sukarno's downfall, Indonesia has joined Thailand, the Philippines, and Malaysia in support of the free enterprise model for development, and the increased regional stability consequent upon ASEAN has attracted massive foreign investment, particularly in the field of oil exploration. Whatever the outcome of the Vietnam War, it seems unlikely that the territories of former Indo-China will be so committed; and it seems likely, therefore, that membership of ASEAN will not grow. Sihanouk and various Vietnamese leaders have talked of the possibility of reviving something like the French-created "Associated States of Indo-China," and it is not too far-fetched to foresee a Southeast Asian division along lines similar to

[17] See, for example, Lincoln Gordon, "Economic Regionalism Reconsidered," in *International Political Communities,* (Garden City, N. J., Anchor Books, 1966).
[18] *Ibid.,* p. 253

those present in Europe: Communist/non-Communist, with Burma studiedly maintaining her neutrality à la Austria. Both the United States and Japan have seen in Southeast Asian regional cooperation a hopeful bulwark against the spread of communism in the area, and both have committed large sums of aid for regional development. But the principal impetus has certainly come from Southeast Asians themselves, and regional pride has been a powerful spur to development. So long as "region building" can be seen to aid "nation building" will regional cooperation be practised, and (it is hoped by the more enlightened politicians of the area) the longer it goes on the more likely it is to become a habit. Southeast Asian regional cooperation seemingly developed not from mutual relevance, but from mutual need.

BIBLIOGRAPHY

Readers interested in further investigation of the subject of this article may wish to consult:

Chuko, William Yen. "Concepts of Regionalism in Southeast Asia," Ph.D. dissertation, New York University, 1965.

Crane, Robert Dickson. "Revolutionary Regionalism in Southeast Asia," *Reporter*, XXXVIII, May 1968.

Fifield, Russell. *Southeast Asia in United States Policy*, (New York, Praeger, 1963).

Foreign Affairs Bulletin (Government Printer, Bangkok). "Association of Southeast Asian Nations," VII, August–September 1967.

Gordon, Bernard K. "Economic impediments to regionalism in Southeast Asia," *Asian Survey*, III, 5, 1963.

——. "Problems of regional cooperation in Southeast Asia," *World Politics*, XVI, 2, 1964.

——. *Dimensions of Conflict in Southeast Asia*, (Englewood Cliffs, N. J., Prentice Hall, 1966).

——. "Regionalism and instability in Southeast Asia," in Joseph Nye (ed.), *International Regionalism*, (Boston, Little Brown, 1968).

——. "Regionalism in Southeast Asia," in Robert Tilman (ed.), *Man, State and Society in Southeast Asia*, (New York, Praeger, 1969).

Hanna, Willard A. *The Formation of Malaysia: New Factor in World Politics*, (New York, American Universities Field Staff Inc., 1964).

Hla, Myint. "The inward and outward looking countries of Southeast Asia and the economic future of the region," *Malayan Economic Review*, XII, 1, 1967.

Jo, Yung-hwan. "Regional cooperation in Southeast Asia and Japan's role," *Journal of Politics*, XXX, 2, 1968.

Kanapathy, V. "Towards a strategy of regional economic development," *Economic Review*, V, 2, 1969.

Keesing, Donald B. "Thailand and Malaysia: A case for a common market," *Malayan Economic Review*, X, 2, 1965.

Leifer, Michael. "Trends in regional association in Southeast Asia," *Asian Studies*, II, 1, 1964.

Mizan, "Regional cooperation in Southeast Asia: Soviet misgivings," IX, November–December 1967.

Morgan, Theodore, and Nyle Spoelstra. *Economic Interdependence in Southeast Asia*, (Madison, Wisc., University of Wisconsin Press, 1969).

Pace, Barbara French (and others). *Regional Cooperation in Southeast Asia: The First Two Years of ASEAN, 1967–69*, (McLean, Va., Research Analysis Corporation, 1970).

Pankin, M. "The position of Southeast Asian countries in the world capitalist market," in Thomas Perry Thornton (ed.), *The Third World in Soviet Perspective*, (Princeton, N. J., Princeton University Press, 1964).

Philippines International Law Journal, "The Federation of Malaya, the Republic of the Philippines, and the Republic of Indonesia: Conference of Foreign Ministers," (documents), II, January–June 1963.

Pollard, Vincent K. "ASA and ASEAN, 1961–67: Southeast Asian regionalism," *Asian Survey*, X, 3, 1970.

Ramos, Nareiso. "Association of Southeast Asia (ASA) and the Philippines," *United Asia*, XVIII, November–December 1966.

Shizuo, Maruyama. "Asian Regionalism," *Japan Quarterly*, XV, January–March 1968.

Sison, Jose Ma. "Prospects for MAPHILINDO," *Eastern World*, XVIII, July 1964.

Taylor, Alastair. "Malaysia, Indonesia and MAPHILINDO," *International Journal*, XIX, Spring 1964.

Vernant, Jaques. "Les états-unis et l'asie du sud-est," *Revue de defense nationale*, XX, April 1964.

Wang Gung-wu. "Nation formation and regionalism in Southeast Asia," in Margaret Grant (ed.), *South Asia Pacific Crisis: National Development and the World Community*, (New York, Dodd Mead & Co., 1964).

Wilcox, Clair. "Regional cooperation in Southeast Asia," *Malayan Economic Review*, IX, 2, 1964.

Yamamoto, Noburu. "The possibility of regional economic integration in Southeast Asia," *Developing Economies*, 2, March 1964.

The Political Economy of Land Reform

JAMES B. STEPANEK

Introduction

Land reform attempts to redistribute rights in agricultural land for the benefit of small farmers, tenants, and farm workers. Admittedly, social inequality and the inefficient use of land do not spring from a maldistribution of ownership alone. Public efforts to educate farmers, to improve their livestock, seed, and to update their techniques are needed as well, and must be included in the broadest sense of the term "land reform." But such matters are excluded from the focus of this paper in order to concentrate on the single topic of the equalization of land ownership. This study, then, is about the redistribution of land titles in Colombia and Taiwan; our purpose is to establish a link between the political process in these countries and the specific social and economic problems that tenure reform was designed to remedy. The inclusion of Colombia and Taiwan as case studies is motivated by my experience as an agricultural extensionist and as a student in first one and then the other of these countries.

Land reform was seriously undertaken for the first time in Colombia and Taiwan to save a political situation. At that particular time in their history both countries faced imminent political collapse. Since the 1948 assassination of Jorge Eliécer Gaitan, leader of the reformist wing of the Liberal Party, Colombia began a ten-year period of unconstrained violence in the countryside between men of the same families and between towns and villages—violence that Orlando Fals-Borda estimates minimally spent the lives of 200,000 individuals and caused immeasurable destruction of rural property between 1948 and 1960.[1] Moderates of both parties saw a relationship between land reform and peace. Accordingly, after the founding

[1] German Guzman Campos, Orlando Fals-Borda, and Eduardo Umaña Luna, *La Violencia en Colombia* (Bogotá: Ediciones Tercer Mundo, 1964), pp. 362–71.

of a new coalition party in 1958 called the *Frente Nacional,* or National Front between Conservatives and Liberals, the government began to attack problems of land tenancy in order to redress grievances in the countryside that were held to be partly responsible for the epoch of *La Violencia.* Another reason for the impetus given land reform was the fear aroused in the Colombian oligarchy by the Cuban revolution.

After Japan was defeated in the Pacific a *Kuomintang* (abbreviated KMT) provincial governor was sent over to reinstate Chinese rule in Taiwan. Governor Ch'en Yi was a typical carpetbagger of that period, whose oppressive government provoked a rebellion among Taiwanese on August 28, 1947. The uprising was quickly subdued, the governor was removed expeditiously from his post, and was later promoted to the governorship of Chiang Kai-shek's home province of Chekiang. However, he was shot a year later as a "communist conspirator." Such were the remarkable twists in that era of Chinese history. In 1949 the Nationalist government was driven to Taiwan leaving the mainland in communist hands. The Nationalist land reform program for Taiwan was launched immediately thereafter and was implemented for reasons similar to the Colombian case in one respect: the government wanted to consolidate its control of rural areas after a period of war in an attempt to prevent another insurrection. In both Colombia and Taiwan agrarian reform was not a *fan shen,* or "turning over," as the Chinese say, but was promulgated peacefully by the party in power.

Agrarian Reform in Colombia

Colombian agriculture today was molded by the land pattern established as a result of the Spanish conquest of the sixteenth century and by population growth in the nineteenth and twentieth centuries. Over a period of time the structure of land tenure has taken on features that appear irrational from the economic standpoint. With the exception of the savanna north of Bogotá and valley land near Medellín and Cali, large estates occupy the flat, fertile valleys and plateaus while small intensively farmed *minifundio* (family subsistence plots of less than .5 hectare) occupy the less productive hillsides. Farms of five hectares or under make up 56 per cent of the enterprises but occupy only 4 per cent of the agricultural acreage; farms between 100 and 500 hectares, however, occupy 33 per cent of the land but only 3 per cent of the enterprises.[2] According to the Economic Research Service, 25 per cent of Colombia's farmers in 1960 were tenants, which is below the average for Latin America.[3] But the remaining owner-operated farms were often so small, fragmented, or poor in quality that their owners were as destitute as tenants and farm laborers.

Under the Colombian tenancy system the landowner leases his land and collects rent in the form of money or produce from cultivators on small holdings who work the land with their own livestock. The rent may be in the form of a fixed amount per hectare or a share of the crop, the latter being by far the most prevalent form. If he is a large owner he may live in Bogotá and collect rents through a hierarchy of agents and subagents. Agricultural management in such instances is dependent on finding a good *mayordomo,* or overseer of the estate, who will consistently deliver a lucrative remuneration without making demands upon the landlord for money to finance capital improvements. Colombia's population growth was, for a period during the 1960s, the highest in Latin America, exceeding an annual growth rate of 3 per cent. Landless peasants who are without work may swell the unemployed urban mass in Bogotá or Barranquilla and contribute to political unrest of the sort already common in São Paulo and Buenos Aires.

Previous to the agrarian reform law a few government agencies had a degree of contact with the countryside. A ministry of Agriculture was founded in 1947, but was impotent and disorganized except in the provinces of Cundinamarca and Antioquia, where it worked actively in reforestation and soil conservation. In the coffee regions of Caldas, Antioquia, Tolima, and the Valle de Cauca a cooperative association, the *Federacíon Nacional de Cafeteros,* has been in existence since 1927 to provide easy credit and the facility of central warehouses to the many small coffee growers who now characterize this industry.

Colombia's Agrarian Reform Law 135 was passed in December,

[2] The International Bank of Reconstruction and Development, *The Agricultural Development of Colombia* (Washington: IBRD, 1955), p. 68.

[3] Economic Research Service, *Changes in Agriculture in 26 Developing Nations, 1948–1963* (Washington, D. C.: Economic Research Service, 1963), p. 37.

1961. It established the Colombian Agrarian Reform Institute (*Instituto Colombiano de la Reforma Agraria,* or simply INCORA), set up a National Agrarian Fund to finance the agency's activities, and provided for the extinction of title to unused lands.[4] To this end the law called for payment for uncultivated lands with 25-year 2 per cent bonds and payment for inadequately cultivated lands partly in cash and partly in non-negotiable government securities repayable in eight annual installments with 4 per cent annual interest. Payment for adequately cultivated lands was partly in cash (a higher maximum cash payment was provided for here), and partly in non-negotiable government securities, repayable in five annual installments with a 6 per cent annual interest.

This law limited the scope of INCORA operations from its very inception. Short terms of payment and large cash and interest payments made expropriation of land on a large scale prohibitively expensive. The law stipulated that only certain lands were subject to expropriation in the social interest. These were lands needed to remedy severe *minifundio* conditions, those needed to help set up farmers on new land due to soil impoverishment of their lands, and third, those in the way of road and irrigation projects.[5] Lands expropriated by INCORA were to be sold to the future owner at their purchase price, plus the cost of any improvements made by INCORA. This might have been a reasonable guideline to follow were it not for the high cost of expropriated land, as we shall see. Furthermore, INCORA was often prompted to invest heavily in the land before it was parceled and sold to farmers, thus raising the sales price to them. The new cultivators, poorly educated and sometimes middle-aged men, were often not competent to extricate themselves from debt in their working lifetime.

Subsequent to the enactment of Law 135, the *Instituto Colombiano Agropecuario* (ICA) was launched with aid from the Ford, Kellogg, and Rockefeller foundations to conduct agricultural research and rural extension activities; and in July 1963 INCORA received from the United States a ten-million dollar USAID loan to begin what has in recent years grown into its biggest program consisting of supervised credit to owner-cultivators.

[4] Ernest A. Duff, *Agrarian Reform in Colombia* (New York: Frederick A. Praeger, 1968), p. 45.
[5] Duff, p. 165.

IMPLEMENTATION OF THE LAW

It was the intention of Enrique Peñalosa, INCORA's first Director, to concentrate the agency's effort on carefully selected geographic regions, rather than to dissipate its resources in an attempt to bring agrarian reform to every corner of the country.[6] Given its limited resources and the animosity directed against it by conservatives, INCORA thought it best to work where there existed a potential for rapid increases in agricultural output and not where rural poverty was necessarily most acute.

In July, 1962, INCORA embarked on one of its first projects. It soon developed problems that are indicative of what it has had to face ever since. Nariño No. 1, as the area was designated, was centered near Pasto, the capital of a southern Andean province. It was naturally divided into two distinct geographic regions, both possessing land well-suited for farming; these were the high savanna near Pasto and the eastern slope of the Andes. INCORA had two goals in mind in planning the project. On the high savanna the basic problem was one of extremely fragmented holdings existing alongside extensively farmed *latifundio,* or giant estates. INCORA intended to buy these estates and later redistribute them on a rational basis, at the same time giving technical help and credit. On the eastern slope of the Andes, INCORA faced the problem of squatters who had occupied public land. INCORA proposed to assist these people by constructing access roads and providing technical assistance, in addition to adjudicating land titles to the squatters. Fifty million pesos was allocated for both areas over a three-year period.

According to *El Tiempo,* the large landowners of Nariño saw the project as a threat to their interests and banded together in mid 1962 in the *Asociacíon de Agricultores* to lobby covertly for its early demise.[7] When echoes of the battle between INCORA and the Nariño landowners reached Bogotá, the *Sociedad de Agricultores Colombianos,* a national society of country squires and land speculators—not cultivators as the name implies—entered the dispute on the side of the Nariño landowners. The *Sociedad,* while affirming its philosophical support of land reform, declared that INCORA was attempting to corrupt the reform in that province by expropriating adequately exploited farms as small as 50 hectares.[8] This prompted an immedi-

---

[6] *Ibid.,* p. 51.   [7] *El Tiempo,* October 17, 1962, p. 4.   [8] *Ibid.*

ate rejoinder from Peñalosa to the effect that negotiations in progress were for the purchase of 94 hectares, that the farms in question were owned mostly by absentee landowners, and that they permitted their land to be farmed extensively. He conceded that a few ranches of less than 100 hectares were slated for purchase or expropriation, but these were instances in which the land was known to be owned by men who had ten or fifteen such ranches up and down the province. Peñalosa was skeptical that strong opposition would materialize, and he is quoted as saying that ". . . these people are getting nowhere. Thanks to the efforts of the Church and others our project in Nariño will be successful." [9] In retrospect, Enrique Peñalosa's estimate of the relative power of INCORA and its antagonists was not at all realistic. Nearly three years after Nariño No. 1 was begun, only 4,287 hectares had been acquired of the 30,000 originally planned for redistribution. The landlords were forcing INCORA into six-month proceedings in almost every expropriation case. When the deadline for the project's completion elapsed, only 151 families had been resettled. The best estimate of the average cost per family settled in INCORA's two earliest parcelization efforts (Tolima No. 1 and Nariño No. 1) came to approximately 60,000 pesos.[10] At this time the Catholic Church officially favored land reform, a decision perhaps made without misgivings, since its vast *latifundio* holdings had been expropriated by the state 112 years earlier.

INCORA'S NEW PRIORITIES

The political climate of the time influenced the direction taken by INCORA in the second half of the 1960s. As early as 1959 the hegemony of the National Front was precarious. The *Alianza Nacional Popular* and the Conservative *Laureanistas* on the right, plus the *Movimiento Revolucionario Liberal* on the left, constituted the "outsiders" in Colombian politics. Their reasons for opposing land reform under the auspices of the moderates fell into the proverbial "too much" or "too little" categories. Conservative pressure upon the government was especially strong during the four years of the Valencia administration (1962–1966), when there was almost a complete halt in the redistribution of land titles. According to one writer, the Valencia government eventually produced INCORA's and Peñalosa's

[9] *Ibid.*, October 21, 1962, p. 1.
[10] Jaime Martinez Cardena, "La Reforma Agraria Colombiana," in *Revista Javeriana* (Bogotá: La Javeriana, 1963), p. 27.

"agonizing reappraisal" of what they thought to be the agrarian problem in Colombia, leading to two astonishing conclusions that, (1) there was doubt as to whether Colombia's land tenure system really created many inequities, and (2) that there was not enough good, un-utilized farm land in western Colombia to justify a program of ex-propriation of *latifundias*.[11] The switch in policy from an emphasis on tenure reform to colonization and other projects is often blamed on a concurrent shift in United States policy toward social reform in Latin America. It is true that the Johnson Administration empha-sized the technical features of land reform under the Alliance for Progress, rather than the expropriation feature written into the charter of Punta del Este. In this particular case, however, a close reading of the popular press of the time and hints from other sources suggest that the change was due to a coalition of indigenous conser-vative pressure groups that were not influenced by United States pol-icy one way or the other.

Since 1966 INCORA has emphasized more high-cost irrigation, road, and land reclamation projects in the Rio Magdalena Valley and elsewhere. This kind of work is, of course, motivated by political factors, for the economic facts of the case would indicate that the idle holdings of large landlords be distributed before farmers are set-tled on barren public domain far from reliable markets, without roads, schools, and government services. Cost estimates by the Ex-port-Import Bank have shown that colonization and reclamation in the less desirable agricultural areas of Colombia require large invest-ments in land, education, and equipment.[12] But these schemes, though costly to society at large, are not politically abrasive. Thus, INCORA projects a "technical" rather than a "social" image for its operations: supervised credit receives top priority and other pro-grams skirt the century-old socioeconomic relationships of the proj-ect areas.

The Taiwan Case

Taiwan represents a country that is ahead of Colombia economi-cally, and one that is growing prodigiously. The rate of economic growth in Taiwan is the highest among the countries in the Far East, with the exceptions of Japan and Korea. Taiwan regularly achieves a

[11] Duff, p. 77.   [12] *Ibid.*, p. 100.

4 per cent per capita growth of national product that is distributed more equitably than it is among the Colombian population.[13] On the other hand, the rate of population increase of 3.7 per cent during the early 1960s surpassed the demographic growth rate of all Latin American countries during the same period. Taiwan's population in late 1969 of 14,312,000 persons was augmented by the influx of 2,-500,000 refugees from the mainland before 1950. The island's population density of 802 persons per square mile is also among the world's highest figures, and represents a concentration of human beings about five times greater than in western Colombia. Until recently the pressure of population on land in Taiwan was alleviated when the doubling of the population was almost matched by a commensurate increase of the farmland from 1905 to 1945. Since the war the population has doubled again, but the amount of arable land has not.

In 1945 Taiwan was retrocessed to China after fifty years of Japanese rule. It is interesting that the colonial period left a feeling of good will between the inhabitants of Taiwan and the Japanese, but this might only reflect the tendency to see them in a better light when their behavior is contrasted with the first *Kuomintang* provincial administration. In 1949 the Chinese Nationalists were routed by the communists except on the offshore islands of Chin men and Ma tzu, and on Taiwan itself, where communism had been kept at bay during Japanese suzerainty of the island. In that year land reform was again thought to be a paramount political necessity, as it had been on the mainland for the past twenty years.

Agriculture in Taiwan is characterized by land-intensive farming and the use of abundant labor inputs. The subtropical and tropical climates in Taiwan permit the production of three or four crops a year on the same piece of land. In addition to the heavy labor demands for seeding, transplanting, weeding, and harvesting the crops, which consist principally of sugar cane, sweet potatoes, and several varieties of rice, the system of year-around cropping employed in most of Taiwan requires labor to replenish large quantities of plant materials into the soil. The frequent application of chemical fertilizer

---

[13] Shigeto Kawano, "The Reasons for Taiwan's High Growth Rate," in *Economic Development Issues: Greece, Israel, Taiwan and Thailand* (New York: Frederick A. Praeger, 1968), p. 125. Also see Lorenz Curves provided by Ernest A. Duff, *Agrarian Reform in Colombia* (New York: Frederick A. Praeger, 1968), p. 102.

and periodic spreading of insecticides by hand are other labor-consuming jobs. Under a system of agricultural exploitation of this kind, extra effort and care by the peasant will often boost the yield substantially, but such marginal exertion is not forthcoming in Taiwan nor is it in Colombia—unless he works under a land tenure system that rewards him fairly.

The Japanese left the rural economy in a state quite changed from what it was in 1895 when they arrived. They encouraged irrigation and advanced the scientific cultivation of rice and sugar cane. In an effort to integrate Taiwan into the Japanese orbit socially and economically, the government subsidized migration from the homeland, and committed itself to harbor construction, roads, agricultural research, and extension work.[14] Japan's contributions to Taiwan's rural economic development that in hindsight have weighed heaviest in succeeding events are: (1) Reliable cadastral records that made an immediate implementation of the agrarian reform program possible in 1949: (2) An early extension service to educate farmers at large. Ideas regarding the exploitation of cash crops, the selection of good seed, and the efficient use of irrigation were widely disseminated and put to use. The response that extension workers in Colombia and Taiwan usually receive among farmers is dramatically different. Alongside the rather torpid Colombian *campesino,* the peasant of Taiwan is indeed a rapacious profiteer. And, (3) the Japanese bequeathed to the successor mainland administration tropical fruit export monopolies, mostly in sugar and bananas, which helped earn foreign exchange in the difficult years between 1949 and 1953.[15]

The land reform agency in Taiwan that corresponds roughly to INCORA in orientation and function, is the JCRR, or Sino-American Joint Commission for Rural Reconstruction. Like INCORA, the JCRR received aid grants from the United States equal to the local currency equivalent of 98 million American dollars between 1950 and 1964.[16] The basic philosophy of the JCRR, set forth by its Chairman Chiang Mon-lin, was that the program should achieve two fundamental principles; social justice, interpreted to mean the de-

[14] Anthony Y. C. Koo, *The Role of Land Reform in Economic Development: A Case Study of Taiwan* (New York: Frederick A. Praeger, 1968), p. 25.

[15] Koo, p. 25.

[16] Douglas Mendel, *The Politics of Formosan Nationalism* (Berkeley: The University of California Press, 1970) p. 69.

mocratization of the control of income of the agricultural sector, and second, an increase in the material well-being of the peasant class by raising the market value of their yields.[17] To emphasize one principle to the neglect of the other was avoided in the belief that ". . . working for social justice alone would achieve but an equalization of poverty, whereas working for increased production alone would widen the gap between the have's and have-not's." [18] Unlike INCORA, however, the JCRR did strike a balance between these two objectives. Its "material well-being" program included many hundreds of diverse projects. The land distribution program per se came in three steps; rent reduction was enforced in 1949, the sale of public land occurred in 1951, and was followed by the land-to-the-tiller program in 1953.

RENT REDUCTION AND THE SALE OF PUBLIC LAND

In April, 1949, a law known as the "Regulations Governing the Lease of Private Farm Lands" was passed by the provincial government of Taiwan. (The Taiwan provincial government is dominated by the *Kuomintang,* but is nevertheless situated in the provincial capital of Chung hsing Hsin ts'un. The "national government" in Taipei still maintains bureaus and committees for the various provincial affairs, and claims adamantly to represent the legitimate seat of government of all 35 provinces on the communist-controlled mainland.) Stage one of the reform provided for the mandatory reduction of the annual land rent from the prevailing 50 to 70 per cent to 37.5 per cent of the main crop. The figure of 37.5 had been adopted by the KMT in 1930 but was not implemented. In places where the rent was already below the 37.5 per cent level it could not be raised. Moreover, leases had to be written and honored for at least six years. All extra burdens on the peasant, such as advance rent payments or security deposits, were prohibited.

How was the first step of agrarian reform to be enforced, given the rather low rent ceiling of 37.5 per cent? Fortunately, the Japanese had made a detailed working cadastral system under which the categories, grades, and areas of private land had been painstakingly investigated, surveyed, and the land rights registered. Perhaps because it had been made by a severe, but fair, colonial power, the objectivity of its records was never disputed by either landlord or tenant. These

[17] Koo, p. 114. [18] *Ibid.*

records were the basis for determining what the rent ought to be by calculating the average yield for all grades of paddy and dry land.

By June, 1949, or after a lapse of only two months, a total of 377,364 contracts for private farmland under lease had been duly revised. The follow-up program included spot inspection by the provincial government for possible violations of new lease terms, and 34,-800 irregularities were discovered and corrected.[19] Landlords often attempted to compensate for a loss in land rent by charging house rent or by inventing other new fees. Uneducated tenants were persuaded not to report themselves as tenants, in which case, since there was no one claiming tenancy rights, the landlord could dictate the contract.[20] But according to most sources the peasants of Taiwan during this time were not easily browbeaten by landlords. In Colombia, however, most tenants are afraid to venture even the most circumspect words about the weather in the presence of the landlord; very few indeed have been able to summon up the courage to challenge him on the important issue of rent.

Since land value is closely connected with the rent landlords are able to command, the reduction of rent in Taiwan had the effect of depressing the free market value of farmland leased to tenant farmers. A study made by the Cabinet Rent Reduction Inspection team found that the average decline in the value of tenanted land after rent reduction was from one third to one half of the pre-reform values.[21] The fall in land prices was significant because it set in motion price changes that may fundamentally alter the Taiwanese rural society. For example, the decline in land values tended to be more precipitous for leased land than for owner-cultivated land. In one locale the value of an owner-cultivated paddy field was about 5,000 Taiwan dollars per acre, while a leased field of identical quality was valued at only 2,920 Taiwan dollars per acre.[22] Such a free market price differential worked to penalize absentee landowners, capital gains tended to accrue to the owner-cultivator, and farmland speculation was less profitable.

[19] *Ibid.*, p. 32.
[20] Bernard Gallin, *Hsin Hsing: A Taiwanese Agricultural Village* (Ithaca, New York: Cornell University Press, 1961), p. 131.
[21] C. Cheng, *Land Reform in Taiwan* (Taipei: China Publishing Company, 1961), p. 45.
[22] *Ibid.*, p. 310.

At the close of the Second World War a total of 434,000 acres of Japanese property was seized. The land represented the former holdings of Japanese immigrants, private industries, and plantations. Under the second stage of land reform inaugurated in June, 1951, a portion of this property was sold to peasants, with preference being given to tenants as a matter of policy. The sales price was set at two-and-one-half times the annual yield of the main crop, repayable in twenty semiannual installments at 4 per cent interest. Peasants numbering 139,688 took advantage of this program to buy farms.[23]

STEP THREE: LAND-TO-THE-TILLER

The last phase of the reform began in 1953 to help tenants become landowners at easy terms, to protect the legal rights of the landlords during the transition period, and, ultimately, to convert the landholdings of the expropriated landlords into industrial holdings. The degree to which the program really gave "land to the tiller," so to speak, is remarkable. Chang Yen-t'ien estimates that in Taiwan about 46.4 per cent of the total pre-reform tenants, including part-tenants, purchased land through the reform program.[24] In all, 143,568 hectares were redistributed. Landlords were paid near market prices for expropriated land and were allowed to retain 7.2 acres of medium-grade land to farm themselves or until they found another livelihood in the city. Of the total compensation to landlords, 70 per cent of the land value was paid in rice and sweet potato bonds (which hedged against inflation and guaranteed a steady income). The other 30 per cent was paid in public enterprise stock. The Taiwan Cement and Taiwan Paper corporations have prospered in the last decade, but shares of the other corporations have declined in value on the stock exchange.

The tenant occupying expropriated land was given the first option to buy it. Installments were to be paid over ten years and no single payment, plus the land tax, was to exceed 37.5 per cent of the annual main crop yield. By the end of stage three, tenure reform in Taiwan had accomplished many of its goals: over 377,000 lease contracts were revised under the tenancy law; about 140,000 families bought

[23] W. G. Goddard, *The Makers of Taiwan* (Taipei, 1963), p. 192.

[24] Chang Yen-t'ien, *Land Reform in Taiwan* (Taichung: The Department of Agricultural Economics, Taiwan Provincial College of Agriculture, 1954), p. 86.

public land during stage two; and in the final step of the reform 106,000 landlords sold their land to the government, which in turn sold it to 195,000 families under the land-to-the-tiller program.

A Comparison of Tenure Reform in Colombia and Taiwan

We shall now contrast the problems that INCORA and the JCRR faced in common and those that were unique to one country or the other, the response of INCORA and the JCRR to these problems, and lastly, the rural society and political milieu in each country.

1) A fundamental difference between the pre-reform agrarian structure in Colombia and Taiwan is that in Colombia the land was there but landlords tried to deny access to it and not, as in Taiwan, simply to charge higher prices for its use. From the start INCORA and the JCRR had to work under different conditions inherited from the old social order. For example, in nearly every case land expropriated in Colombia did not have the facilities for agricultural exploitation; roads, wells, fences, homes, and schools had to be constructed *in toto,* usually by farmers unfamiliar with many aspects of their new surroundings, particularly the soil and market. In Taiwan during steps one and three of land reform the JCRR gave farmers legal title to the ground they already occupied (in the majority of cases) where capital investments in land terraces, water works, homes, and bridges had been made over generations.

2) If land-tenure reform is compromising and gradual there is a greater likelihood that high costs of expropriation will be incurred. In the words of Doreen Warriner, "The more scope for exemption, the more scope for litigation and corruption." [25] The speed with which INCORA and the JCRR acquired land deserves special attention.

The JCRR swiftly took possession of all property above 7.17 acres that was not personally cultivated by the owner and his family. Land acquired by the JCRR was offered for resale on the same basis as farmland it compulsorily purchased—namely, at a price 2.5 times the total amount of the annual main crop yield for the respective land grades. In retrospect, the unequivocal way the JCRR executed

[25] Doreen Warriner, *Land Reform in Principle and Practice* (London, England: The Clarendon Press, 1969), p. 19.

steps one and three of the reform helped to communicate to the landed gentry in a credible way that it was useless to resist. The sense of panic among landlords led many of them to sell their land quickly, and in many cases cheaply, to get the entire proceeds in cash. They feared this would not be so if they waited any longer. During this period in Taiwan many tenants and poor farmers bought paddy and dry land they could never have afforded before or since then.

INCORA did not move with any haste. A year elapsed before it opened its central headquarters in Bogotá, and many more months passed before it opened offices in the provinces. In April, 1962, the first major land parcelling project began in eastern Tolima, but it had adjudicated land to only 581 families by 1966. In other provinces today plans to expropriate large tracts of private land have been shelved or left unfinished. Among inveterate cynics it has even become a matter of dispute as to which group benefited most by this limited expropriation of land. Was it the recipients of the land or the expropriated? Some landowners undoubtedly used INCORA to dispose of unwanted and unused lands at prices above the market price. Rumors abound concerning landowners who correctly assessed the probability of expropriation, set a high bargaining price for their land accordingly, and reaped profits from the sale to INCORA. A study made for INCORA by the Agustin Codazzi Geographic Institute showed that in ten municipalities in Tolima, Huila, and Norte de Santander, where INCORA projects were either begun or imminent, the evaluation of rural farmlands undertaken by the landlords produced an average increase in evaluation of 143 per cent.[26] However, the study did not persuade INCORA that it was enriching expropriated landlords. By not asserting their presence in the countryside quickly, the landlords had time to muster a strong counterattack politically and in the courtroom, which should have been foreseen in a country that boasts a lawyer in every family.

3) It is sometimes feared that the fragmentation of land holdings into smaller ones will cause efficiency to fall. But too many factors bear on the question to permit one to make the neat dichotomy that land redistribution spells disaster for "modern," that is, large-scale, agriculture as it is known in North America. For example, a large ranch encompassing thousands of hectares may still be unable to em-

26 CIDA, *Tenancia de la Tierra*, p. 406, Table M-3.

ploy modern machinery efficiently if the owner permits only the lot behind his house to be cultivated so that the rest can be pasture for bulls. In this case, land parcelization may lead to a statistical drop in the size of the average enterprise. But in fact something quite different may have transpired if there had been an increase in the number of farm units cultivating cash crops extensively.

Tenure reform in Taiwan has redistributed title to land already highly fragmented both physically and legally. There has been a trend, accelerated by the land reform program, for the size of the holdings to get smaller. This trend has continued into 1971. Today the average Taiwanese farming household tills just under one hectare.[27] According to Dr. T. H. Lee, Chief of the JCRR's Rural Economics Division, steps are now being taken to reverse this trend so that more farm units can profitably use new Japanese wet farming techniques and machinery.

Since many ranches in western Colombia are too large in relation to the absentee owner's ability to manage or invest in it, the expropriation of these large properties and their distribution into family farms may lead to an increase in production by putting comparatively good soil under cultivation. The belief that agrarian reform means the division of efficient large farms into inefficient small ones is generally not true, because in the fertile highlands of western Colombia, where the population is concentrated, the large under-utilized ranches persist. In any case, the farm size which maximizes output per farm laborer is a variable dependent on several factors, such as the density of farm population expressed in the man–land ratio, the type of land—determined on the one hand by the grade of soil and on the other by the market—and by methods of production which should reflect the relative scarcity and productivity of agricultural inputs. In the province of Boyacá INCORA imagined it was possible to scientifically determine almost to the square meter the optimum size of a family farm. It has proceeded to invest in canals, drainage facilities, walls and fences of trees—all of which means that IN-CORA engineers are making decisions based on a priori assumptions about future market price relationships. Many people in Colombia acquiesce in the prevailing wisdom so current in poor countries that what is small scale is antiquated. According to Professor Duff, the

[27] Provincial Government of Taiwan, Department of Agriculture and Forestry, *Taiwan Agricultural Yearbook: 1970 Edition* (Chung Hsing Hsin ts'un: The Provincial Government of Taiwan, June, 1970), pp. 32 and 48.

optimum size for the majority of agricultural enterprises in Colombia is the farm that can be tended by one man and his family, with perhaps one or two hired hands.[28] This statement is persuasive if we interpret it to apply to Colombia today and not ten years hence.

4) INCORA and the JCRR were not given the financial resources to transform the countryside, and it is inconceivable that they will get the appropriations to do so. Thus, the extent to which they have motivated farmers to invest more of their own resources to improve agricultural productivity is more important than their own modest investments in public works. If agrarian reform does not increase the incentives of those who till the soil its results may be provisional.

Many policies have been tried in Colombia to inculcate *campesinos* with a "modern" innovative mentality (including the conscious policy of doing absolutely nothing). Patriotism, for example, was tried, but the admonition popular in early INCORA broadcasts, "Ask not what your country can do for you but what you can do for your country," was considered a disingenuous appeal by peasants, who thought it was an excuse not to help them and a pretext to exploit their own meager resources by raising taxes. Nor did paternalism succeed, as typified by free tree nurseries once maintained by the Ministry of Agriculture. But when farmers were rewarded for hard work, when the benefits of better farming accrued to themselves, as they did in the coffee regions of Colombia for some time, the results have been as good as they were unexpected. Tenure reform is a common-sense way to ensure that hard work and favorable prices benefit the farmer and his family. This is not usually known to happen in Colombia when the cultivator and owner are different individuals. The basic idea is reflected in Arthur Young's well-known remark about the magic of ownership turning sand into gold.

But the problem is more complex than this. Not all Colombian farmers are necessarily motivated in the same way as were the industrious farmers of Belgium who inspired Young's words. Nor is the problem in Colombia merely one of tenancy. It involves *minifundistas,* or small landowners, who cannot live on the miniature farms they own without sinking into debt. Economists are forever perplexed that sociological phenomena, which can be difficult to define let alone measure, inexorably enter the problem under study to the detriment of tidy predictions. This is such a case. Will land that is

---

[28] Duff, p. 106.

redistributed in Colombia or Taiwan necessarily be farmed profitably by the new owner? A partial answer is that it depends largely on what sort of fellow this new owner is. The attitude of the beneficiary toward independent farming and material rewards is an important question because these are the incentives associated with ownership. This attitude, related to the desire for land ownership, often reflects the social institutions of a feudatory past; from experience in Colombia it seems possible to distinguish between the attitudes characteristic of *campesinos* (a broad term that designates the vast rural population of share croppers, part-owners, small independent farmers, and even tenants) and *peónes* (serfs who work for a landlord without a cash wage in exchange for the chance to husband the remaining top soil in the most undesirable part of the landlords domain). Although *peónes* form a small percentage of the rural population, they are conspicuously poor. The *campesino,* with ample land to support a family comfortably, and the *peón,* with no education, land, or inheritance whatsoever, represent the uncommon extremes. Each group, and those in between, plays a slightly different social and economic role and is likely to have acquired different values from the prevailing rural society. The experience of many observers in Colombia can be synthesized thus: that *campesinos* who own some land are possessed by an insatiable craving to become independent farmers for reasons of income, security, independence, and also for reasons of status. *Peónes* are at the bottom of the social scale (but still above Blacks) and are unlike *campesinos* in that they want to be free from the need to work, except to the extent necessary to subsist. Once basic needs are met the incentive to work drops off sharply. If a former *peón* receives land he may use it to feed himself, consuming more and marketing less. Here there exists a possible conflict between social equality and increased production. Former serfs and old peasants too aged or feeble to adapt to new ways have therefore been largely excluded from INCORA programs because they are a high risk.

Tenure reform may not only encourage farmers to work harder on land they own but may encourage them to be more attentive to the details of farm management. The Regional Director of INCORA, economist Alberto Carro, argues that this is the case in his country. A tenant may be cognizant for years of a simple way to increase the harvest, a small technical innovation perhaps, but he does not use it while under the surveillance of the landlord who may raise the rent when the tenant is seen living better than a tenant is expected to live.

There is a statute in Colombia to protect tenants against extortion, but it is not taken seriously by the authorities.

The incentive mainspring of agricultural development in Colombia has scarcely been tapped by INCORA. The large under-utilized ranches, frequently endowed with Colombia's richest soil and near highways and cities (transportation and markets), represent a logical place to settle tenants and *minifundistas.* Statistics on farm size and productivity suggest that wide-scale expropriation of idle land would increase output more than the present colonization schemes. For instance, small farms (from 0 to 5 hectares) account for 20 per cent of Colombia's total agricultural production by value, despite the fact that they comprise a mere 6 per cent of Colombia's farmland, while estates of 50 to 200 hectares produce but 19 per cent of the country's agricultural output, even though they constitute 25 per cent of the total farm acreage. The most productive class of farmers are the small owners of between 5 and 50 hectares who produce 46 per cent of the country's agricultural produce by value on 23 per cent of the land.[29]

Today INCORA extends credit, technical assistance, and in other ways concentrates its resources on the technical and financial aspects of land development. The research stations of ICA have already achieved impressive results with new strains of barley, wheat, rice, potatoes, and forage crops. When these are disseminated widely it may inaugurate a "green revolution" comparable to the spectacular increases in wheat yields in Mexico and in the production of rice in the Philippines. It may exaggerate the inequality between rich and poor in Colombia (the above-mentioned high-yield strains require large capital investments) and create unforeseen political problems that overshadow the short-run gains in agricultural productivity. Finally, INCORA projects tend to be expensive in terms of their opportunity cost. There are tens of thousands of capable Colombian farmers who aspire to own their own land but cannot for a variety of economic and psychological reasons. The high per capita cost of technical assistance may be related to the feeling of despair and resignation many of them feel toward their livelihood. Two educational foundations that work in rural areas north of Bogotá, SENA and *La Fundacíon de Antonio Puerto,* reported that they spent approximately 400 pesos or 24 American dollars, per person during every

[29] *Ibid.,* p. 121.

ten-hour session of their joint outdoor demonstrations that averaged eight men per class. According to the report the farmers felt that the techniques they learned could not realistically be used on their own land, where fertilizer sacks had to be hoisted up the mountain by donkey, the supply of water was irregular, and such primitive agricultural implements as the hoe and sickle proved more suited to cultivation on the parched hillsides than more modern equipment advertised by the foundations. A follow-up survey revealed that few farmers had applied their new knowledge to improve their crop yields. Perhaps the cost of investment in education is not as closely related to the lack of information as to the disinclination to use it. Investment in people, in their education, and so forth differs fundamentally from investment in land and machinery; crops, it is observed, respond in a predictable way to irrigation or to the application of specific doses of fertilizer, but education does not elicit an automatic response from the human mind. Without the proper incentives farmers will not respond to new techniques, regardless of the sum that is lavished in their instruction. Many writers concur with Theodore Shultz in the conviction that the job of dissemination becomes much easier if farmers are "ready" to have it. A further suspicion we can infer from the evidence is that tenure reform accelerates the "readiness" of farmers by years and perhaps decades. When tenure reform places the soil resources of the nation into the hands of the most highly motivated farmers, then the infrastructure-building now carried on by INCORA may have greater effect at less cost. Both are essential in agricultural development but production is likely to increase most if they are carried out simultaneously.[30]

The Directors of the JCRR did not hesitate to act upon the belief that land ownership would provide greater incentives to the Taiwanese peasantry. By 1970, 79 per cent of the farm families in Taiwan were owner-cultivators, 11 per cent were part-owners, and only 11 per cent were tenants.[31] This was achieved by redistributing large land holdings to tenants and part-owners. The land was redistributed immediately; no investments of any significance by the JCRR were made between the time land was expropriated and the time the new proprietor was legally invested. The new owner was charged a price for the land equal to 2.5 times the total yearly main crop yield. Accordingly, the annual installments over a ten-year period were equal

---

[30] Warriner, p. 29.   [31] *Taiwan Agricultural Yearbook,* p. 49.

to one-quarter of the total annual harvest. Significantly, this was a measure of land value easy for the farmer to grasp. Also, when the 7.5 per cent land tax was added to the installment the farmer still paid less out of his crop yield than did the tenant (32.5 per cent as against 37.5 per cent). The JCRR was more sensitive to the role of incentives than INCORA. They also believed that the farmer's idea of ownership is less abstract than the lawyer's. Having the land title in his name can not assure that greater incentives to work necessarily follow. There may be shades of ownership in the mind of a farmer, depending on the degree to which income derived from the land is his to enjoy and to reinvest.

Statistics assembled by Professor Anthony Koo support the contention that the incentive-effect of land ownership has increased aggregate agricultural production as the JCRR said it would. Koo observed, first, that tenure reform not only provided incentives to owner-cultivators to increase the amount of labor and capital inputs but also prompted them to improve the quality of these inputs. After becoming landowners farmers were far more eager to find out the latest information on new seeds and on techniques of insecticide application.[32] Also, by using the aggregate data of input and output for the agricultural sector as a whole and looking at productivity of the main crops the findings indicate

a general increase of agricultural productivity in the past decade (1950–1960), with the increase of capital input being a more important element than either the increase of labor input or technological progress. . . . We do not contend that land reform is the sole contributory factor in this achievement. Rather it is significantly correlated with such other factors as improved rice varieties and the dissemination of technology in the use of fertilizers and insecticides.[33]

Delbert A. Fitchett has compiled before-and-after statistics on Colombia's aggregate annual agricultural output. His figures for 1962—the first full year of the agrarian reform law—showed an increase in agricultural production of 5.2 per cent. The increase in 1963 was 3.3 per cent, while that for 1964 was 5.3 per cent. The average increase for the period 1956–1960 was slightly less than 3 per cent.[34] These figures, however, do not prove that land reform has

[32] Koo, p. 64.   [33] *Ibid.*, p. 77.
[34] Delbert A. Fitchett, "A Short Survey of Colombian Agricultural Development in Recent Years," (Santa Monica, California: The Rand Corporation, 1966), p. 5.

stimulated agricultural output in Colombia because other factors may have strongly influenced the trend, such as the cyclical rise in international coffee prices during the mid and late 1960s, and the investments of public and private agencies in the agricultural sector. Ernest Duff does assert that agricultural output increased after the early 1960s, but he does not attempt to correlate the work of INCORA to this development either.

5) In addition to its economic objectives the three-step tenancy reform program in Taiwan also tried to create a less hierarchical rural society. Here again experts familiar with Taiwan project a strongly favorable image of the reform's achievements. For lack of facts to the contrary in authoritative material, this account is hard to challenge.

Before 1949 a tenant was prevented from showing open support of land reform by outright intimidation from his landlord. If a tenant engaged in political activity of such a radical nature his friendly personal relationship (known to the Chinese as *kan ch'ing*) with the landlord was upset and his tenancy rights on the land jeopardized.[35] After 1949 Bernard Gallin described the state of affairs this way:

Village affairs are being profoundly affected as many former large landlords (who were the traditional local leaders) transfer their economic interests and activities away from the land to new outside business interests. When a landlord gives up his major economic interest in the area, it is usually not long before he also loses interest in and becomes unwilling to spend time and money on village social, religious, and political activities. Because the personal advantage is gone, he no longer is concerned with maintaining his status or leadership role. He may even move his residence out of the village in order to be closer to his new economic interests.

In those villages where such a situation has developed the villagers have reacted in two different ways to fill the vacuum created by the withdrawal of the landlord. The first reaction has been one of apathy, a reluctance to occupy positions of formal village leadership. The other reaction has been for villagers who have more time and money than their fellows and who perhaps aspire to improve their status to assume formal village leadership.[36]

Corroborative evidence can be found in the statistics compiled by Frank Bessac. They show that after Taiwan's land-reform tenants tended to participate approximately twice as often in village, district,

---

[35] Gallin, p. 128.   [36] *Ibid.*, p. 187.

and provincial elections (but not at the national level which, of course, the dictatorship of Chiang Kai-shek precludes). This illustrates the relationship between higher status and political participation at the local level. "The average increase in voter participation for the village mayor," he writes, "was 85.9 per cent; that of the tenants for village mayor was 83 per cent. The average increase in voter participation for all the local elected administrative personnel was 117 per cent while the average increase among tenants in voting for elected administrative personnel was 184 per cent." [37] A more accurate idea of the impact of the land-to-the-tiller program can be gained by comparing his statistics for voter participation by tenants in the 1948 election for provincial representatives with the 1965 turnout of owners and part-owners, and noting the jump in voting presumably caused by a change in status from tenant to owner. Using this method we get a voting increase of 241 per cent among those who received land during the land-to-the-tiller program.[38] Other changes in the social hierarchy can be illustrated by two examples. When Bernard Gallin lived in a Taiwanese village in the period following stage one of the reform he noted that:

With the tenant's security on the land protected it was no longer necessary for him to kow tow to his landlord or attempt to maintain good *kan ch'ing*. Today it is common to hear a tenant, who formerly was courteous to his landlord whether he liked him or not, actually curse the landlord when the latter comes in his own wagon to pick up and load the land rent. Formerly the tenant delivered the rent to the landlord.[39]

Another example comes from a series of interviews with Taiwanese farmers conducted by Professor Bessac. He writes that:

An official is now not given respect merely because of his status; he must also be considered a worthwhile official. One informant stated that before the land reform one had to treat officials with great politeness and offer them the best of the house. At present, he said, we farmers not only refuse to offer tea or cigarettes to officials who drop by but who are not properly introduced to us by the village mayor, but we let the dogs loose upon them.[40]

The sentiment of this farmer probably reflects the higher status some peasants now feel vis-à-vis the official class.

[37] Frank B. Bessac, *An Example of Social Change in Taiwan Related to Land Reform* (Missoula, Montana: The University of Montana Press, 1967), p. 18.

[38] Bessac, p. 18.   [39] Gallin, p. 133.   [40] Bessac, p. 26.

The changing status of women is another manifestation of a less rigid social hierarchy. Before, women were not allowed to be seen working in the fields, but now they are permitted to work in the fields with everybody else. When men were requisitioned by the Japanese army to help fight a war the women cared for the fields and continued to work at the side of their husbands when they got back. Before, growing vegetables was strictly a woman's job, but when vegetables became a highly prized cash crop in parts of the island, the men joined the women in this important undertaking. Today women tend to be seen more frequently at the sides of their husbands in the fields and in the towns. Due in part to land reform, which is reputed to have made farmers work longer and harder (eight days longer per year according to one source) the fuller economic role of women and the greater sharing of domestic responsibility may have been encouraged.[41]

If the rise in status of former tenant farmers contributed to a more egalitarian social order, then it follows that the relative impoverishment of the former landlord class also contributed to that end. A survey of 500 ex-landlord households by Martin M. C. Yang showed that land reform hurt the majority of them severely.[42] But a tiny minority profited immensely at the expense of other landlords. In another survey by Professor Yang it was found that over 90 per cent of the landlords sold their stocks in corporations soon after they received them due to the rumor that was circulated, perhaps spread intentionally, that all the companies were headed for bankruptcy. The average stock was sold 40 per cent below par value.[43] The buyers of these stocks were mainlanders and a few former landlords. The point should be made, if only in passing, that land reform in Taiwan was incomparably successful in democratizing ownership of the agricultural sector of the economy but at the same time it facilitated the inequitable concentration of industrial wealth.

Revolutionary forces have likewise begun to shake the foundation of Colombian society, but land reform can not seriously be grouped among the chief catalytic agents, except perhaps in the hopes and frustrations it inspires. In the four years between 1949 and 1953, 335,000 families in Taiwan became landowners. By contrast, only

[41] Gallin, p. 133.
[42] Martin M. C. Yang, *Socio-Economic Results of Land Reform in Taiwan* (Honolulu: East-West Center Press, 1970), pp. 264–65.
[43] Yang, p. 232.

47,688 Colombian farm families were sold land by INCORA during the four years from 1962 to 1966.

From the point of view of the landlords, INCORA showed demonstrably good sense by not tampering recklessly with the fabric of society. One can easily understand why, out of reasons of habit and education, the landlord feels more at ease in a hierarchical society where he sits upon the apex and old forms of ceremonial deference converge upon him. For all its many shortcomings the old order still favors his income relative to the peasantry's. It is important, though, not to oversimplify the rural Colombian society and imply, by endlessly recounting the gross inequities of the system, that there are two antagonistic classes clearly arrayed before each other in battle dress. In fact, were a landlord to treat his tenants, workers, and servants the way a severe but benevolent father would treat a child, then he might be praised in parts of the country as an exemplary *patrón*. One commonly hears peasants complain that their *patrónes* do not play their role well anymore. To forsake one's duties in the traditional Colombian society constitutes iniquitous behavior, as it does in Confucian society. Many landlords are profoundly religious men who detest the abuse of power. They do only what propriety calls for. For instance, when a serf on an estate is swindled by the *mayordomo* out of most of his harvest, the *mayordomo* may be rebuked; when his son is injured on the work gang the next messenger to remind him of a 40 per cent interest payment on a debt he owes will surely bear word of the master's sincerest condolences; when he approaches death at the age of forty a priest will be dispatched at no cost to the dying man, and his widow will be dismissed with generous advance notice. It is not true that the obsequious peasant will always remain so. Now he occupies a social role by birth that he must play as best he can. The Taiwanese peasant, we have seen, found a degree of freedom in land ownership, and soon learned the role that typifies the independent farmer in that country.

In most of Colombia's eighteen provinces the institution of landownership can be compared to a prism through which passes the income from land. This prism exists today in a state so aberrant from equity that it breaks the rural society into a wide spectrum of classes clearly demarcating the social position of the extremely rich and poor. A stratified society of this sort does not foster an ideology affirming the right of all men to enter politics. Nor is this in fact so. Colombian farmers who are not substantial landowners in their community know it is prudent to defer to the will of landlords when they vote in village, provincial, or national elections. Under this system the initiative for any change whatsoever must come from individuals whose interests are not ill-served by the status quo. Without changing the system of land tenure INCORA cannot radically change the way a community chooses its own leaders.

6) There were notable differences in the political situation as it existed in Colombia and Taiwan. A political history of the Nationalist regime on the mainland and on Taiwan (from 1945 to 1949) presents a picture of a government that was split by feuds to its very top and not enthusiastically committed to reform measures. Yet, after studying land reform in Taiwan one is forced to hypothesize that it could not have succeeded to the extent it did had not the government been to a degree honest, efficient, and fully committed to land reform. The paradox is not resolved in the abundant literature on the subject of land reform in Taiwan. One finds comments attributing success to the "determination" of men like Ch'en Ch'eng, who was provincial governor at the time, to the "willingness" of peasants to modernize, and to "favorable antecedents" of the reform, such as the material heritage of agricultural development left by the Japanese. These factors are certainly important but may only bear on the matter obliquely. The political situation from 1945 to 1953 may contain more relevant clues. A number of facts stand out. The Nationalist Chinese arrived on the island with a beleagured but experienced army that was useful in putting down rebellion and consolidating KMT authority in Taiwan. The Nationalists brought the principal members of their own bureaucracy with them to Taipei. Perhaps this bureaucracy had not coexisted with the indigenous landlord class long enough to establish a political alliance. Such alliances run at cross-purposes to the implementation of tenure reform and have obstructed it in Colombia, where top INCORA personnel have been related on many occasions to the same people that have had land designated for expropriation. Also, none of the KMT leaders owned land in Taiwan at this time.[44] Land reform was therefore conducted in Taiwan under very exceptional political circumstances, yet writers on land reform continue to single it out as a model other countries can successfully emulate. Finally, the government may have wanted to reduce the power of the native Taiwanese landlords by confiscating their lands. The landlords were the social elite in every community

[44] Mendel, p. 70.

and many among them were known to have been active in the 1947 revolt.[45] In any case, the government proceeded to buy land so quickly (the entire program ran 26 months) that a political alliance among landlords themselves could not arise. The organization of landlords in Nariño, Colombia, to block INCORA action in the region is a case in point.

It seems to be clear that land reform has a better chance of success if it strengthens the hand of a constituency favoring further execution of the policy. Small farmers and the landless must benefit immediately by the policy; in addition, they must perceive that they have been helped. Otherwise those in the government who favor tenure reform will not have a constituency to fall back on when the landlords mobilize their friends in high places. Many of the men who governed affairs of the Colombian Liberal Party were well-intentioned, but they feared what might happen if they threw open to more and more uneducated peasants the traditional closed preserve of political decisionmaking. From its inception *La Reforma Agraria* made no demonstrable headway against an antiquated tenure system on a scale that aroused vocal support. Given the aloof and distrustful mentality of *campesinos,* their support can often be enlisted by deeds, but not by promises. Invariably, the electioneering slogan "No más engaños!" ("no more deception") finds its way into all political campaigns. Voter disenchantment with land reform and other National Front programs clearly manifests itself in national elections. In the past the protest vote went to the mildly radical party of Lopez Michelsen on the left, but now it goes overwhelmingly to the party of ex-dictator General Rojas Pinilla. With the exception of the large body of INCORA technicians and bureaucrats that now exists, an outspoken constituency in support of INCORA did not develop out of the Agrarian Reform Law.

BIBLIOGRAPHY

Readers interested in a further investigation of the subject of this article may wish to consult:

Bauer, Peter T., and Basil S. Yamey. *The Economics of Underdeveloped Countries.* Chicago: The University of Chicago Press, 1957.
Bessac, Frank B. *An Example of Social Change in Taiwan Related to Land Reform.* Missoula, Montana: The University of Montana Press, 1967.

[45] *Ibid.*

Boorman, Howard L. (ed.). *Biographical Dictionary of the Republic of China.* New York: Columbia University Press, 1967.

Chang Yen-t'ien. *Land Reform in Taiwan.* Taichung: The Department of Agricultural Economics, Taiwan Provincial College of Agriculture, 1954.

Chen, C. *Land Reform in Taiwan.* Taipei: China Publishing Company, 1961.

Committee for Economic Development. *Economic Development Issues: Greece, Israel, Taiwan, and Thailand.* New York: Frederick A. Praeger, Publishers, 1968.

Duff, Ernest A. *Agrarian Reform in Colombia.* New York: Frederick A. Praeger, Publishers, 1968.

Economic Research Service. *Changes in Agriculture in Twenty-Six Developing Nations, 1948–1963.* Washington, D. C.: Economic Research Service, 1963.

Fitchett, Delbert A. "A Short Survey of Colombian Agricultural Development in Recent Years." Santa Monica, California: The RAND Corporation, 1966.

Gallin, Bernard. *Hsin Hsing: A Taiwanese Agricultural Village.* Ithaca, New York: Cornell University Press, 1961.

Goddard, W. G. *The Makers of Taiwan.* Taipei, 1963.

Hirschman, Albert O. *Journey Toward Progress.* New York: The Twentieth Century Fund, 1963.

INCORA. *Cinco Años de la Reforma Social Agraria: Informe de Actividades.* Bogotá: INCORA, 1966.

Joint Commission on Rural Reconstruction. *General Report.* Taipei, Taiwan: JCRR, 1970.

Kerr, George H. *Formosa Betrayed.* Boston: Houghton Mifflin Co., 1951.

Koo, Anthony Y. C. *The Role of Land Reform in Economic Development: A Case Study of Taiwan.* New York: Frederick A. Praeger, Publishers, 1968.

Mendel, Douglas. *The Politics of Formosan Nationalism.* Berkeley: The University of California Press, 1970.

Parsons, Kenneth H., Raymond J. Penn, and Philip M. Raup. *Land Tenure. Proceedings of the International Conference on Land Tenure and Related Problems in World Agriculture Held at Madison, Wisconsin, 1951.* Madison: The University of Wisconsin Press, 1956.

Provincial Government of Taiwan, Department of Agriculture and Forestry. *Taiwan Agricultural Yearbook.* Chung hsing Hsin ts'un: Provincial Government, June 1970.

Schultz, Theodore W. *Transforming Traditional Agriculture.* New Haven: Yale University Press, 1964.

Tang, H. S., S. C. Hsieh, "Land Reform and Agricultural Development in Taiwan," in Walter Froehlich (ed.) *Land Tenure, Industrialization and Social Stability.* Milwaukee: Marquette University Press, 1961.

T'ang Hui-sun. *Land Reform in Free China.* Taipei: Chinese-American Joint Commission on Rural Reconstruction, 1954.

United Nations. *Progress in Land Reform.* New York: UN, 1966.

Warriner, Doreen. *Land Reform in Principle and Practice.* London, England: The Claredon Press, 1969.

Yang, Martin M. C. *Socio-Economic Results of Land Reform in Taiwan.* Honolulu: East-West Center Press, 1970.

Biographical Sketches

STEPHEN ADLER was born in London, England, in August 1948 and was educated at Orange Hill Grammar School. After attending the Hebrew University in Jerusalem for a year as a special student in 1966–1967, he went up to Exeter College, Oxford University, where he obtained a degree in philosophy, politics, and economics. He is currently studying for a Master's degree at Columbia University's School of International Affairs, where his particular interests are international politics and the Middle East. He is one of the editors of the *Journal of International Affairs* for the year 1971–1972.

MICHAEL K. BLAKER, doctoral candidate in the Department of Political Science (International Relations) and the East Asian Institute, was graduated from the University of Southern California (B.A. Political Science, 1962; M.A. International Relations, 1967), studied in Japan at the Inter-University Center for Japanese Studies in Tokyo 1964–1965, and as a U.S.C. Harris Fellow in Japan during 1965–1966. The recipient of NDFL Fellowships in Japanese 1964–1968 and East Asian Institute Research Assistantships 1968–1970, he was Instructor in Japanese at Manhattanville College 1969–1970 and the East Asian Institute's Japan Bibliographer for the newly established Japan Documentation Center 1970–1971. He served as Administrative Assistant for the Conference on Japanese-American Relations 1931–1941 held near Lake Kawaguchi, Japan during July, 1969, and co-edited its *Proceedings*. He is currently completing a doctoral thesis dealing with Japan's techniques of international negotiation before World War II.

MICHAEL J. BUCUVALAS is a graduate student working toward his Ph.D. in Comparative Politics, with specializations in Greek politics and ethnic politics in the United States. He graduated from Columbia College in June, 1970, as a Political Science major, and in his senior year was appointed the David Rose Senior Teaching Assistant for the Department of Political Science. In addition to his continuing interest in Greece, he is presently engaged in research relating to ethnic differences in political styles at the grassroots level in various neighborhoods in New York City.

NORMAN LOUIS CIGAR, a Phi Beta Kappa graduate of the State University of New York, Buffalo (1970), received his Masters in International

Affairs from Columbia University and Certificate from the Middle East Institute in June 1972. Concentrating in French and Arabic as an undergraduate, Mr. Cigar was granted a scholarship for independent study in Tunisia. He is fluent in Italian, French, Russian, and Arabic. At present he is continuing his studies of the Middle East at Oxford University.

FELICE D. GAER received her B.A. with Distinction in Political Science in 1968 from Wellesley College, where she was also a Wellesley College Scholar. She is presently a certified Ph.D. candidate in Political Science at Columbia University. She obtained an M.A. in Political Science from Columbia in June, 1971, at which time she also received the Certificate of the Russian Institute. Miss Gaer, whose major field is comparative politics, has been especially concerned in her studies with the interaction of science and politics. She is currently writing a dissertation on the impact of cybernetics and computerization on Soviet politics. Miss Gaer has been the recipient of two National Defense Foreign Language Fellowships (1969–70, 1970–71) and has recently been awarded the Vita Dutton Scudder Fellowship from Wellesley College for continued graduate study in political science (1972–73).

DAVID A. J. MACEY emigrated to the United States from England in December 1964, after having served for several years as an officer in the British Merchant Navy. In 1965 he entered Brooklyn College, from which he was graduated in 1968, *summa cum laude* and with honors in history. He was also elected to Phi Beta Kappa. A Woodrow Wilson nominee and winner of a Herbert H. Lehman Fellowship, he entered Columbia's Graduate Department of History and the Russian Institute as a Fellow of the Faculty and holds an NDEA Title IV fellowship. Awarded a Certificate of the Russian Institute in December 1970 and an M.A. degree in French history in February 1971, he is now studying for a Ph.D. in Russian history with a minor field in Modern European history. He has begun work on his dissertation in the field of Russian agrarian history between 1906 and World War I. He is married and has one child.

MARIE L. ROCCA received her B.A. degree, *magna cum laude,* in June 1969, from St. Joseph's College, Brooklyn, New York. A member of Sigma Iota Chi Honor Society, she also received a New York State Regents Teaching Fellowship. At Columbia University she is studying Latin American History as a Fellow of the Faculty and received a National Defense Foreign Language Fellowship for 1969–1970 and again for 1970–1971. During the summer of 1970 Miss Rocca participated in the Summer Field Training Program of the Institute of Latin American Studies and under a fellowship did research on the Yaqui Indians of northwestern Mexico. She is now working for the Ph.D. degree in the Department of History and for the Certificate of the Institute of Latin American Studies at Columbia University.

MARGARET ROFF is a New Zealander. She took her Bachelor's degree at Victoria University of Wellington, and her Master's degree at the University of Malaya, Kuala Lumpur. After teaching for two years at the University of Melbourne, Australia, she returned to the University of Malaya to teach in the then recently established Faculty of Economics and Administration. Mrs. Roff first came to the United States in the fall of 1969 when her husband joined the faculty of Columbia University's History Department. She has published more than a dozen articles in such journals as *Asian Studies, Journal of Southeast Asian History,* and *International Studies.* At present she is in Southeast Asia completing research for her doctoral dissertation to be presented to the Political Science Department of Columbia University.

JAMES B. STEPANEK has spent half his life abroad, having lived as a dependent three years in China, two years in Indonesia, two years in Burma, four years in India, plus two years in Colombia as a Volunteer with the Peace Corps. Graduating *cum laude* (1967) from the University of Colorado, Boulder, where he concentrated in international affairs, Mr. Stepanek is now working on a Ph.D. in economics at Columbia University. His special interest is the economic development of the Far East.